Lucullus

Lucullus

The Life and Campaigns
of a Roman Conqueror

Lee Fratantuono

Pen & Sword
MILITARY

First published in Great Britain in 2017 by
Pen & Sword Military
An imprint of
Pen & Sword Books Ltd
47 Church Street
Barnsley
South Yorkshire
S70 2AS

ISBN 978 1 47388 361 1

Printed and bound in England
by CPI Group (UK) Ltd, Croydon, CR0 4YY

Pen & Sword Books Ltd incorporates the Imprints of Pen & Sword
Archaeology, Atlas, Aviation, Battleground, Discovery, Family History, History,
Maritime, Military, Naval, Politics, Railways, Select, Transport,
True Crime, Fiction, Frontline Books, Leo Cooper, Praetorian Press,
Seaforth Publishing, Wharncliffe and White Owl.

For a complete list of Pen & Sword titles please contact
PEN & SWORD BOOKS LIMITED
47 Church Street, Barnsley, South Yorkshire, S70 2AS, England
E-mail: enquiries@pen-and-sword.co.uk
Website: www.pen-and-sword.co.uk

For Katie,
with respect and appreciation

Contents

Preface and Acknowledgments

The present volume is one of a relatively small number of books devoted to the Roman republican military and political figure Lucius Licinius Lucullus. Among these titles, the most extensive scholarly treatment of Lucullus is that of Arthur Peter Keaveney, *Lucullus, a Life*, which was originally published in 1992 by Routledge. A second edition from Gorgias Press in 2009 offered a new postscript that takes account of the Lucullan scholarship that appeared in the seventeen years since the original printing (this second edition reprints the main body of the 1992 work without edit).

Keaveney's book is a masterful treatment of a complicated time and a difficult life. It is aimed at a scholarly audience, with extensive documentation of sources both primary and secondary. Keaveney's work assumes a certain familiarity with the history of the Roman Republic, in particular the political and domestic challenges of the first half of the first century BC. It seeks to offer solutions to several seemingly intractable problems in the timeline and investigation of Lucullus' career, and to disentangle the thornier knots posed by contradictory sources. It is a valuable, indeed indispensable companion to any study of its subject, as the number of references to it in this work attests. Keaveney's work has largely eclipsed the most comprehensive biography available before it, van Ooteghem's French language *Lucius Licinius Lucullus* (Brussels: 1959), which still retains its usefulness on a number of points. Manuel Tröster's *Themes, Character and Politics in Plutarch's Life of Lucullus: The Construction of a Roman Aristocrat* (Stuttgart: Franz Steiner Verlag, 2008) is mostly concerned with Plutarch's biographical treatment of Lucullus. Neither van Ooteghem nor Tröster offer the degree of coverage of all aspects of Lucullus' life that Keaveney provides. It might also be useful to note that Keaveney, van Ooteghem and Tröster are not always easily obtainable, especially by students (let alone the general reader).

From the start, I should make clear that my work on Lucullus does not in any way seek to replace, or even to supplement Keaveney's. Rather, it seeks to make Lucullus more accessible to a wider audience of readers, in particular to students and devotees of military history and Roman military science. Certainly it seeks to offer fresh appraisals of the same problems that Keaveney and other scholars have researched and appraised. But scholars will want to turn first to Keaveney. The present book seeks to focus more closely on Lucullus' military career than his political, in keeping with the nature of the series of Roman military biographies in which it appears. At the same time, it also endeavours to present relevant commentary on that career from Lucullus' literary and artistic pursuits, in particular with respect to the question of Lucullus as a Roman Alexander, and of Lucullus' relationship to Epicureanism. Throughout, it does not so much aspire to say something new about its subject, as it hopes to make a major figure of republican Rome better known to a wider audience.

But why Lucullus? First and foremost, because among the figures of the military and political world of the late Republic, he is among the most underappreciated. Both personal achievements and the benefit of historical hindsight have made Caesar, Pompey and even Crassus appreciably more famous and familiar to later generations. Lucullus is all but forgotten, even among those with at least a passing interest in Roman republican history. This relative obscurity does not accord with the accomplishments of the man, both in the forum and the field; this almost studied neglect does not reflect the résumé of a man for whom, we shall see, the title 'Last of the Republicans' is not inappropriate (Keaveney would confer the label on Lucullus' spiritual father Sulla). In the life of Lucullus, we may well find a microcosm of many of the problems that confronted Rome, both domestically and internationally; Lucullus' life is emblematic of his age, and both his successes and failures attest to the particular realities of Roman republican life to a remarkably transparent degree.

Another reason for a new consideration of Lucullus is that even after Keaveney, many passing mentions of Lucullus in works on Roman history, in biographies of his great antagonist Mithridates of Pontus and in volumes on republican military science refer to Lucullus as essentially a failure in his military and political quests in Asia, and, ultimately, a synonym for hedonist and decadent pleasure-seeker. This crude appraisal of the man remains all too common in otherwise praiseworthy treatments of the period. Lucullus' enemies, one might almost think, performed exceedingly well in their enterprise of discrediting the man. Keaveney's work was groundbreaking in its reconsideration of an old stereotype that may well never die out entirely; the present volume seeks to expand on that re-evaluation of a man whose last years were a testament not so much to decadence as to acceptance of a fate that was undeserved and unmerited (Keaveney, we should note, has also done great work in treating the somewhat similar problems posed by the life of Sulla).

The abiding conviction that undergirds this book is that Lucullus deserves wider fame and appreciation for his deeds. A student of mine once commented that all she knew of Lucullus was the mention of him in Stanley Kubrick's 1960 film *Spartacus*. I could not criticize her for the inaccurate observation; Kubrick's film was the first time I too had heard of Lucullus. And, like her, I did not realize at the time that the film referenced his brother, Marcus Lucullus, and not the more accomplished Lucius. In hindsight, the inadvertent 'error' of both my student and myself is instructive and worthy of reflection. Lucullus has been largely forgotten in comparison to his more storied rivals and colleagues. It is my conviction after spending many months with his life and story that he deserves wider fame. Both he and his brother achieved much in a difficult age; they became the glories of their family and were a credit to the Republic that nurtured and inspired them. Lucullus and his brother also stand forth as almost lonely examples of fame from their family; before them, their lineage could boast a scattered sampling of note-worthy figures – and after them, there is almost nothing to report.

Lucullus, too, offers a case study in the particular circumstances and the polit-ical and philosophical underpinnings of the collapse of the republican system in which he was so invested. To study Lucullus is to appreciate better why the Republic collapsed, and also to investigate closely how and why Rome expanded its power so dramatically toward the East. It is a story of incalculable significance for the later history of Turkey, Armenia, Syria and Greece; it is an adventure that is both eminently Roman and hauntingly Alexandrian. The relationship between Rome's eastern expansion and the eventual transformation of the Roman political system from a predominately republican to a predominately imperial experience is at the heart of understanding the career of Lucullus. He was one of the most inveterate defenders of the 'old' republican system, of the traditional structures of Roman government and societal management. In investigating his life closely, we may discover along the way that his work in eastern realms contributed to the metamorphosis of that ancient system into what would eventually become the 'Roman Empire' of post-Caesarian, post-Augustan realities. In some circles it is popular to speak of 'liminal' figures. In the case of Lucullus, the trendy adjective is appropriate. Lucullus bridges the Republic and the Empire. He is a tragic figure in that he helped to bring about a world in which he would not have felt at ease. He also bridges the worlds of Sulla and Caesar, the one man his mentor and political and military father, the other an upcoming, rising star on the Roman stage who represented so much of what Sulla and Lucullus opposed. To understand better the life and motivations of both Sulla and Caesar, one may turn to Lucullus, the almost forgotten intermediary figure between the horrors of the Sullan Age and the no less transformative (and oftentimes violent) experience of the Caesarian.

Lucullus was inextricably connected to the literary and philosophical worlds of his day. Cicero was certainly his acquaintance and, at times at least, friend; the poet Lucretius was likely among his associates as well. Given how today Lucullus is bet-ter known as the source of a *recherché* adjective ('lucullan') connoting luxury and decadence, it is profitable to consider his life in terms of his contemporary Roman experience of Epicureanism, a philosophical school that has often suffered the same imprecise, ultimately unfair characterization that has besmirched Lucullus' own reputation. The study of Lucullus' life and work offers the chance to see first-hand the delicate and sometimes tense interplay between political and military exigencies on the one hand, and the clarion call of poetry and philosophy on the other. Lucullus was a man of letters as much as he was a man of battle, sieges and financial administration. Somewhere along the path of exploring his life, we may hope to achieve a better understanding of the place of literature and the arts in the late Republic, and we may see in Lucullus a man who found it difficult to compartmentalize conveniently these seemingly disparate aspects of his life. The Lucullus that emerges will be a man of profound conviction – especially in the area of loyalty to family and friends, the exercise of the Roman virtue of *pietas* – and also a man who may well have been singularly unsuited to the demands of power and prestige in his age. His failure, such as it is, is the failure of his class and the system it had forged in the course of centuries of Roman political life. Beyond all this, Lucullus' work and catalogue of accomplishments merit more than an advanced vocabulary item that references luxurious dinners and potent palatables – even if we shall see that the result of this caricature of the man is an abidingly happy memory among the descendants of the Greeks in particular, whose lands and people he so loved. The phihellene Lucullus remains a popular figure in the Greek world, even if only in circles gastronomical – and given the trajectory of his life, it is possible that he would have been content with this positive memory.

If there is anything remotely novel in the treatment of Lucullus in these pages, it is perhaps to be found in the reappraisal of this consummate Roman politician and general as a man of letters and perhaps even a devotee of Epicurean philosophy, and as a man deeply invested in certain aspects of the Alexander myth. The Alexander image may serve, in the end, to unify certain seemingly contradictory facets and aspects of Lucullus' life. We shall see how both Lucullus' engagement with the Alexander legend, and his study of different Greek philosophical schools and the lessons of Epicureanism in particular, were recast in a republican reality that was not necessarily well suited to their lessons. Put another way, to the degree to which Lucullus was devoted to the maintenance of the Roman Republic, he was also stymied in his *de facto* attempts to emulate Alexander and to pursue the teachings of Epicurus. Lucullus was enamoured of and loyal to a system that did not permit the free exercise of both his military and philosophical passions. His failure was in part the attempt to reconcile the irreconcilable. It was perhaps mostly in his sense of *pietas* that he found himself unable to make the compromises that in several important regards characterized the work of Pompey and Caesar.

In an important sense, the present work is an adventure story of the old-fashioned, perennially popular sort. It begins in an Italy that was convulsed by the ravages of civil strife in the so-called Social War, and continues in the mythic lands of Athens and the Greek islands, though not without sojourns in North Africa, Egypt and

Cyprus. From there it proceeds to the Asian continent, to the site of the ruined city of Troy and beyond into Cappadocia and distant Armenia. It ends where it began, in Italy – in a Roman Republic that was irrevocably changed from the political and social reality whence Lucullus first set out. Like the work of Plutarch on which we rely for so much of our knowledge about our subject, it is a biography that seeks to understand better the motivations and accomplishments of one figure within a system that was both at its height of glory and in peril of lasting ruin.

For the military historian, Lucullus' life offers the chance to explore certain aspects of Roman military practice, both on land and sea. Lucullus was among the few Roman military commanders with a credible, indeed impressive record for victories achieved in both naval and ground combat. Indeed, his career falls within a period in which Roman naval power was increasingly needed to surmount the continuing plague of piracy in the Mediterranean. In ground operations, Lucullus was skilled in both infantry and cavalry management, and in the prosecution of siege warfare. To study Lucullus' campaigns is to receive an education in the complete range of tactical military operations. The greatness of our subject is confirmed when we consider that his military successes were wedded to a keen eye for financial administration and diplomatic engagement. And the backdrop of Lucullus' own wars is a canvas of battle: the Sertorian War in Spain; the Spartacus War in Italy; the aforementioned struggle against the pirates of Cilicia. The story of Lucullus' life is the story of a Republic that had outgrown Italy before it could say it had fully mastered even that peninsula.

Lucullus was undeniably a literary man, a man deeply invested in the romantic tradition of Greek epic as well as history and philosophy. He was well aware of the mythical adventures of Achilles and Alexander alike, of the lore of Homer and the Macedonian monarch. The world of Achilles and Alexander alike could not have been more removed from that of Lucullus' Roman Republic. To appreciate the tension between two diametrically opposed world views is to begin to understand something of the enigma of Lucullus.

This book is the result of the happy process of collaboration and consultation with a wide range of colleagues and friends. As ever, Philip Sidnell is a remarkable editor and wise counsellor, and to him I owe a continuing debt of gratitude. My first exposure to Roman history came at The College of the Holy Cross, where Professor Blaise Nagy remains a constant source of assistance and advice on all matters historical. Work on Lucullus has been an exercise in remembering the teaching and example of Professor Gerard Lavery, himself a scholar of Lucullus and Roman military and political history. I have also benefited from the historical writings of my former teacher Thomas R. Martin. Shadi Bartsch has been a source of encouragement and inspiration in my ongoing scholarly endeavours; so also Alden Smith, Michael Putnam and Richard Thomas.

Every other spring, I have the great pleasure to offer a lecture course on the history of the Roman Republic. The forty to fifty undergraduates who enroll in that class, and in its sister course on the Empire, are a constant source of encouragement and challenge on all manner of topics in the study of the history, literature and thought of the ancient Romans. To those many classes I owe a special debt. So also to Sarah Foster, major in Classics and chair of our student board for Classics, who has provided help and valuable advice in the course of both writing and lecturing on Lucullus, and who has never failed to remind me of the value of the study of the Classics for a better appreciation of our contemporary world and its political challenges. I am also grateful to my students Annie Roth and Emily Blaner for their assistance and help in the fall semester of 2016 in particular. So also to Elise Baer.

The greatest debt I have is to my talented and tireless photographer, Katie McGarr. Katie studied Roman history and Classics with me at Ohio Wesleyan University, as part of her work for a degree in Humanities and History. She has travelled extensively in the territories (both mainland and insular) of the Roman Empire (by airplane, train, bus, car, ferry, hot air balloon – and of course on foot). In modern Greece, Cyprus and Turkey, she followed the steps of Lucullus and visited a wide range of sites connected to his life and work, especially in the Greek islands and Cappadocia. She has also had the opportunity to dine at and visit with the owners and managers of several of the restaurants in the eastern Mediterranean that are dedicated to the memory of Rome's famous epicure.

The photographic illustration of this book shows but a part of the rich coverage and artistic interpretation of the ancient world that has characterized Katie's work. Her artistry extends beyond the photographic to engagement with the lasting influence of the Romans on the lands and peoples once under their domination; her insights into classical reception and history have been a sustaining influence on my work. Katie encouraged me to pursue this and related projects as part of the ongoing mortal quest to preserve the memory of great men and their deeds. As the first publication in which her colour photography has appeared, this volume is fittingly dedicated to her.

Lee Fratantuono
Delaware, Ohio, USA
November 2016
In festo S. Caeciliae

Chapter 1

From the Dawn of an Optimate Life

Culinary Relics

There is a *taverna* on the so-called Old Market Street in Chora on the Greek island of Naxos that is named the 'Taverna Lucullus'.[1] It is one of several such dining establishments scattered across the eastern Mediterranean.[2] These restaurants serve as a curious survival of the popular memory of an almost forgotten hero of immense significance to Roman military, political, literary and, yes, gastronomical history.[3] (Indeed, outside of the world of ancient military history and Classics, it is possible that the most enduring legacy of Lucullus is in the culinary arena.) The English adjective 'lucullan' has endured as a lasting lexical tribute (after a fashion) to the Roman statesman and general. The onomastic memory of Lucullus is thus centred on his association with the joys of a luxurious, even decadent table; his great accomplishments in Asia Minor – from Cappadocia to Pontus to Armenia – seemingly take second place to the fame of his table. This enduring memory of the man is rendered all the more striking by the fact that not a single hint of definitive information survives as to exactly what was served of either food or drink at the allegedly lavish dinners that Lucullus hosted. And the gastronomic memorial gives no credit to Lucullus' many achievements in the worlds of both Roman politics and military adventure.

A Man of His Age

The present volume is a study of the life and (in particular) military achievements of one of the lesser-known figures of the Roman Republic, at least in the popular imagination. For many students and even scholars of Roman military history, Lucullus is little more than a notable republican of vague significance. But Lucius Licinius Lucullus (118–57/56 BC) represents in some ways the consummate hero of the Roman Republic.[4] He was a military general of extraordinary ability, with an impressive résumé of achievement.[5] He was also an inveterate patron and devotee of the arts and literature (a fact that may have played into the hands of his rivals and critics). His travels were among the most extensive of any Roman of his age; in some ways he may be considered an incarnation of the spirit of infectious enthusiasm and resolute determination that characterized Roman Republican colonization and overseas adventure – he simply saw and experienced more of the world than many of his contemporaries. There are negative attributes, to be sure, in the sum appraisal of his life – but no one who has taken the time to study the period closely has seriously called into question the significance of the tremendous victories he won over Rome's Eastern enemies, no one either of his contemporaries or of subsequent historians of the Republic. Lucullus could well have become the Roman Alexander the Great; if Pompey was destined for the title, Lucullus paved the way. Among the great military and political figures of the late Republic, Lucullus also had a claim on the title of the most literary and philosophically inclined. Today, some might call him a Renaissance man, a polymath of astonishing range.

Lucullus has also been shrouded in relative obscurity and unfamiliarity, largely due to the eclipse his fame and glory suffered in the wake of younger rivals and contemporaries, in particular Pompey and Caesar. In some ways he was fortunate in seemingly knowing when best to exit the stage of Roman history (this is something that was recognized even in antiquity); his ultimate fate could easily have been as violent as those that befell his more storied Roman colleagues. Instead, we shall find that Lucullus' final years are more closely associated with rumours of luxurious decadence, mental decline and eventual dementia; part of our task will be to evaluate the evidence for these charges.[6] He may well have been a victim of Alzheimer's Disease, as some have speculated; he may have been accidentally poisoned. His end, in any case, will prove an interesting story in itself.

Our task will be primarily to examine the remarkable military career of a man who travelled to the distant Roman East and helped to establish a more or less lasting order throughout many of its more troubled realms – and, throughout, to study what factors contributed to the making of a Roman military genius. Along the way, we may discover that Lucullus deserves far more credit and praise for his military acumen and mastery of the arts of strategy and tactics than he has received. If Caesar is still a household name, and Pompey and Crassus relatively famous even among those with limited knowledge of Roman history, Lucullus has experienced a far less sympathetic treatment from the ravages of time and lost memory. If anything, Lucullus' reputation hovers today between obscurity on the one hand, and the increasingly unfamiliar meaning of such references as 'lucullan' in matters of luxury and decadence. Throughout, our task will be to evaluate the charges brought against him, and to assess the validity of the indictment.

But some questions deserve to be asked from the start and throughout our investigation of this military hero. We may ask why Lucullus failed in several important facets of his political and military careers. We may wonder what qualities in the man served him well, and which aspects of his personality and behaviour may have done him harm. We may seek to identify critical moments in his life, where a different decision might have spelled incalculably different consequences for the history of the Republic. These are the same problems that all biographers tackle; they stand at the heart of the ancient tradition of recording Lucullus' life and memory.

In an important sense, the story of Lucullus' military life is a microcosm of the problems of the Republic in what some might call its dying years. It was an age of immensely talented men of arms, public speakers and indeed literary and poetic voices. It was a time of extraordinary expansion of the borders of the Roman world, of consolidation of gains and testing of new relations with foreign neighbours. It was an age of massive internal upheaval and turmoil, not least because of the eruption of the Spartacus slave war in Italy. For many of the more troubled and controversial periods in question, Lucullus was blessed to be far off in Asia. It is possible he stayed there too long – and equally possible that he did not stay long enough. Lucullus remains an enigma, though an enigma we do well to investigate closely. Along the way, we may discover some useful insights into the slow and inexorable collapse of a political and military system that had long ago outgrown the borders of the Italian peninsula.

Lucullus' life is reasonably well documented in surviving literature, though significant problems of interpretation of the evidence remain. We shall see that we are not able to be certain of the definitive chronology of select key events in Lucullus' life, or of the motivation and rationale behind several important twists of fate. These difficulties, however, are relatively minor and do not impede an appreciation and better understanding of this quintessential late republican life.

Military Acumen

The main focus of the present work is on Lucullus' military achievements, most notably the conduct and prosecution of his wars against both Mithridates of Pontus and Tigranes of Armenia. It will be demonstrated that Lucullus was one of the finest military commanders of his age, a strategist and tactician of immense talent and ability, a versatile leader in the business of combat operations on both land and sea – indeed, perhaps the finest 'amphibious' commander in Roman military history, with only Pompey for serious rival. The Lucullus of military history will emerge as an underappreciated master of Roman military science, a general whose diplomatic skills were equally honed and finessed in the course of the long wars in the Roman East. And, we shall see, in terms of the lasting import of Lucullus' work, the disposition of affairs beyond the Bosporus and the Euphrates for years to come would largely be the result of the achievements won by this protégé of Sulla.

Names and Origins

We may begin – as so often in the study of Roman personages – with names. 'Lucius' is one of the relatively few Roman 'first names' or *praenomina*; it is derived from the Latin noun *lux*, 'light' (and so our title 'from the dawn of an optimate life' for our subject). The *nomen* 'Licinius' refers to the clan or *gens* 'Licinia', a plebeian *gens* whose origins may have been Etruscan.[7] 'Lucullus' is a *cognomen*, the third part of a Roman name that referred to a particular family. Some Romans are more commonly known today by their *nomen* (cf. Virgil, Ovid), and others by their *cognomen* (e.g., Cicero). Lucullus is in this latter category. Besides the Luculli, the Licinian clan could also boast the Crassi, the most famous of whom was Marcus Licinius Crassus (c. 115–53 BC), Lucullus' almost exact contemporary – and another Roman who would find adventure in the East (with rather more fatal consequences).

Lucullus was, strictly speaking, a plebeian – as were Crassus and Pompey. But as we shall see, many noble plebeians were more akin to traditional patricians in their political dealings than to the *plebs* or 'common people'. Conversely, while Gaius Julius Caesar was a patrician (and one who could boast descent from Aeneas' son Iulus and, ultimately, the goddess Venus), his sympathies were most decidedly popular and not traditional or senatorial.[8] Lucullus was a plebeian, but his sensibilities and manner through his life were patrician (in contrast, his brother-in-law and antagonist, the patrician Publius Clodius Pulcher, would actually eventually pursue adoption into a plebeian family).[9] Lucullus was no innovator (at least to any appreciable extent) in the political or social realms; his talents lay elsewhere. He was what we may label a traditionalist; his sympathies were with the preservation of senatorial prerogatives and the defence of the *ancien regime*, as it were. And unlike some of his contemporaries, Lucullus never wavered in his allegiances; a traditionalist optimate he was, and a traditionalist optimate he remained. Consistency and loyalty were high in his list of virtues; scholars may question whether these attributes played a part in the ultimate failure of some of his enterprises.

The Evidence of Plutarch

Lucullus is not infrequently cited in extant Greek and Latin literature. But our principal surviving source of evidence for his life is the biography of Plutarch (c. AD 46–120), the Greek scholar and man of letters who is justly celebrated for his parallel lives of noteworthy Greeks and Romans.[10] Plutarch's life of Lucullus is paired with his account of the Athenian statesman and military master Cimon (c. 510–450 BC); we shall return later to the significance of this comparison in terms of Lucullus' military record.

Plutarch offers the most complete extant account of Lucullus' life; it is the single most important source of information we have for his military and other exploits. And that life encompassed some of the most tumultuous and dramatic years in the history of the Republic; Lucullus lived through the first half of a century that would witness what some would consider the death of the Republic. In some regards it is a paradigmatic life of a republican Roman; the history of Lucullus' life is inextricably linked to the history of the Republic he served well in both peace and war. Like all ancient sources, it must be evaluated for its reliability and candour, its biases and prejudices. But without Plutarch's life, our knowledge of Rome's great Republican general would be unquestionably impoverished.[11] As we shall see, Lucullus was one of those subjects of biography who held a special significance for Plutarch because of his connections to the author's native Chaeronea in Boeotia. In the more general programme of Plutarch's treatment of the Republic, Lucullus' life is one of the key elements in the biographer/historian's unfolding of the complicated story of the fall of the Republic.[12] We do well to consider how improverished our undestanding of the man would be in the absence of the Plutarchan life.

There are problems, however, that are attendant to having only one major surviving source. For many episodes of Lucullus' life, we are essentially dependent on Plutarch's account, and reliant on the biographer's accuracy in forming a fair portrait of Lucullus' life and experiences in both the political and military arenas.[13] In other cases, we must resort to comparing Plutarch's version with the accounts of others – in other words, the normal work of source criticism and analysis. For Plutarch, the life of Lucullus falls more or less neatly into two phases – first a long period marked by industry and careful planning and work, and the second a period that was defined by the luxurious decadence for which 'lucullan' has become a watchword, however increasingly abstruse and *recherché*. But even the binary division of Lucullus' life by Plutarch is not without controversy; the biographer is ready, we shall see, to pass critical judgment on the last part of his subject's life, but without clear indication that the criticism outweighs the positive qualities of Lucullus' earlier life. We are left with an enigma, a strange Republican life that will prove to be replete with lessons about the military and political realities of the age in which it was lived.

The Virtue of *Pietas*

How does Plutarch commence his biographical portrait of a man who will emerge as something of a mystery? Plutarch's Lucullus is presented from the start as a man outstanding for what to a Roman would be defined as the virtue of *pietas*. The English derivative 'piety' does not satisfactorily render or translate the untranslatable. *Pietas* defines the ideal relationship between human beings and the immortals; it provides a framework for organizing and defining familial connections and ties of kinship and friendship. In the case of Lucullus, *pietas* was manifested in the young Roman's decision (in concert with his brother Marcus, who was one or at most two years younger) to seek to prosecute the man who had prosecuted his father. There is a moral dimension to Plutarch's record; certain defining traits and characteristics of the man are presented from the start. For Plutarch, these characteristics fashioned and shaped Lucullus' reactions to a variety of situations throughout his life, and in the end they may prove to be as much emblematic of an age as of an individual.

Further, Plutarch notes in the very opening lines of the life that Lucullus was the grandson of a consul, and the nephew of the consul Quintus Caecilius Metellus Numidicus (c. 160–91 BC)[14] – but the son of parents of somewhat less glorious a record. Lucullus is implicitly presented, we might think, as a study in contradictions. He was born into a family and social *milieu* that afforded examples of both good and bad – the Roman *exempla* of achievement and moral excellence, and of depravity, crime and infamous disgrace. The navigation of those opposites would be the challenge that would confront the young plebeian noble. By the end of his relatively long life (at least by ancient standards), Lucullus would offer both positive and negative *exempla*, and stand forth as a seeming study in conflicting displays of character and behaviour.

We may observe that Lucullus' formative years and entry into political and public life were accompanied by questions of loyalty and duty. Toward the end of his career in the military and his difficult return to Rome after the long campaigns in Asia and Armenia, it is possible that Lucullus suffered deeply from a sense of a lack of appreciation of his talents and devotion to obligation, and a feeling that the virtues that had marked his early years and career were no longer so valued in Republican Rome. Lucullus was born into a difficult age and a family that had enjoyed a checkered reputation, yet by the time of his death, he could at least lay claim to the unquestioned title of being the most notable scion of his line.

The Defence of His Father

Some salient details and conclusions may be offered here. Lucullus' introduction to public life was firmly invested in the traditions of familial *pietas*, of a son's defence and support of his father, an image that for the Romans had its origins in the Trojan hero Aeneas' rescue of his father Anchises from the burning ruins of Priam's fabled city. The brothers Luculli failed in their attempt to prosecute successfully the man who had driven their father into exile – but the fraternal attempt at filial *pietas* did not go without notice and reward. It was an act of daring in a troubled political climate, a deed invested with the spirit of devotion to one's parents that so inspired the Roman imagination. For the Romans of Lucullus' day, filial respect mattered more than the question of whether or not Lucullus Senior was guilty and justly condemned; the devotion of a son to his father transcended any concerns with what we might label a vendetta, or revenge for revenge's sake.[15] Servilius had been responsible for the prosecution and disgrace of Lucullus Senior; the question was not one of the father's guilt, but of the duty of his sons to show respect and honour to their *paterfamilias*, notwithstanding his crime. And in the wake of Lucullus' father's exile, the son assumed the burden and responsibility of being the head of the household.

What exactly had happened?[16] Lucullus' father – confusingly for students of Roman history, both the father and the grandfather had the same name as their more famous descendant – had been sent to Sicily in 103–102 BC to quell the uprising that would later be known to history as the Second Servile or Slave War (his son Marcus Lucullus would have the chance to restore something of his father's honour in his part in ending the Spartacus War years later – indeed, if Lucius is an undeservedly unsung hero in some circles, his brother has suffered even more in this regard).

Lucullus Senior had served as urban praetor (*praetor urbanus*) in 104, and was propraetor when he went to Sicily. He seems, one might think, not to have found the task of suppressing the Slave War entirely to his liking, and at any rate he was not ultimately successful in his commission, despite the apparent achievement of a brilliant victory – the historian Diodorus Siculus argues that because of either laziness or bribery, the victor refused to finish his task.[17] He was replaced in 102 by one Gaius Servilius, whose complaints about his predecessor led at least in part (if not directly) to the efforts of his cousin Servilius the Augur to prosecute the former commander.[18] Lucullus Senior was charged 'officially' with extortion (the full Latin term for the offence was *res repetundae pecuniae*).[19] Convicted of the offence, he was condemned to exile when his son was barely 16 – the age when a Roman youth traditionally assumed the 'toga of manhood' or *toga virilis* that signified his having reached the age of maturity. The Lucullus brothers thus made their entrance into adult society in the shadow of family disgrace and upheaval. There is every reason to believe that the boys' father was indeed guilty of some sort of offence, as he would never be recalled from his exile and fades in shame from the pages of history.

The *pietas* of the Luculli brothers may have been all the more striking in light of the fact that Lucullus Senior was not aided in his hour of need by his wife's powerful relatives, the Metelli. We are not entirely sure why his in-laws abandoned him (Arthur Keaveney cites the cryptic note at *De Viris Illustribus* 62.4 that seems to refer to an offence taken by Metellus Numidicus to some aspect of Lucullus' conduct of his praetorship).[20] Lucullus Senior had few friends in the crisis of his life; he was able, however, to count on the loyalty of his two sons – a loyalty that would perhaps serve the brothers more effectively than the doomed father. The brothers would be together again at the end of Lucius' life, when in his declining years he would depend on Marcus for sustenance and support.

Lucullus' Early Life

But what of the son's life in the years before his father's Sicilian disaster, and in the immediate wake of the father's trial and conviction? Admittedly we are without anything much in the way of information about Lucullus' childhood. He may initially have been privately tutored at home (a common enough practice for wealthier families). If he travelled abroad in his youth, no record remains. Sometimes, classical personages who went on to achieve glory and renown would be remembered for offering signs of future achievement even in infancy and early youth. No such lore seems to have survived for Lucullus. Essentially, he first appears in the context of his father's career-ending debacle (this is admittedly the result of our need to rely on Plutarch for a comprehensive account of his life; another biographer or historian might have made other emphases in describing his early life). We have no certain knowledge of whether or not the young Lucullus was aware of the military adventures that marked his youth; his childhood saw the war against Jugurtha that broke out in 112 BC, and the years surrounding his father's disgrace were the same ones in which Gaius Marius won his victories over the Teutones and the Cimbri (102 and 101 BC). Indeed, Carthage had been destroyed less than thirty years before his birth (146 BC). Rome was well established as an international power, and Roman military and political affairs already stretched across the Mediterranean and far into the unsettled and often troubled regions to the north of Italy. And there were the first major engagements in the East, in the Greek world and in modern Turkey – a region that was, as any literate Roman knew, the mythological home of the Trojan ancestors of the Romans, the realm of Priam, of Aeneas and his son Iulus.

Literary and Cultural Influences

Some evidence, however, does survive to fill out the picture of the young Roman's formative years – though of a more reflective, literary sort. Cicero's speech in defence of the Greek poet Archias – the celebrated *Pro Archia Poeta* oration of 62 BC, to which we shall return as an important source of relevant testimony about the life of Lucullus – notes that Archias arrived in Rome in 102 BC, and that he was warmly received by the Luculli first of all.[21] In fact, Archias is said by Cicero to have accompanied Marcus Lucullus to Sicily; the date of this mission is uncertain, as is the exact rationale for it.[22] Some have concluded that Archias was a tutor of the brothers Lucullus, but this is nowhere stated in the surviving evidence – and we do well to remember that Archias was himself an adolescent at this time. The intimate connection of the Greek poet to the Lucullus family cannot, however, in any way be exaggerated. When Archias became a Roman citizen, he took the name of the family that had shown him such favour and patronage.[23] And, as we shall soon enough see, Archias accompanied Lucius Lucullus on his quaestorship in the East, and remained a loyal friend of the family to the end.[24] Many leading Romans of Lucullus' day were particularly interested in Greek literature and the patronage of the literary arts. Lucullus seems to have been more given over to these pursuits than others, which may eventually have provided his enemies with an avenue of criticism and attack. Simply put, an educated Roman could be a lover of Greek literature – but there were limits of tolerance for phihellenism, and Lucullus may have provided an easy target for those who wanted to charge him with the alleged vice.[25]

Lucullus' early life, at any rate, was imbued with the spirit of Greek language and literature, and with the presence of a poet of some talent whose influence and inspiration were likely considerable.[26] Bright and energetic, the young Lucullus was immersed in a world of epic, history, tragedy and lyric, as well as the vast treasure of Greek philosophical writings. The house of Lucullus was perhaps something of a small centre for the infusion of Hellenic culture into the Roman Republic; Lucius and Marcus Lucullus had a ready contemporary with deep knowledge of the vast tradition of Greek literature. Educated young Romans would soon become familiar with the martial and adventure epics of the ancient Greeks (especially Homer), the great corpus of tragic verse and the mammoth histories of the wars between the Greeks and the Persians, and the city-states of Athens and Sparta. Lucullus was introduced to the vast panorama of Greek literature and history, replete as it was with lessons for a young Roman aristocrat – lessons that the eager young reader would soon enough be able to put into practice in his own life.

Talent in Forensic Oratory

Rhetoric and oratory were also staples of the Roman educational system for young boys. In the business of avenging their father's disgrace, Plutarch compares Lucullus and his younger brother Marcus to whelps or pups of good breeding, noble hounds that set out to hunt down and destroy the wild animals which had maligned and wronged their father. We do not know exactly when the brothers made their legal attack on Servilius; the charge levelled against the augur was perhaps that he had misappropriated public funds while serving as quaestor – but in fact we cannot be sure what exactly Servilius was accused of having done. We do know that violence broke out at the court proceedings; there were multiple injuries and even deaths in the chaos that attended the case. Plutarch's comparison of the brothers to young dogs in ferocious attacks on feral beasts may reflect something of the physical altercations that disrupted the trial. But if Plutarch can be trusted – and in this instance there seems to be no compelling reason to think not – Lucius and his brother made a strikingly positive impression on the audience. Their entry into Roman public life did them no discredit, violent episodes notwithstanding. Lucius Lucullus did much with his education; talent in public speaking was a hallmark of a promising political career, and also had undeniable advantages in the military arena in terms of persuading one's soldiers to follow one's orders – an area in which, we shall see, Lucullus would eventually have difficulty, though not for lack of oratorical skill. For now, Lucullus was an acknowledged talent at one of the hallmark virtues of Roman public life, and he had all the appropriate credentials and trappings to embark on a public career.

A Credible Historian

For it seems that despite the acquittal of Servilius, the Lucullus brothers were admired all the same for their rhetorical skills and ability, and that they did not suffer any handicap for the loss. Plutarch proceeds at once in his narrative to focus on the results of Lucullus' literary and historical training. The young Lucullus became fluent in both Greek and Latin, and was credited with outstanding speaking and writing abilities both in and out of the world of politics and government. Some even credited him with composing a history of the Social War (91–88 BC) in Greek, no small feat for a native speaker of Latin. The subject matter, too, we might think, was no easy topic for historical composition. Indeed, to this day, scholars are often left without reliable ancient evidence for the bloody, bitter conflict; the Social War seems not to have attracted the attention and talents of Rome's great historians – not surprisingly, given the subject matter and its inherent lack of glory.[27]

The tradition of Lucullus' authorship of a history on the harrowing experience of the Social War – a war in which he would serve – is that the decision to compose a Greek history was the result of a lot or game of chance (the question was whether the work should be a prose history or an epic poem, and indeed whether it should be in Greek or Latin; the interlocutors with Lucullus were said to have been the orator Hortensius and the famous historian Sisenna – the greatest Roman historian of his age). The history of the Social or Marsic War is the only historical work credited to Lucullus in our sources. Plutarch claims that the history was extant in his time, but no trace of it has survived. Perhaps predictably, the argument has been made that Lucullus wrote no such book, or that the work of another was unjustly ascribed to the famous general. The Social War is among the least well-documented of Roman military engagements. By its very nature it was not the sort of conflict in which one could hope to achieve the sort of glory that could be attained by foreign conquest, settlement and plunder. It is perfectly reasonable to conclude that Lucullus was sufficiently fascinated by the formative military conflict of his youth to endeavour to write a history of the period. The composition of an account of the Social War would blend the young Roman's cultural and military/political pursuits. In short, we have no reason to doubt the report of Lucullus *historicus*.

There is a fascinating detail about Lucullus' literary and historical aspirations in a letter of Cicero to Atticus (I.19.10).[28] Cicero notes that Lucullus was in the habit of making deliberate mistakes in Greek in his historical composition, so that a reader might more readily recognize that the work was by a Roman hand. It is unknown to what works of history Cicero might be referring; it could be to the treatment of the Social War mentioned in Plutarch. Plutarch further notes that Lucius Cornelius Sulla (c. 138–78 BC) dedicated his memoirs to Lucullus, noting that Lucullus was better skilled at composing and arranging such a work of history.[29] The context of Cicero's comment on Lucullus is a passage where he notes that he is sending Atticus a sketch of his Greek work on his consulship. In contrast to Lucullus' alleged deliberate use of solecisms, Cicero notes that any mistakes in *his* Greek were entirely unintentional. A Latin version is also promised, and a poem.

A Book in His Honour

Cicero also famously named a book after Lucullus – the second of his so-called *Academica* or treatment of epistemology, the theory of knowledge. We possess this 'Book II' of a work that was eventually reissued in four books, of which only part of the first survives.[30] It would appear that Cicero's work – which opens with a brief survey of certain aspects of Lucullus' life – was a major influence on Plutarch in the composition of the opening of his biography of the general. Cicero notes that Lucullus gave no indication in his youth of the likelihood of a promising military career; he was, instead, a powerfully gifted orator and legal practitioner. Cicero credits Lucullus with having an especially gifted memory for the retention of facts and details, information that could be recalled at an instant for use in some interlocution or exchange of words. Cicero takes great effort to underscore Lucullus' devotion to literature and philosophy.[31] *Magnum ingenium L. Luculli* – the 'great talent [or native ability] of Lucius Lucullus' – is the subject of Cicero's praise of the man. One almost receives the impression that Cicero saw in the young

Lucullus a kindred spirit, something of a similarly gifted individual who might have won great fame in the courts – were he not to have travelled with Sulla to the East. Cicero's Lucullus hones his skills and enhances his knowledge by ready conversation with those who were acknowledged as experts in different fields – and in the reading of military history. Lucullus stands in the proud tradition of those military figures who were avid readers of the deeds of their predecessors. For Cicero, the principal result of this education was the splendidly diverse skill of the man. Lucullus is credited with great ability in sieges, sea engagements, land warfare and even the mundane business of outfitting and provisioning an army in the field. One imagines that Cicero is being completely honest when he says that he laments that Lucullus' manifold talents and gifts were absent for too long from Rome, with the great administrator and wise and just statesman unable to exercise his abilities in the capital. Cicero ascribed the motive of *calumnia* or calumny to Lucullus' enemies, enemies who are labelled *inimici* – the Latin word for a personal enemy. These hateful individuals are blamed for delaying Lucullus' triumph when he returned from the Third Mithridatic War.

The Loyalty of the Brothers

Literary skill and interest are seamlessly blended by Plutarch into an account of Lucullus' *pietas* that encompasses not only duty to his father, but also love for his brother Marcus. Lucius is said to have waited for the younger Marcus to 'catch up' with him in years for the sake of running for political office.[32] For a young man born into a challenging and often tumultuous age in the history of the Roman Republic, Lucius Lucullus was endowed both with a strong sense of family loyalty, and attentive devotion and concern to the timeless pleasures and educational wisdom afforded by literature and the arts. Lucius and Marcus would remain loyally devoted to each other. The younger brother would be responsible one day for overseeing the requiem for the older, indeed for taking care of his brother in the final stage of his life, when he suffered mental defect and disability.

Lucius Lucullus was from the start, then, a man of both deeds and words. His training would have been firmly rooted in the traditions of classical antiquity, of Greek and Roman literature and the arts.[33] In this education he is universally attested to have excelled. Lucullus' eloquence, we might note, is also among the signal qualities attributed to him in the only other extant biography from antiquity, the brief life in the aforementioned *De Viris Illustribus*, a late Latin work of uncertain authorship and provenance.[34] Eloquence follows nobility there in the short account of Lucullus' *vita*; we do well to remember that he came of age in a time when there were many men of competitive skill levels in the art of oratory and declamation (Cicero and Caesar prominent among them). Lucullus was born into an age with no dearth of exceptional, outstanding public speakers, writers and scholars, and so the praise of his skills that we find in our ancient sources can be taken as indications of an especially gifted mind and ability.

The Pursuit of the Beautiful or the Good

We may also note that Plutarch ascribes to Lucullus a devotion even from youth to the ideal of the 'beautiful' or 'good', or in Greek, τὸ καλόν.[35] This Platonic ideal may have been an especially attractive, appealing quality in his Roman subject. It speaks to an aesthetic and philosophical goal that stands in striking relief to the travails of republican political life. It is an eminently complimentary detail from the biographer about his subject. One of the important aspects of Lucullus' life to consider will be the question of whether or not the noble-minded youth would succumb to decadence and ill-repute later in life – the problem of the general's alleged descent into luxury and more hedonistic pursuits.[36] Along the way, we shall also find it useful to investigate the philosophical schools to which Lucullus was most inclined to give his support and allegiance. Lucullus maintained a close relationship throughout his life with the poet Archias, among other men of letters, and literature and the arts were always dear to his heart.[37]

Sulla the Mentor

Plutarch associates Lucullus' steadfast constancy and mild disposition with the trust that Sulla put in the young plebeian almost from the start.[38] Sulla was thus in some sense responsible for Lucullus' introduction to military life and training; Lucullus first served in the devastating, bloody war between the Roman Republic and several Italian city-states – the so-called Social War (from the Latin *socii*, 'allies').[39] The first war that Lucullus may well have experienced would appear to have furnished the material for his first foray into the literary and historical arts. If we can believe our extant sources – and there are no good reasons for doubting them on this point – Sulla was impressed with his young protégé both in military and civilian arts. Lucullus would impress his mentor both in his bravery and martial intelligence, and in his measured, eloquent expression and writing. The devoted friendship of the two men extended beyond the grave, as Sulla would leave the guardianship of his son to Lucullus as a provision of his last will and testament.[40] Lucullus' early life offers a somewhat odd juxtaposition of the mild and the violent; he may have had a reputation for the former, but he was witness on more than one occasion to the worst expressions of the latter. His defence of his father's and family's honour against Servilius demonstrated amply, too, that his mildness was not the result of a lack of resolution or cowardice.

The Sole Loyal Quaestor?

The opening of Plutarch's life of Lucullus, then, presents a devoted son and brother, a man of great literary and forensic talent, who soon enough becomes a loyal subordinate to a military commander of unquestioned ability, notwithstanding the serious controversies that would attend Sulla's life and political career. One of the most damning of the criticisms that would be levelled against Sulla was that in 88 BC he marched on Rome itself in an effort to defeat his domestic opponents. The Greek historian Appian offers a tantalizing note in his account of the Roman civil wars (I.57) that all of Sulla's senior officers abandoned him in his entry into Rome at the head of his armed forces – with the sole exception of a single quaestor. Scholars have considered the possibility, if not the likelihood, that Lucullus was the 'loyal' quaestor who remained steadfast to Sulla even in this most controversial and dramatic of military gestures.[41] Sulla was some two decades older than Lucullus, and may well have served as a surrogate father for the young man in the early stages of his pursuit of the Roman *cursus honorum*. We certainly have every reason to believe that Lucullus remained devoted to Sulla until the latter's death in 78 BC. [42]

If Ernst Badian and others are correct in asserting that Appian's mysterious sole quaestor is to be identified as Lucullus, than the 29 or 30-year-old officer may presumably have aroused some mixed reactions and feelings from his peers at his decision to join Sulla in the dramatic step of marching on Rome. For some, decisions such as this are what would have engendered the apparent suspicion of many of his contemporaries that Lucullus was something of a degenerate, suspicions that may have been responsible for his ultimate failure to rise to the same first ranks as Crassus, Pompey and Caesar.[43] Did some consider Lucullus' loyalty to Sulla to be another example of the same sense of *pietas* that inspired him to avenge his father, guilty though he may well have known his sire to be of the charges lodged against him? One noted modern historian has written: 'The revolutionary nature of the step [i.e., of Sulla's march on Rome] may be seen from the fact that only one of his officers followed him, L. Licinius Lucullus.'[44] If loyalty to a commander was to be praised, than Lucullus was worthy of approbation. The problem was whether or not Sulla deserved the fidelity.

If Lucullus was the only quaestor of 88 BC to enter Rome with Sulla in that fateful year, we have no idea what he did in the aftermath of his superior's taking control of the situation in the city. We are told that the Marian supporter, Sulpicius, was betrayed by one of his own slaves and subsequently killed. Sulla rewarded the slave by emancipating him, only to have him hurled from the Tarpeian Rock for the crime of having betrayed his master. Was Lucullus privy to this correction of what Sulla and he would have considered an unforgivable breach of *pietas*?[45]

What are we to make, at any rate, of Lucullus' earlier life and the possibility of military experience before his involvement with Sulla, the Social War and the quaestorship that would in the end last from c. 88–80 BC? We have no definitive evidence for any military campaign experience prior to the Italian War, though some have speculated that there must have been something on his *curriculum vitae* before he attracted the favourable attention of his famous commander (below we shall explore the evidence for his military tribunate). Like many heroes of the military and political realms, Lucullus was favoured by the time of his birth. Rome was in the opening movements of what would be the slow and inexorable decline and eventual fall of the Republic, a period in Roman history that afforded ample opportunity for valorous deeds and courageous acts, not least in the complicated arena of foreign affairs, where the domestic problems of the Republic found a twin peril in the clashes of Roman military forces with neighbours in both the East and the West. Lucullus spent some of these complicated, difficult years in the East, and others in Rome. On the whole, we shall see that his time in Asia was perhaps the most successful period in his life, and that overall he achieved far more in foreign affairs than he ever did in domestic.

An 'Optimate' Life

Lucullus entered what we have called his 'optimate' life as the grandson of a consul. *That* Lucius Licinius Lucullus served in 151 BC as a so-called *novus homo*[46] or 'new man', the first in his family to attain the consulship.[47] Lucullus was thus a *nobilis* or noble, though not, strictly speaking, a patrician. His family, after all, was not descended from the Trojan exiles under Aeneas who had made their way to Italy in the misty shadows of the mytho-historical past (we may compare Caesar's alleged descent from Aeneas' son Iulus). Tradition had it that the Luculli were descended from a king of Illyria, that vast region of the western Balkans that figured prominently in Roman expansion and colonization both during the Republic and Empire.[48] Lucullus' consular grandfather had a chequered career in Spain, the provincial playground in which he established the fame and fortune that would so benefit his descendant.[49] If anything, Lucullus would outshine both his father and his grandfather in the upright rectitude and reputation of his ways. While he certainly profited from his status as the grandson of a consul and his unofficial rank as a 'noble' plebeian, he would more than earn the honours that would accrue to the name he shared with his sires. Without question, he would be the most storied member of the Lucullus family. The fact is, however, that we do not know Lucullus' exact family tree.

The first Lucullus whose name survives in historical citation is a Lucius Licinius Lucullus of 202 BC, who served as curule aedile. No member of the family seems to have achieved anything of special note until the winning of the consulship by Lucullus' grandfather in 151. As we have seen, the son of the consul fared rather less well in political life, and it would be for the grandson to achieve the greatest renown for his family. We do not know for certain if the consul of 151 was the son of the curule aedile of 202, or of another Lucullus who served as *tribunus plebis* or 'tribune of the plebs' in 196. Lucullus' mother was one Caecilia Metelli, the sister of two consuls; Plutarch memorably describes her as simply being a bad woman, and there is evidence that her history of scandalous escapades led to divorce and certain ill-repute. Lucullus himself would have bad luck with women in his family, as both his first and second wife are said to have been of questionable moral reputation. We may wonder if any of this marital difficulty contributed to the husband's eventual reputation as a hedonist. Lucullus could certainly never claim to have a peaceful, virtuous home life.

Lucullus' grandfather had experienced significant difficulties with the plebeian tribunes in consequence of his actions as consul, and his grandson would become firmly associated with the so-called *optimates* or *boni* (we might think of editorializing labels such as 'best' or at least 'good' men), traditionalists who sought to uphold the prerogatives of the senatorial aristocracy. Noble plebeians like the Luculli were allies of the patrician old guard in this movement; their opponents constituted the *populares* or 'popular' assemblies. What some would deride as hypocrisy could sometimes be found in the different 'sides' that individual Romans took in the republican squabbles that contributed so much to the downfall of the whole system. Lucullus' grandfather had been a *novus homo* (cf. also Cicero himself), and yet both men were allied with the *optimates*. In general terms, the *optimates* were defenders of what they considered to be the *mos maiorum*, or the customs of their ancestors. There was a fair amount of *pietas* connected to all this, and given his history and what had befallen his family, there is absolutely no surprise in Lucullus' aligning himself with the traditionalists.[50] Events in the first half of the first century BC may also have contributed to a certain hardening of positions for Lucullus: the traditionalist may well have become far more traditional as Rome drew inexorably nearer to the Age of Pompey and the Age of Caesar.

We may take stock at this juncture of certain aspects of the training, education and background of the young Lucullus. His family stood at the intersection of the two great divisions in Roman political life, the patrician and the plebeian. In some ways, the Luculli were patrician in all but blood lines and name. The family traced its legendary origins to Illyria on the doorstep of the Roman East, and the noblest ancestor of young Lucius served as consul in the distant Roman West, in Spain. Professional difficulties vexed the lives of Lucullus' father and grandfather; both Lucius and his brother Marcus came of age in a world teetering on the verge of major change and the hazard of governmental instability, if not collapse. The first war in which Lucullus certainly participated bore all the marks of a civil struggle that threatened to tear apart the very fabric of Italy. His early career was dominated by the turmoil between the supporters of Sulla and his great rival Marius, and by the rising threat from Rome's increasingly aggressive enemies in the East. Lucullus' career was formed in the spirit of the domestic and civil uprisings that threatened to tear apart the fabric of the Republic. It would be developed and reach maturity in the nascent imperial aspirations of Rome in the distant East of the dream of Alexander.

Early Life

Did Lucullus know hardship or financial struggle because of his father's exile? Some scholars have cited the evidence of Pliny the Elder, who records a stray comment attributed to Marcus Varro to the effect that Lucullus never saw a lavish banquet at his father's house in which Greek wine was served more than once.[51] But we have no good reason to believe that the Luculli suffered inordinate harm from the banishment of their father. Marcus Lucullus was adopted by one Marcus Terentius Varro (not, as scholars hasten to note, the more famous Roman scholar and author of the same name). The reason for the adoption is unknown.

One additional, important shred of evidence about the early career of Lucullus comes from the world of inscriptions. *Inscriptiones Latinae Selectae* 60 praises Lucullus as the victor over Mithridates and Tigranes; it notes that he served as *tribunus militum*, or tribune of the soldiers.[52] The military tribunate had become an office more political than military after the army reforms of Marius of 107 BC,[53] but Lucullus' tenure in the position points to something of a military career prior to his service under Sulla in the Social War.[54] Once again we are without firm evidence for a particular date, though shreds of evidence offer clues of a more or less conventional approach to a Roman political and/or military career.[55] Lucullus may have served as tribune in 90–89 BC. At the very least, we can say that the son of a disgraced father had found a model for military acumen and martial science in one of the finest minds for war that Rome had ever seen. If Sulla's own résumé were to be examined, his patronage and promotion of Lucullus would surely stand forth as one of his most impressive accomplishments on behalf of the Republic. If Lucius Lucullus had a father after the events of 102 BC, it was Sulla.[56] Under Sulla's patronage, Lucullus would receive training in foreign service, an extended time abroad that would contrast with the domestic horrors of the Social War, not to mention the turmoil in Rome and Italy occasioned by the civil strife between Sullans and Marians.

Lucullus had the perfect optimate training in his service as quaestor under the consul Sulla in c. 88 BC. The quaestorship was the lowest rung of the Roman ladder of public offices, essentially a financial and economic occupation, with responsibility for treasury transactions and maintenance. The author of the Lucullan life in the *De Viris Illustribus* states the fact clearly: *Lucius Licinius Lucullus nobilis, disertus et dives, munus quaestorium amplissimum dedit*. Lucullus was not only eloquent (*disertus*), but also wealthy (*dives*) – and he more than adequately discharged his quaestorial duties. While there were the aforementioned, serious domestic challenges that confronted both Sulla and his young officer, there was also a far more perilous threat in the Roman East – the advance of King Mithridates VI of Pontus that threatened the stability of Roman holdings in both Asia Minor and Greece. Whatever Lucullus had done to merit the confidence of his superiors in Italy, he would soon rise to the occasion presented by war in the eastern Mediterranean in a manner that would leave no doubt as to his merit and resourceful achievement.[57]

Arrival in Greece

Greece enjoyed a long and storied history for countless centuries before Sulla and Lucullus arrived there in what was probably early 87 BC. While Rome was convulsed by the aftermath of the Social War and the *de facto* civil war between Sulla and Marius, Greece suffered the threat of yet another invasion from an eastern potentate – Mithridates had launched a wide-ranging, full-scale attack on his western neighbour, the doorway to Europe. Events in Rome arguably demanded Sulla's attention – but in the absence of bilocation, the pressing problems of the East could no longer be ignored either. With 'peace' more or less restored in the aftermath of his march on Rome, Sulla proceeded to Greece – as did Lucullus. It seems likely that Lucullus arrived first, perhaps as part of an advance, reconnaissance embassy to gauge the situation on the scene before the arrival of the new commander. Our knowledge of the early events of what would become a long and protracted engagement in the East – and the real chance for Lucullus' abilities and mettle to shine forth – comes largely from Plutarch's life of Sulla.[58] Quintus Bruttius Sura was the Roman commander in the service of Gaius Sentius Saturninus, the praetor of Macedonia. In 88 BC, he had engaged Mithridates' commander, Archelaüs, in at least three encounters over three days at Plutarch's hometown of Chaeronea in Boeotia – the famous site of the battle in 338 BC where Alexander the Great's father, Philip II of Macedon, decisively defeated the Greek forces allied against him.

Sura did well (in Plutarch's estimation at least) against Archelaüs; though Sura commanded a moderate force and was surrounded by potential threats and hostile forces, he acquitted himself well and may have provided the only real challenge at this point to Mithridates' advances into the region. Again, Lucullus seems to have arrived in Greece before Sulla. He proceeded to Sura's camp and announced that

Sulla was now taking command of the overall struggle against the Pontic threat. Sura withdrew to Sentius, his moment of glory now past. Chaeronea would prove soon enough to be the scene for another engagement of the Mithridatic war – and this time, Sulla would receive the credit and fame for what would prove to be a decisive Roman victory.

Appian provides some further details about the engagement of Sura and Archelaüs in his record of the war against Mithridates.[59] Sura is attested there as having performed well in a naval encounter against one of the king's commanders. In the subsequent land engagements, the contest was evenly matched until Lacedaemoneans and Achaeans came to the aid of Mithridates' forces. Whatever the exact history of his military achievements, Sura fades from the pages of the records of war, and Lucullus announces the arrival of the optimate general, who would now prosecute a war that had already cost thousands of Italian military and civilian lives across the East. The first record of Lucullus' activities in the East comes in the significant role of serving as spokesman for Sulla. The man who may well have been the lone senior officer to accompany his superior in the fateful march on Rome would now serve as his precursor in the midst of the chaos and tumult that was Greece in 87 BC.

There are some mysteries, however, about Lucullus' activities in and near Chaeronea in this period. It is not entirely certain that Sura's campaigns against Archelaüs occurred only in 88 BC; they may have extended into 87. A larger problem is the narrative of Lucullus' reaction to the sensationalized 'Damon drama' that we find at the very start of Plutarch's life of Cimon (the biography paired with that of Lucullus in his collection). The Roman commander of a cohort based near Chaeronea had fallen madly in love, it seems, with a young local named Damon. Damon eventually raised a small force of friends and companions, sixteen in all. While under the influence of alcohol, they assaulted the Roman and several of his associates, and killed the lot of them. They fled the city out of fear of repercussions and reprisals, and were subsequently condemned to death in absentia by the townsfolk (who feared Roman revenge for the loss of the commander and his men). Damon and his gang had apparently had a taste for blood; they returned under cover of night to Chaeronea and killed the magistrates and their friends – revenge for the condemnation. Damon's outlaw rebels escaped yet again, with more blood and murder on their hands.

Soon enough, Lucullus is said to have arrived in the area with an army. He launched an investigation into the whole affair, and ruled that the people of Chaeronea were victims and not guilty of any wrongdoing. He took away the Roman garrison that was present in the city, and continued on his way. Damon was meanwhile ravaging the surrounding countryside, and was a greater threat to Chaeronea in the absence of the Roman occupation force. The citizens offered a deal: Damon would be made gymnasiarch (the official technically in charge of training athletes) if he returned to the city. But soon after his acceptance of the amnesty, he was murdered in the bath – a significant local problem now solved.

The whole sordid matter might have ended right then and there, had not the Chaeroneans' neighbours – the Orchomenians – decided to take advantage of the controversy to do harm to their rivals. They suborned perjury from a Roman informer to testify that the citizens of Chaeronea were to blame for the death of the Roman soldiers Damon had assassinated. The city was compelled to invoke the name and aid of Lucullus, who agreed that the citizens were quite innocent. A marble statue was placed in the town market in honour of the saviour of what would later be Plutarch's hometown; the commemorative tribute was placed right at the side of a statue of the god Dionysus. The people of Chaeronea had been saved from the threat of terrible Roman reprisals by the intervention of Lucullus. If the biographer can be trusted – and again, we have no good reason to argue to the contrary – the Roman commander treated the local population with measured sobriety and respect.

The narrative is classic Plutarch, with more than a bit of local pride and respect for the Roman who had acted so honourably in his salvation of the imperilled city. The problem is that we are uncertain of the year of the events. The dates proposed for the Damon story are wildly divergent.[60] Some would prefer 87 or 86 B.C. Part of the difficulty of establishing the chronology is knowing exactly what Lucullus was doing in the area when he was distracted by the case of the slain commander and the Chaeronean rebels. Plutarch's life of Lucullus glosses over the whole period; we have seen that the *Sulla* biography offers the detail about Lucullus' virtual deposition of Sura as part of the advance mission of the officer to Boeotia. It is not clear why Lucullus would have been taking soldiers away from Chaeronea, though the simplest explanation would be that they were needed elsewhere on the front in a tense time.[61] Lucullus' adjudication of the Chaeronea case presumably would have taken place some years after the original incident. The soldiers involved in the Damon affair were almost certainly men under the command of the deposed Sura.[62]

Currency in His Name

Plutarch also notes *en passant* the economic acumen and skill of the young Lucullus in the winter of 87–86 BC, when he was credited with the minting of the money that was used in southern Greece during the war with Mithridates, money that was even named after the young quaestor (the so-called Lucullea).[63] Lucullus' fame spread widely abroad due to the swift circulation of the currency that bore his name.[64] Soon enough, the economic official would dramatically and appreciably expand his résumé of military accomplishment and victory, and Lucullus would not need coins to spread his name and fame. He would become a worthy candidate for the mantle of the Roman Alexander.[65]

Chapter 2

The First Mithridatic War

The city of Athens was the only Mycenaean settlement in Greece to have escaped the widespread devastation and social upheaval that heralded the advent of the so-called Dark Ages in Greece.[1] While the circumstances of Athens' relatively unscathed survival are unknown, what is certain is that the city of the virgin goddess of war Athena rose to tremendous prominence in the Classical Age, only to suffer untold misery and ruin in the Peloponnesian War that convulsed Greece in the later part of the fifth century BC. Athens was the city of the Parthenon, the great temple to Athena – and of the literary and cultural influence of Aeschylus, Sophocles, Euripides and Aristophanes, to name only the luminaries of classical drama. Athens had come to know phenomenal power and prestige in the heyday of Pericles and the great building projects in the years before the war with Sparta – just as it had known honour and renown for the great victories over the Persians in such immortal military engagements as Marathon and Salamis. While a shadow of its former self, Athens in the days of Lucullus was still a place of mystery, magic and mystique.

The storied city of Athens was an obvious prize in the Roman war with Mithridates. The Pontic monarch was in firm control of the locale and its excellent harbour facilities. Sulla, for his part, was in serious need of financial resources to finance his major military undertakings. Lucullus was a key figure in the economic work that made the siege of Athens both possible and a realistic operation for an army that was weary and far from home. Mithridates was interested in attacking Athens, just as the Persians of the fifth century had set their sights on the fabled region of Attica. Control of Athens and its harbour facilities would enable the wily king to pose a credible threat across the Aegean Sea. Possession of the Piraeus, the harbour district of Athens, would allow for extensive military operations that could threaten Roman grain shipments from Egypt, as well as general commerce and economic exchange. Mithridates, in short, was not content merely to control the Asian side of the map – he wanted a foothold, and a significant one, in Europe.

At this juncture, then, Sulla was not only in need of money – he also faced an enemy who had a significant geographic advantage. Plutarch makes clear what the problem was: Sulla was able to apply superior force on land, but Mithridates and his subordinates had control over the sea routes that were critical to the resupply of his forces in Athens.[2] Greece is a jumble of islands, both Ionian and Aegean, and

Mithridates at this point was more or less the master of the Aegean. The Romans had no real choice other than to engage with Mithridates in naval battles – and Lucullus was once again the man of the hour, the saviour for Sulla who would find the necessary means to ensure a Roman victory over the increasingly irritating Eastern enemy. Rome and Italy had only of late emerged from a state of serious crisis and near civil war, and the threat of an outbreak of renewed violence in the capital was very real. But for now, Mithridates was the pressing threat to Roman interests – the Republic was well on its way to becoming an Empire, and Greece could not be surrendered to Pontus, especially not the cultural if not juridical capital of Athens.

We should note that the Romans were in a significantly weaker position than Mithridates due to a relative lack of naval power. Mithridates had been able to seize Aegean islands and to threaten mainland Greece precisely because he had a credible naval force, against which the Romans had very little to muster. Mithridates could transport and supply his forces with little threat of hindrance from his Roman adversaries. The Romans, conversely, were constantly under threat whenever they tried to take to the high seas. Sulla recognized that if Mithridates was to be defeated, he would need the hardware and resources to challenge control of the sea lanes. Lucullus would be tasked with this immense responsibility.[3] Sulla's actions might also be a significant benefit for the situation in Italy, as pirates and Mithriadatic warships did their part to choke off Roman grain from the breadbaskets of Egypt and the East.

Overseas Mission

According to Plutarch, Lucullus was sent by Sulla to Egypt and Libya with the command to secure naval vessels and supplies from Africa. Egypt was at the time an independent kingdom, something of a remnant of the struggle for empire and world war that had erupted in the aftermath of the death of Alexander and the subsequent division of his realms. It was the possession of the Ptolemies, though by the time Lucullus would have visited the kingdom, it was really a protectorate of Rome – squabbles and internecine fighting between family factions had seriously weakened the standing of Egypt in the eastern Mediterranean. Libya had been fully under Roman domination since the final collapse of Carthage in 146 BC, and the whole area was thus more or less secure under Roman control – the closest and most natural source of military aid that Sulla and his emissary could invoke in the struggle against Mithridates.

Appian also records the embassy of Lucullus in search of support for Sulla's efforts.[4] Appian notes that Lucullus was sent on a secret mission to Alexandria and Syria, to secure naval assistance from local potentates who were famous for their people's prowess in sea combat. On the return voyage to Athens, he was to join forces with Rome's allies from the island of Rhodes. It was a long and dangerous mission; the seas were hardly pacified, and there was no guarantee that Lucullus would find a friendly, warm reception at all ports of call. It was in several important regards Lucullus' introduction to the challenges of the vast territory of the eastern Mediterranean, and the first experience the young officer had in dealing with the varied peoples of Rome's eastern borders: client kings, Greek colonists and provincial administrations.

The fact that the philosopher Antiochus (on whom we shall say more shortly) accompanied Lucullus on this mission has received some commentary from scholars. For the cynical, this was more evidence of tendencies in the man that were open to criticism, that Lucullus was more interested in the life of Greek philosophy than the hard demands of contemporary Roman military and diplomatic life.[5]

Crete

Plutarch notes that Lucullus left on his mission in winter (87–86 BC); the time of year was unsafe, indeed hazardous for navigation – a clear sign of the urgency of the mission. The waters were also by no means free of the threat of both piracy and Mithridatic naval forces. The first stop that Lucullus made on his mission was the great island of Crete, the storied home of the Minoan civilization that was famous for the legends of the minotaur, the labyrinth and the intervention of the Athenian hero Theseus in rescuing the youth of his realm from death at the hands of the monstrous bull.

Crete was not an entirely civilized and tranquil place in the early first century BC. It was a notable refuge for pirates, and the population of the island was not considered particularly trustworthy in the matter of supporting Roman imperial ambitions in the eastern Mediterranean. Crete was in fact still some twenty years away from complete Roman conquest. It is interesting to note that Lucullus apparently made a quite positive impression on the islanders. Crete was a poor place and unlikely to be able to supply much in the way of quantifiable aid to the Romans – but at the very least, the island could be persuaded not to side with Mithridates, and to remain effectively neutral in the forthcoming struggle. The history of the island had changed much from the days when it was the centre of the so-called thalassocracy of King Minos.

One interesting extant source of information on the part played by Crete in the military and political intrigues of the period is the geographer Strabo (64–63 BC – c. AD 25), who records (X.4.9) that Crete had anciently been a well-governed, well-managed realm (i.e., under Minos and his legendary thalassocracy), only to succumb to anarchy and piracy. Strabo blames the Cretans for doing more damage to Roman interests in the Mediterranean than anyone else except the Etruscans. Rome is said finally to have subdued the threat of Cretan piracy, and also the peril posed by the Cilicians of southern Asia Minor, who more or less succeeded the Cretans as the main danger to safe navigation in the region. Whatever the exact circumstances in Crete in the winter of 87–86 BC, it is likely to Lucullus' credit that the island would pose no threat to Rome during the Mithridatic War. Rome had good reason to be afraid of perils emanating from the ancient land. The Cilicians had essentially allowed themselves to be Mithridates' navy, or at least a key part of it, and Crete was more or less open to use for Cilician naval bases.

Scholars argue over the exact point of not only the visit to Crete, but more generally of the entire naval tour of Lucullus on behalf of Sulla. It is conceivable that one focus of the mission was solidifying support for Sulla at a difficult time in domestic affairs for Rome. But the priority was certainly the war with Mithridates and the pirate peril that was closely, indeed inextricably linked to the king's machinations in the eastern Mediterranean. It would not be for Lucullus to solve the pirate problem, and certainly not at this moment in history – his rival Pompey would eventually receive the glory for protecting the seas of the East. But if Lucullus was not destined to receive the glory for extirpating the pirate scourge, Mark Antony's father, as we shall soon see, would find not merely an absence of glory, but lasting disgrace for his failure to tame the problem.

North Africa

From Crete, Lucullus made his way to the south-west to the coast of Libya and the city of Cyrene – the so-called Athens of Africa (not far from the contemporary Shahaat). Cyrene was the legendary home of the great Hellenistic poet Callimachus (311–240 BC), and could boast an impressive literary pedigree and history in the Hellenized world that had emerged from Alexander's conquests. Cyrene is famous in Christian lore as the home of the Simon who helped to carry the cross for Christ. It was also the birthplace of Eratosthenes (c. 276–195/194 BC), the Greek mathematician, astronomer and philosopher who is famous as the author of the *Catasterisms*, a collection of star myths.

Here in Plutarch's account, we find another hint of the literary and cultural work of Lucullus.[6] No doubt Lucullus was delighted to visit a city of such literary and philosophical renown. But there were more pressing matters to occupy Sulla's legate, and he tended to them with skill and speed. Lucullus found Cyrene in a state of disorder and confusion, and he reminded the people of an oracle about the locale that was attributed to Plato – namely that Cyrene was difficult to govern when fortune and luck were good.[7] Once again, Lucullus is said to have been successful, quelling the trouble in Libya and receiving a warm welcome from the inhabitants. We have no idea exactly how Lucullus settled the affairs of Cyrene. From Plutarch's account, however, there emerges a picture of an eminent statesman, of a man who was able to impart a sense of peace and direction to a troubled realm. No doubt Lucullus' interest in Greek culture and civilization aided him in his settlement of affairs among the Greeks of North Africa. If circumstances in the eastern Mediterranean made it advisable for Lucullus to stay longer than he might otherwise have wished in Cyrene, it certainly would have served him well to be on good terms with the local population and ruling class. But he never had to pretend to be a lover of Greek culture; one imagines that his time in Cyrene was enjoyable, and certainly preferable to hazarding the dangerous seas en route from Libya to Egypt. Lucullus may well have been compelled to stay in Cyrene longer than one with the benefit of hindsight might have wished, but Cyrene was, admittedly, not an unpleasant place to visit.

Up to this point in the miniature tour of the eastern Mediterranean that Sulla had enjoined on him, Lucullus had experienced no hostile threat. That changed, apparently, when he departed Cyrene for Egypt. Plutarch relates that his vessels were attacked by pirates, and that most of his ships were lost. The biographer does not record what supplement (if any) Lucullus had received from Crete and Cyrene, but does note the initial fleet that had left Athens: three light Greek sailing vessels and three Rhodian biremes – a not particularly impressive flotilla, and one that might easily have been overwhelmed by a pirate force. Plutarch presents Lucullus as succeeding in escaping, and there is no hint that a better commander might have saved the day or won a victory. Appian observes (XII.33) that Lucullus travelled through hostile waters in a fast sailing vessel, changing from one ship to another in order to conceal his movements; nothing of this trick is in Plutarch. Again, this period in our subject's life is the stuff of classic adventure. Lucullus risked life and limb on his quest to support Sulla's efforts to secure Roman interests in the East. Lucullus was very much an underdog – and he was acquitting himself appreciably well under challenging circumstances.

Alexandria

When Lucullus arrived in the port of Alexandria in Ptolemaic Egypt, he was welcomed as a king, and became the first foreigner to be received as an overnight guest in the royal palace.[8] One might well think of the very different reception that would be accorded to Pompey, and to the eventual arrival of Julius Caesar at the height of the sibling tensions between Cleopatra and her brother Ptolemy XIII. Lucullus would in many regards end his career in a distant second place to Pompey, but at least his arrival in Alexandria would not cost him his head.

The Mithridatic hostilities had left the eastern Mediterranean in a state of convulsion and upheaval. And indeed Egypt was in a state of disarray, no less than its neighbours. The king in Alexandria was Ptolemy Soter II, who had the distinction of being the Egyptian monarch three times – his brother and rival serving in the intervening periods. Ptolemy had just taken the throne for the third time in 88 BC, and would remain in power until his death in 81. His brother Ptolemy Alexander I had left the kingdom of Egypt to Rome in his will; his brother had good reason to fear that Lucullus would insist that the inheritance be honoured, and that Rome be allowed to take possession of the realm.

Plutarch here offers more insight into his characterization of the morality of Lucullus. Ptolemy offered the Roman commander an amazingly rich assortment of treasures and great wealth, but Lucullus accepted only what was necessary for his expenses. He was offered the chance to visit the great landmarks of Egypt, the splendours of Memphis and elsewhere in the ancient kingdom, but he refused, citing the grounds that his commander Sulla was sleeping under the open air on the very front line against Mithridates. We are very far from the portrait of Lucullus that would be painted by his enemies; our Lucullus is a young commander of unquestionable loyalty to his commander, the quintessential Roman who is concerned with honour and sobriety.

Ptolemy was a not unintelligent king. He recognized the great peril in which he found himself, and the fact that he was trapped between the uncertain situation in Rome under Sulla, and the equally ambiguous situation of Mithridates' eastern exploits and would-be conquests. No one could have been more generous and lavish in his reception of Lucullus, but there would be no tangible aid or help from Egypt either. Lucullus would depart from Alexandria with nary a ship to support his fledgling naval operations. He was promised the security of Egyptian aid in sailing as far as the island of Cyprus, that fabulous, storied land where the goddess Aphrodite was said first to have stepped dry-shod from the sea. Ptolemy knew that the Alexandrians were the only power in the region that could hope to provide a counterbalance to the Cilician pirates and Mithridates' naval grip in the East. Ptolemy realized that he was in a unique position to serve as something of a balance between Rome and Pontus – at any rate, caution was no doubt the recommendation of his court.

Lucullus may have been immune from the hazards of bribery and any succumbing to luxury, but he was also shrewd. As he prepared to depart from Egypt, Ptolemy is said to have presented him with an expensive emerald. Once again he refused the ostentatious gift. But the king noted that the stone bore his own likeness, and Lucullus realized that to reject the present was to expose himself to the charge that he was an enemy of the king. He thus accepted the stone and the royal offer of aid for the journey to Cyprus – and along the way to the great island he planned to try to secure the precious support of additional naval forces. What is uncertain is the exact status of the relationship between Egypt and Rome at the time that Lucullus departed from the court of the Ptolemies. It is unknown whether a formal treaty was struck, or, if so, what exactly the terms of such a treaty might have been.[9]

There is a significant detail about Lucullus' quaestorship that is preserved by Cicero in his *Academica*.[10] Cicero notes that Lucullus was devoted to the study of philosophy and literature, even while immersed in his military and diplomatic responsibilities. As we have noted, Lucullus is said to have kept Antiochus of Ascalon (c. 125-c. 68 BC) as his companion in this period. Antiochus was an Academic philosopher and a student of Philo (Antiochus would also be a teacher of Cicero in Athens).[11] According to Cicero, Antiochus would speak with Lucullus about various books that the Roman would then eagerly devour. Lucullus' great memory is said to have served him well as he mastered the doctrines he was taught by his learned companion. Alexandria was famous for the library that had been established by Alexander's general and successor in Egypt, Ptolemy I Soter. One imagines that Lucullus and Antiochus took the time to visit the great wonder of the ancient world, to consult its riches and bask in the accumulated scholarly glory of the Greek world. First Cyrene, and then Alexandria: no Roman of literary tastes could visit the East and not be expected to indulge in the rich treasures of its cities and libraries.

Piracy

If the Cretans had had a reputation for piracy, they had been significantly eclipsed, we have noted, by the Cilicians. Cilicia was something of a lawless land at various points in the long history from the death of Alexander to the advent of Roman power in the eastern Mediterranean. At one point, the region had been a part of Ptolemaic Egypt. It later fell to the Seleucid monarchy of Asia Minor, though that house had never been able to maintain effective control over the entire region. It is perhaps no surprise that pirates soon found a ready reception in the coastal waters due north and north-east of Cyprus.[12]

Lucullus faced a significant threat from the Cilician pirates, and had already suffered one great defeat to Mediterranean brigandage. This time, he was both prepared and focused on either evading or ending the pirate threat. Lucullus displayed sound, practical skill in logistical organization and creative execution of a daring plan.[13] Essentially, he tricked the pirates into thinking that he planned to winter on Cyprus. He contacted the cities of the island and asked for support in just such a hibernation plan – and was as warmly received by the island authorities as he had been in Alexandria. Cyprus was a secure part of the Ptolemaic dominion, and was more or less 'safe' territory for a Roman visitor – but Lucullus had no plans for a long sojourn on the island. Instead, he intended at once to take advantage of favourable winds and sail by surprise for Rhodes, enforcing a full sail departure by night, with daytime voyaging under low sail to give the impression that he was lingering in the vicinity.

Lucullus thus avoided a direct engagement with the Cilician pirates. They would have had the advantage of fighting in their territory, and with superior numbers. Lucullus could not count on any serious reinforcements from Cyprus, especially not in difficult temporal straits. And in the general progress of the war against Mithridates, the Cilician pirates were at best an annoying sideshow, a tedious delay that could sap strength from Lucullus' forces and render him unable to assist Sulla in the primary goal of defeating the Pontic king. Having suffered one loss to marine marauders, Lucullus had no intention of suffering an even more serious setback in the waters beyond Cyprus and the Asian coast – he was on the 'homeward' arc of his return to Sulla.

Rhodes

Scholars cannot precisely delineate what Lucullus was doing from 86 into 85 BC. Some think that he must have spent some time in Rhodes during the winter, his clever plan for avoiding any defeat at the hands of the Cilicians having succeeded. For from Cyprus he certainly proceeded to Rhodes, the largest of the so-called Dodecanese islands – and another legendary place of literary associations (it was the home island of Apollonius of Rhodes, the third-century BC Greek epic poet who authored the *Argonautica*, a mythological epic in four books on the quest of Jason in search of the Golden Fleece). Rhodes was an island of rich history and conflicted foreign allegiances, and at present it was under naval siege and blockade from Mithridatic forces. We learn from Plutarch that Rhodes supplied Lucullus with more vessels, the implication being that the commander was able to defeat Mithridates' naval units.[14] Rhodes, in any case, was famous for its naval strength and the marine acumen of its sailors; a Rhodian naval contingent would be a most welcome aid.

The Lucullan victory in the waters off Rhodes was soon joined by two other major achievements to the general's credit: the securing of Cnidus on the coast of modern Turkey, and the Greek island of Cos, for Sulla's cause. Both Cnidus and Cos had gone over to Mithridates, but now reversed course and pledged allegiance to Rome through Lucullus' diplomatic overtures. The Cnidians and Coans agreed to supply more forces to support the Roman advance against Mithridates. Both the king and his Roman adversaries were pressing a war on both land and sea. Sulla was at present engaged in the prosecution of the land war in Greece, and his deputy Lucullus in braving the seas – and thus far, things were not going badly for the young commander. He had faced little in the way of resistance, and had successfully brooked many dangers. If his achievements were not the stuff of military legend, they were certainly evidence of a competent, careful prosecution of a difficult and challenging war. No one could say that Lucullus had not acquitted himself well. It is perhaps important to note, too, that we have no clear evidence for what Lucullus might have learned about the advances in the Sullan campaign, as communications must have been difficult (though not impossible).

For the time being, though, Lucullus was invested in island work. It was 85 BC, and he was on his return journey back to Sulla.

Cnidus was a Greek city that, like Cos, was of Dorian origin. Together with Lindus on Rhodes, it comprised half of the so-called Dorian Hexapolis, six nearby Greek locales that were linked by common Dorian ancestry and the worship of the god Apollo. Cos is the most populous of the Greek Dodecanese islands after Rhodes, and the third largest in size after Rhodes and Carpathos. The Greek medical writer Hippocrates is perhaps the most famous inhabitant of the island, which was otherwise quite well-known for the silk trade in which it enjoyed prominence due to its close proximity to the East. Both Cnidus and Cos had suffered the depredations of pirate raids and the threat from Mithridates' forces that had seemingly induced them to side with him. It was a time and place of conflicted, shifting alliances and frequent resentment of foreign powers and domination. Lucullus deftly managed the challenges posed by a confused and confusing map of allegiances. He had reason to be especially tolerant of the local population on Cos, as they had earned a modicum and more of respect from Rome for having resisted the demands of Mithridates to kill the Roman population of the island. Every new island presented a risk that Lucullus would suffer critical losses to his forces, a slow and inexorable wasting of men and materials at a time when reinforcement was difficult if not impossible. But Lucullus consistently showed himself to be a competent administrator and more. In some ways, this island sweep was the most successful of his military endeavours – it had a fixed goal, and he attained it.

Samos

According to Plutarch, Lucullus intended to use his Cnidian and Coan reinforcements to assail Mithridates' forces on the Greek island of Samos.[15] The biographer also notes that Lucullus successfully drove the Mithridatic military out of the island of Chios, without any assistance. Chios - celebrated as the birthplace of the poet Homer - had sided with Mithridates, no doubt under serious duress, but the comparative ease with which Lucullus apparently subdued it attests to a strong local sentiment in favour of Rome. To this same period Plutarch assigns Lucullus' invasion of the coastal Greek city of Colophon (in modern Izmir Province, Turkey), where he expelled and arrested the tyrant Epigonus. One may well imagine that Lucullus associated his work on Chios with the liberation of the birthplace of the greatest of Greek epic poets; once again, the literary interests of the general coincided with the military.

Plutarch is not informative about what happened in the attack on Samos. Some scholars have argued that Lucullus and his Cnidian and Coan allies suffered a reversal and were defeated by Mithridates' forces. Certainly the laudatory context of Plutarch's biography might have plausibly induced reticence as to the defeat – though the biographer was willing to note that Lucullus had suffered a defeat to pirates when he was in admittedly less powerful a position. Appian speaks of a pirate attack on Samos (XII.33), but it is not clear when exactly this may have taken place. It may well have been that the Samians were more inclined to support Mithridates than the Romans. But if there was a defeat or setback, it does not seem to have troubled Lucullus too greatly.

Whatever happened at Samos, the next major development in Lucullus' life in arms would be yet another example of the Roman general's sense of loyalty and *pietas*. Simply put, while Lucullus was in search of allies and engaged in naval combat, his superior, Sulla, had been destroying Mithridates on land. Athens had fallen, and the king of Pontus had suffered a series of setbacks that threatened the security not only of his invasion plans, but also of his very empire. Mithridates would lose his war against Rome, though the enemies of both Sulla and Lucullus would point out that he would be permitted to regroup and resume his anti-Roman shenanigans – indeed, by the time he breathed his last when committing suicide, he would have seen not one but three more or less discrete wars against Rome.

The Rebellion of Fimbria

At this juncture in the Mithridatic War, the spotlight turned on one Gaius Flavius Fimbria. Fimbria was a committed partisan of Gaius Marius (he was the son of Gaius Flavius Fimbria, who had served as consul with Marius in 104 BC), and an inveterate opponent of Sulla. In 86 BC, he had been sent to Asia as a legate to Lucius Valerius Flaccus, the provincial governor.[16] Flaccus was the *consul suffectus*, or 'suffect consul', who had finished Marius' term of office in 86 BC; he was the younger brother of Gaius Valerius Flaccus, who had served as consul in 93. Flaccus was an unpopular commander, and Fimbria took advantage of the situation by stirring up a revolt that resulted in the death of the governor and his legate's assumption of control over his military – which turned at once against Mithridates. It is not entirely clear why Fimbria was so hostile to Flaccus; some have speculated that Flaccus was seen as too friendly to Sulla. Certainly the whole matter was an ugly sideshow to the drama that was unfolding in Rome in the wake of the conflict between Marian and Sullan partisans.[17]

Fimbria, we might note, is cited in Saint Augustine's mammoth work *De Civitate Dei* (III.27), where he is given the dubious credit for having seen to the slaying of certain members of the Julian *gens* during the civil war.

The Pontic king soon found himself trapped in Pitane in Aeolis. Fimbria sent word to Lucullus to note that while he himself had a sizeable ground force, the latter had an impressive navy. Together, the two Romans could conceivably close the vice on Mithridates and capture the wily king. This is one of those moments where students of alternative history may have a field day with potential developments.

From the military point of view, Fimbria's logic was unassailable, and we have every reason to believe it would have succeeded. Mithridates could indeed have easily been destroyed by the combined land and sea forces of the two Romans. Lucullus, however, would in no way consent to assisting such a man as Fimbria. There was the question of loyalty to Sulla, to be sure – but also of Fimbria's fomenting of revolt and the death of the governor Flaccus. Lucullus was perfectly willing for Mithridates to escape, rather than to have his honour sacrificed by participating in a joint action with the murderous rebel Fimbria.[18] It may be significant that in Plutarch's account of Fimbria's overtures to Lucullus, the rebel general noted that if the two of them were to defeat Mithridates, the victories of Sulla would be eclipsed in fame and glory. If Fimbria hoped to persuade Lucullus to turn traitor, he had no sense of the best way to achieve his goal. Again, it was a matter of *pietas*; for Lucullus, Fimbria had demonstrated that he lacked this cardinal virtue. The fact that Mithridates was almost certainly doomed if Lucullus joined forces with Fimbria was of less account than Lucullus' no doubt natural recoiling from the idea of allying with such a man.

Naval Engagements and Tenedos

Although Lucullus was not interested in the proposed 'alliance', he did engage with the king's naval forces off Cape Lecton (Latin, Lectum) in the Troad (modern Baba Burnu in western Anatolia). Lucullus won another naval victory, which would prove to be a mere prelude to a greater marine achievement. Mithridates had another naval force near the island of Tenedos, larger and posing more of a threat. It seems that Lucullus himself was in a vessel that was under the command of an experienced Rhodian sailor, one Damagoras; bravely and memorably, the Rhodian ship sailed forth against Mithridates' commander, Neoptolemus, who sought to ram Lucullus' ship in a head-on attack. Damagoras skillfully avoided the deadly blow, and was able to orchestrate a successful victory over the Mithridatic vessels, which soon found themselves in flight from a conquering

Lucullan navy. Mithridates' naval forces in the Aegean were now in full retreat, scattered and disorganized. There was no longer a serious threat to Roman interests in the eastern Mediterranean from any projection of Pontic power over the waters. One imagines that the literate, eminently cultured Lucullus was more than aware of the significance of the waters in which he was doing battle with the forces of the Asian king; this was the vicinity of Troy, and these the waves off the coast where Danaan heroes had advanced against Priam's Trojan and allied hosts. It would not be the last time that Roman naval units would engage with the king's vessels in these waters.

The Price of *Pietas*

Fimbria lost his one great chance to enter the annals of lasting fame; Lucullus would not help him, and Mithridates would escape. Fimbria's own eventual death by suicide would serve only to highlight the hazards of living a reckless political life.

Some have seen in Lucullus' decision not to associate with Fimbria and cooperate in destroying Mithridates a delict approaching the level even of *maiestas* or treason.[19] The degree to which one accepts such a verdict on Lucullus is in part a measure of exactly the same question of the premium to be placed on *pietas* that would prove so central to Lucullus' own navigation of the realities of his contemporary Rome.[20] Of course one might find ready criticism of Lucullus in those who were opposed to the principles and actions of Sulla. To the degree to which one was hostile to the mentor, one would be eager to indict the loyal pupil.

Geographically, at least, the spirit of Troy, in any case, was everywhere in the air – not least in how Fimbria was noted for having massacred the inhabitants of Ilium as part of his general practice of slaughtering or at least severely mistreating those who either rebelled from Rome or sided with Sulla. But in Lucullus' present, Roman reality, Mithridates had escaped to fight another day, and indeed he would fight both long and hard for years to come, engaging Roman forces again and again in what at times would come close to seeming a rabbit chase. Ultimately, the great loss of Lucullus' career would be his failure to resolve the Mithridatic problem. One imagines that in hindsight Lucullus must have occasionally wondered what would have happened had he sided with Fimbria – but one also can reasonably conclude that Lucullus' sense of honour and Roman *pietas* would never have allowed him to sacrifice principle for expediency, even if the expedient might have spelled a very different and better future for both Lucullus and the Roman Republic. His enemies would have much to criticize in hindsight, yet his friends would expect nothing less of the man.

Taking Stock

Lucullus had spent the better part of two years in mostly naval enterprises, with a balance sheet that on the whole showed a positive set of gains for his Roman cause. He had proven his absolute devotion to Sulla, a gesture that would have endeared him to some at Rome even as it would have enraged others in a time of tense civil strife. He had acquitted himself well in the matter of luxury and succumbing to decadence, and had proven himself capable both of bravery and of creative trickery and subterfuge. We have no clear sense of what communication might have been possible between Lucullus and Sulla in this period, but there is every reason to believe that the two men would not have been able to be in touch about events in their respective theatres.

The so-called 'Valerian' legionaries who had served under Lucius Valerius Flaccus, later under Fimbria and at last under Lucullus, are a good example of the problem faced by commanders who expected their legionaries to serve more than the normal six-year minimum period.[21] By the end of their service, the Valerian/Fimbrian legionaries must have been among the most experienced soldiers in the Roman Army, and they had also seen more than their fair share of treachery and mutiny. Disloyal to Flaccus; untrustworthy with Fimbria; unreliable and mutinous with Lucullus – it was a sordid history for a military unit in the Roman Army, and a good example of the hazards of keeping men in arms in distant lands for too long. It was also a case study in the potential problems attendant on the development of a professional armed force.

Reunion with Sulla

Lucullus found Sulla in the Chersonesus, the modern Gallipoli of military fame. We have no clear sense of why Lucullus headed there; perhaps he had received word that this was to be the point of rendezvous to meet with his commander. It was now 84 BC, and both men no doubt had much to share with the other about the adventures of the preceding year and a half. We do well to remember that we have no definitive information about how much contact was exchanged between mentor and mentee during the long months of the Lucullan naval operations. Sulla had vanquished Mithridates' ground forces in Europe and was preparing to cross into Asia, as so many military commanders had dared or dreamed to do down the course of the ages. An agreement had been reached that Sulla would meet with Mithridates to discuss the terms of a settlement. The defeated king had escaped the Troad and made it to Mytilene on the island of Lesbos; he would now return to the Asian mainland and have a parley with Sulla. Militarily, it would seem that Lucullus had little now to do, the original purpose of his long voyage to Africa and the islands having become obsolete. There were significant problems brewing in Italy, and Sulla had no time to spare in a lengthy Asian campaign. There was no consensus on the Roman side as to what exactly should happen in the wake of what history has come to call the First Mithridatic War. As had happened with Carthage in the wake of the First Punic War, the Romans had achieved success, but no satisfactory resolution. The mid-80s BC were years of serious domestic as well as foreign troubles for Rome, and Sulla was squarely in the unenviable position of having to balance the two conflicting arenas of Roman endeavour.

Students of military history might well cite the settlement of 84 BC – the so-called Peace of Dardanus – as a good example of what happens when martial and political problems are left less than perfectly resolved.[22] Dardanus allowed Mithridates to remain as King of Pontus. Admittedly he would surrender Asia to the Romans, and both Bithynia and Cappadocia would be ruled by their own kings – but even at what the historian Memnon (chapter 25) fixes as the cost of eighty triremes and 3,000 talents, he would keep his kingdom (and his head).[23]

Mithridates would indeed live to fight yet more wars against his inveterate Roman foe, so it is no surprise that some have criticized Lucullus for his refusal to join forces with Fimbria in destroying the king once and for all. As we have noted, one can only speculate on what siding with Fimbria against Sulla would have meant for Roman republican history. We do well to remember that nobody could have foreseen clearly in 84 BC how long and drawn-out affairs in the East would become; how Mithridates would eventually join forces with his son-in-law, Tigranes of Armenia, and pose an even greater threat to Roman interests than he had in the days of the First Mithridatic War. Sulla may well have been eager to leave the East and return to the pressing problems in Italy, but he could not be faulted for leaving Lucullus to manage his foreign affairs. The alternative to the Peace of Dardanus would have been to pursue the king as far as he wanted to flee – and the time for that sort of frustrating game would come soon enough, for the man who was now Sulla's loyal and competent manager.

Financial Administration

Lucullus was responsible for overseeing the safe passage of Sulla's forces from Europe into Asia. He had proven his success at naval warfare, and now he was able to enjoy a moment of satisfaction at overseeing the triumphal march, as it were, of his commander into Asia. Soon enough Lucullus was compelled to make the transition from military officer to occupation force administrator. Having already proven his acumen in financial affairs in his service as quaestor, he was now entrusted with the oversight of the settlement that Sulla arranged for Asia Minor. Plutarch notes that Mithridates sailed off into the Euxine (today's Black

Sea); Rome would soon enough hear from him again. Sulla needed money, and quickly; the indemnities and other fines and taxes he levied on Asia – and for which he trusted Lucullus to assist in collecting – would be essential for his success in the forthcoming challenges he faced in Rome.[24] In the immediate moment, Sulla needed a financial administrator more than he needed a military conqueror. The uncertainties of domestic affairs in Rome no doubt weighed more heavily on his mind than the fact that the King of Pontus was soon to be ensconced once again in his kingdom, nursing a grudge and dreams of revenge against Rome. Sulla would never again meet any of Mithridates' forces in battle, although Lucullus would have more than ample opportunity to reacquaint himself with the king and his armies. Lucullus was reliable and trustworthy, and no doubt Sulla heard all about the Fimbrian plan to trap Mithridates. We can be certain that Sulla would have been pleased with his subordinate's filial loyalty to the Sullan cause and optimate refusal to side with such a man as the Marian Fimbria.[25]

If Lucullus had met his end in 84 BC, he might have been remembered as a military figure of moderate competence and reasonable success, a subordinate commander whose ultimate capabilities and potential were left untested and unproven. The complicated events that surrounded a major chapter in the decline and fall of the Roman Republic would soon provide a more than ample staging ground for the optimate plebeian to demonstrate his talents in the political arena. And the survival of Mithridates to fight another day would offer yet more opportunities for displays of military prowess and exceptionally versatile skills.

Chapter 3

The Aftermath of War

If Sulla acquired a reputation for severity and harsh treatment of his opponents, Lucullus' management of Roman affairs in Sulla's name redounded to his credit – at least for a time. Plutarch does well to remind us that the task that confronted Lucullus was inherently unappealing and liable to cause discontent. What was impressive was that Lucullus managed to calm the resentful, near rebellious spirit of his Asian charges and establish a modicum of peace in the wake of the travails of war. Sulla departed from Asia in 84 BC (he had some six years left to live), and Lucius Licinius Murena was made governor of Asia (he had already been governor in Cilicia, and his appointment in Asia was a direct result of the Fimbria fiasco). Murena would become famous not only for war against the Cilician pirates, but also for the brief, so-called Second Mithridatic War – a conflict that started because of the alleged efforts of Mithridates to rearm and prepare for renewed action against the Romans (83–81 BC). Lucullus was not involved in these engagements. Murena invaded Pontus, though some might say the progress of the war was rather desultory (it would eventually end when Sulla ordered his governor to cease further strikes against the king). By all accounts, Lucullus enjoyed a respite of calm government and management of civilian affairs. Later in life, however, Lucullus' devotion to Sulla would be remembered. He would forever be associated with the reactionary forces that had for a relatively brief moment secured the peace in Rome by brutal, unprecedented means. Lucullus may have kept his hands free of the blood, but the stain of Sullan association would remain. And some would say that the Peace of Dardanus was little more than a pause in a conflict that never really ended.

Mytilene

Peace was certainly not to reign everywhere in the East. Mytilene – the capital of the island of Lesbos – had sheltered Mithridates when he escaped from Fimbria's grasp. The island was not exactly ready to surrender to Sulla; it was a lone pocket of resistance to Roman domination in the north-eastern Aegean (at least if by 'Roman' we mean 'Sullan'). We are not sure of the exact chronology, but it seems that the Mytilenean rebellion lasted for some time, perhaps as long as two years.[1] If Plutarch can be trusted, Lucullus was at first quite patient in dealing with the

Lesbians, until finally even the magnanimous commander's tolerance of insurrection was tested too far.

Lucullus launched an attack on Mytilene, defeating their military units in a pitched battle before the walls of the city. Forced inside their fortifications, the Lesbians were compelled to undergo the hazards of a siege – always a costly and time-consuming endeavour for the attacker.[2] We have no details on the tactics by which Lucullus won his ground battle victory, but we do know that he once again displayed his talent for playing tricks on his enemies. Lucullus pretended that he was giving up the whole business of laying siege to the city – many commanders would have abandoned such a thankless task after all – and he sailed away. The Mytileneans opened their gates and proceeded to plunder the remnants of the Roman camp. Right on cue, Lucullus returned and defeated the Lesbians in another ground engagement, this time a far more decisive victory. We are told that 500 of the enemy were killed, with 6,000 sold into slavery – not to mention the fact that it was now Lucullus who was able to plunder the wealth of the island's capital.[3]

Lucullus had displayed calm and reasonable patience in the face of resistance; when pushed beyond his limits, he demonstrated amply that he could seize an island city and subjugate it in short order at minimal risk to his own forces. The diplomat was still a ready and able military presence. Some have argued that Lucullus did not, in fact, actually subdue Mytilene. If this is true, then he merely won a skirmish of sorts before the walls of the city, and then withdrew again and left the city to continue its resistance. But did Mytilene really lose 6,500 people to death or slavery and still manage to hold out?[4] Were there in fact two sieges of Mytilene, the first an inconclusive one under Lucullus, and the second the decisive victory?

The so-called 'Siege of Mytilene' is famous to history for another reason. It was at this time that Gaius Julius Caesar was serving in Asia and had his first taste of military combat.[5] The biographer Suetonius reports that Marcus Minucius Thermus awarded Caesar the *corona civica*, or 'civic crown', for his performance during the siege.[6] The crown was the second highest decoration in the Roman military box of honours. As the name indicates, it was awarded for the salvation of a fellow citizen in battle. Caesar is said to have proceeded to Cilicia for further service; he would return to Rome after the death of Sulla in 78 BC. Caesar had been the subject of gossip and criticism for his conduct at the court of Bithynia (where he was accused of being involved in a homosexual liaison with King Nicomedes), but his performance at Mytilene did much to salvage his reputation and establish his name as a respectable young Roman patrician of his age. Suetonius is our only source for the part played by Thermus in the siege. Is it possible that his attack was conducted in concert with Lucullus, as part of the same general sequence of events? Arthur Keaveney argues that Lucullus' siege of Mytilene occurred in

82 BC, and that Lucullus returned to Rome with Murena in 80 (in this chronology, he would have left Asia in 81 or even 82). In 79 BC, Thermus arrived as governor and completed the work of reducing Mytilene. Caesar would have been present for this second, successful siege – and not the unfinished Lucullan one.[7] It is arguably improbable that Lucullus won so sizeable a victory over Mytilene as Plutarch records, only to leave the city in a state of continued resistance that would be quelled definitively only three years later. The evidence we have does not seem to permit a definitive conclusion; certainly Plutarch seems to credit Lucullus with the defeat of Mytilene.

What is clear and deserving of emphasis here is that the available evidence supports the view that Lucullus was exceedingly patient and tolerant of the peoples Sulla had entrusted to his oversight. Lucullus was scrupulous to avoid crippling financial sanctions and impossible burdens on defeated populations – so scrupulous, in fact, that he would suffer grievously for his reasonable disposition. Mytilene was a significant headache for Lucullus, though not one, it would seem, that would cause lasting harm to his career. We may note in passing that like so many other places that Lucullus visited in these years, Lesbos was associated with literature, specifically Greek lyric poetry. Mytilene was the home of the seventh-sixth-century BC poet Alcaeus, and Lesbos was famous as the birthplace of the celebrated poet Sappho.

Return to Rome

Plutarch notes too that it was to Lucullus' great advantage that he was in Asia at exactly the time when Sulla and Marius were subjecting Rome to the horrors of civil strife and atrocity.[8] Indeed, an important theme of Plutarch's treatment of Lucullus is the question of fortune and luck in the timing of certain events in his life. The first hint of trouble for the hitherto successful young Roman comes when the biographer notes that Sulla preferred Lucullus to Pompey in the matter of the guardianship of his son Faustus and daughter Fausta in his will. Plutarch notes that both Lucullus and Pompey were eager for fame, and that the death of Sulla and the reading of his will occasioned the start of the jealousy and resentment that was to plague their subsequent relationship. Lucullus had been something of 'the Long Quaestor', serving for longer than the norm no matter what Asian chronology one prefers. One can easily imagine that on his return to Rome, he was eager to advance to political distinction and achievement.

We know that he served as aedile in 79 BC, an office he held with his brother – again; the story goes that out of *pietas* he delayed his candidacy until the two could serve together (of course he was also preoccupied with affairs in the East). As for Sulla's will, besides the fact that Lucullus was a cousin of Sulla's wife, the fact is that he was older and more established than Pompey at the time of Sulla's death. While there may well have been an intended slight (or at least clipping of the wings) of Pompey in Sulla's testament, there was also a natural place for Lucullus. If Sulla had a mentee, it was Lucullus; if Sulla could count on someone's unquestioned loyalty, it was Lucullus. It may well have been the case that Sulla did not live long enough to do all that he could to ensure a more secure political future for his protégé, though for the moment, Lucullus' advancement was not exactly thwarted or retarded. Lucullus' return to Rome in 80 BC was the start of a new phase in his life, a phase that in some ways would be an interlude between his foreign apprenticeship and his foreign command – and an interlude in which he would find both success and frustration. He may have been all too well aware that he left the East in a state of transition and potential disorder.

Curule Aedile

The fact is that we know precious little definitively about what Lucullus was doing in Rome in the last years of Sulla's life, and our knowledge is mostly derived from general information about the work of curule aediles. The office was mostly concerned with public works and the management and organization of the Roman games. Inevitably, the job was an invitation to secure one's popularity with the people by a lavish display of gladiatorial combats and the like. We know that Lucullus was subsequently allowed to serve as praetor in 78 BC – the year that would be most famous for the death of Sulla – even though technically he should have had to wait for a two-year period to expire before he could hold another office.

By all accounts, it would seem clear that Lucullus performed exceptionally well in the climate of late Sullan Rome. He and his brother were apparently popular civic officials, and no doubt Lucullus' achievements in Greece and Asia brought him significant praise and even glory. He had incurred no outstanding failures to besmirch his record, and he had no areas where by Sullan or other expectations he had failed to achieve some goal. His record might well even be favourably placed in comparison with those of other notable Romans of the same age. Some might conclude that he had shown ample evidence of great promise; if anything, his greatest asset seemed to be an ability to move equally well in foreign as well as domestic service. There can be no serious question that Lucullus was aided in his work in the *cursus honorum* by Sulla's patronage. Sulla had of course arrived back in Rome first, and no doubt his faithful, loyal subordinate Lucullus was one of the men whose careers he was interested in promoting, in part as a support to his own hold on power. A Roman optimate had expectations of office, of duty and political life, and Lucullus was of a disposition to execute his obligations to the best of his ability, both for the Republic and for his family's own reputation and honour.

Most scholars concur that Sulla's decision not to name Pompey in his will may have been a direct result of the dislike that most certainly seems to have arisen between Lucullus and his younger rival.[9] It is possible that too much has been made of the relatively scanty evidence of the Sullan testament. Pompey and Lucullus were able to work alone in quite different theatres for many years of their careers, one in Spain and the other in Asia. In large part, whatever tensions would arise between them had more to do with when Pompey was finished with Sertorius and, later, the pirate menace – and with the respective attitudes of the two men toward senatorial prerogatives and the pursuit of their own ambitions within the republican system. But it is also possible that of all the young men of promise who were left in the wake of Sulla's death, the old republican – the one some would call the last republican – trusted most in Lucullus. And the most trustworthy of his protégés would be the obvious choice for the enrusting of his family and the management of his estate.[10] Sulla may not have realized that by favouring Lucullus over Pompey, he was setting the stage for what might admittedly have been an inevitable conflict of rivals.

Provincial Options

One episode from this period is cited by historians as a telling fragment of evidence about Lucullus the man. Our source is Dio Cassius' Roman history (XXXVI.41.1–2).[11] Dio notes that Lucullus was finishing his term as praetor in 78 BC when he was chosen by lot to serve as governor of the island of Sardinia. He refused the commission on the grounds that too many of those responsible for managing provincial affairs were corrupt and given to financial greed and mismanagement.[12] It is possible of course that such sentiments were expressions meant to do credit to his reputation, even as he was really interested in a different or more prestigious post. Whatever the true reason, it worked to the benefit of his reputation.

A Broken Chair

Dio also indicates that when Manius Acilius Glabrio demanded that Lucullus' chair be broken because Lucullus did not stand in respect when Glabrio (who may have been a tribune; it is uncertain what office he held, or what dignity, that required the honour of a sign of respect) passed by, Lucullus did not protest, but in all humility stood and rendered his decision with his praetorial colleagues while standing – a mark of his great willingness to admit when he was wrong, and to submit humbly to correction. It is another anecdote, another tale of the calm disposition and easygoing nature of the man – a striking contrast to Sulla, and to the young Pompey for that matter. But for those who might unfavourably compare

Lucullus with Pompey, or Caesar for that matter, the anecdote might be telling. Lucullus was perhaps too enamoured of republican sensibilities and grace for an age in which it was increasingly unrealistic, if not impossible, for one man to aspire to be the champion of an ever sicker and more enfeebled Republic.

The late and notoriously problematic source the *De Viris Illustribus* (74) gives us another fragment of information about this period. Lucullus may have turned down Sardinia, but he did go to serve as governor in Africa once his praetorship was concluded. All we know about his conduct in Africa is that he performed his work ably and justly: *Africam iustissime rexit*. A superlative description for an apparently exceptional governor and administrator. Africa may have been a quite peaceful province, and no real challenge for the talents of a man who had already courted danger and seen action in the East. What is less clear is how exactly it came about that Lucullus was assigned to Africa, and agreed to go. Why did he refuse Sardinia (if we can believe Dio), but proceed to Africa? We have no conclusive answers to these questions. It may be significant that Plutarch essentially passes over the period from 78–74 BC, offering nothing in the way of summary even about Lucullus' career.[13] Despite his successes, he may have been viewed as something of a mediocrity (especially by his rivals), a loyal enough Sullan, to be sure, but perhaps not quite deserving of the signal honour that Sulla had bestowed on him by making him the legal guardian of his children. He was certainly not as ambitious a figure as the younger Pompey (or even the still younger Caesar). But by c. 70 BC, while Lucullus was still an ardent Sullan, Pompey had certainly distanced himself from the controversial legacy. Indeed, through the course of his life, Lucullus would prove remarkably steadfast in his views. While Pompey, Caesar and even Crassus seemed willing to conform to the spirit of the age, Lucullus would increasingly seem to be a throwback to an earlier time – perhaps to a time that existed only in the idealized, mythic memory of optimate traditionalists.

Africa Proconsularis

The Roman province of Africa was a proconsular province that had been established after the defeat of Carthage in the Third Punic War (146 BC). Vast in size, it stretched across parts of modern Algeria, Tunisia and Libya. It was a wealthy province, of great natural and human resources; Pompey had been governor there before Lucullus (82–79 BC). Africa was an especially popular province for retired veterans, who flocked to the territory to take possession of tracts of farmland that were part of the Roman military pension programme. If there is any answer to the question of why Lucullus preferred Africa to Sardinia, it may rest with the wealth of the province, and possibly with increased cultural opportunities.

Whatever his rationale for rejecting Sardinia, Lucullus did serve in Africa, and if he discharged his responsibilities with justice and upright conduct, he also appears to have done nothing of note – indeed, there may have been nothing noteworthy for him to accomplish. We cannot be sure, even, of how long Lucullus was in Africa. At the very least he served there in 77 BC. We next hear of him as consul in 74; if he returned to Rome in 76, we are forced to conclude that he spent a considerable amount of time essentially doing nothing of historical significance before attaining the highest office of the *cursus honorum*. Some would thus prefer to imagine that he spent more than a year in Africa, perhaps returning to Rome in 75 BC to run for office. Some have concluded that there likely is a gap in Lucullus' career, and one that can even be considered circumstantial evidence that he was not particularly ambitious or aggressive in his political pursuits – but this seems to be a hasty conclusion based on the tradition of Lucullus' later descent into indolence and luxury.

We do well to remember how uncertain we really are about various dates in Lucullus' career, and where exactly he was at a given moment of crisis. It is quite possible that the reason for Lucullus' apparent lack of involvement in certain major episodes in republican history was his absence from Rome at the time when positions were being canvassed and assigned. One might even dare to say that Lucullus spent both too much and too little time in Rome; certainly he knew his greatest successes and fulfillment away from the capital. Then again, his most productive years were some of the most difficult in the life of the city. Lucullus had served in the East, and now he had ruled wisely in one of the most important of the western provinces – even if it was also one of the relatively sleepier corners of the increasingly imperial republic. Still, the admittedly younger Pompey had served there too – there was no discredit in Lucullus' tenure in Africa Proconsularis, either in the assignment or in the execution of his commission. But of course it may well be true that Lucullus had interests in other positions, and that Africa was not high on his list of desired posts. We have no way to know for certain.

Nuptials

We may with confidence date Lucullus' marriage to this period as well. His bride was Clodia Pulcher, the daughter of the patrician Appius Claudius Pulcher (who died in 76 BC; the girl's brother gave permission for the marriage) and sister of the notorious Publius Clodius Pulcher.[14] We may glean some information about the nuptial union from Plutarch. Lucullus' wife was apparently of ill repute, and her husband would eventually divorce her. If she had a positive quality, it was said to have been her appearance and not much else.[15] There was even a report of incest between the wife and her brother.[16] Once again there is something of an orderly, even mundane progress to our subject's career, for despite his acknowledged talents and signal accomplishments, the steps taken toward the consulship were fairly routine. A marriage union was expected, and sometime after his return to Rome from Africa, Lucullus contracted it. In hindsight, Lucullus would rue the union; the Clodii/Claudii were a problematic lot, to be sure (the most famous members of the family, after all, were Lucullus' ill-fated, aforementioned brother-in-law Publius Clodius Pulcher, and his sister-in-law, who has been associated with the 'Lesbia' of the poetry of Catullus).[17] If Lucullus were known for his praiseworthy conduct and restraint, he certainly did not marry into a family of equal reputation. He would eventually divorce Clodia and marry again – although as we shall see, his second marriage would not be much better.

The most obvious advantage to Lucullus of the marriage was that the optimate plebeian had now entered into a patrician marriage alliance; the plebeian was now closer to the traditional haunts of power, and had a certain respectability added to his relatively humble origins. Some scholars have argued that like not a few patrician families in the late Republic, the Clodii/Claudii were in difficult financial circumstances, money problems that an alliance with Lucullus might have helped to soothe. We cannot be certain. We do know that Lucullus was willing not to accept the customary dowry for the hand of Clodia, but the reason for his generosity is unclear.[18] He may well have been smitten with the beautiful Clodia. If so, the day would come when he would sorely regret the infatuation. A Roman optimate was expected to marry, and to marry with an eye to political and financial gain. Whether besotted or misled, Lucullus certainly could have done better in the signing of his marriage contract.

Consul

The height of the *cursus honorum* was the consulate. Lucullus served as consul with Marcus Aurelius Cotta, the half-brother of Aurelia Cotta, the mother of Julius Caesar. In 74 BC, the situation in the increasingly imperial Roman Republic was markedly unstable. In some regards the world was a significantly more dangerous place than when Lucullus had departed for the East in the days of the First Mithridatic War. Now there was the threat of renewed war in the East with Mithridates. There were the perennially problematic Cilician pirates. And in Spain, Quintus Sertorius had waged a bitter campaign against Sulla's optimates that had stretched on for years with no sign of resolution.[19] Pompey had been earning fame and renown in the Spanish campaigns, but the situation was far from concluded – and so Rome faced threats in both the distant east and the west. Lucullus' provincial allotment was Cisalpine Gaul, 'Gaul on this side of the Alps' – the part of 'northern Italy' made famous in later years for its Rubicon border that Caesar would cross. Cisalpine Gaul was arguably the key province in the defence of Italy from any Spanish threat. If Sertorius was to mount an attack on Italy, Rome would need a strong defensive force in Hither Gaul. For the moment, though, there was no potential for real excitement and glory in the province, and Lucullus might well have thought the job was nothing in comparison to what Pompey could hope to achieve in Spain. We are told by Plutarch that Lucullus was quite worried that Pompey would eventually be awarded the command of the Roman forces that were increasingly inevitably seen as soon to engage Mithridates. In an ideal situation for Pompey, he would achieve victory over Sertorius in the western theatre and then proceed to vanquish the problem king in the East – and this is in fact exactly what would happen. The Lucullan nightmare of 74 BC would come true in but a few years, precious years in which Lucullus would have the opportunity to solve Rome's eastern problems for good and all.[20]

Unsurprisingly, when Pompey appealed to Rome for help in the struggle against Sertorius, Lucullus was adamant that he should be supported. The apparent fear was that Pompey would carry out his threat of returning to Italy unless he were properly funded and supplied for military operations in Spain. Lucullus was of a mind to do all he could to keep Pompey engaged with Sertorius. It is not clear if there was any definitive plan beyond this (e.g., what course of action should be followed if Pompey won a great victory and then returned in triumph). If anything, in 74 BC Lucullus must have seemed able and competent as an administrator, and less than impressive in terms of his résumé of military achievement – at least in comparison to Pompey. Plutarch notes that Marcus Cotta argued that the war with Mithridates had never really ended. The fledgling administration of Lucullus and his colleague was truly caught between two potentially massive external threats, with serious resultant implications for the political situation in Rome so soon after the Sullan-Marian civil war.[21] The Republic was not functioning in the manner for which it was designed – there were too many potential military commanders jockeying for supreme power in this or that theatre. And the rise of a professional army had spelled out its own consequences for Rome.

A Plea from Pompey

Pompey's appeal to Rome for help is cited in one of the more substantial surviving fragments of Book 2 of Sallust's *Historiae*.[22] Sallust notes that both Lucullus and Cotta were greatly distressed by Pompey's letter, partly because of the seriousness of the situation in Spain, but also because of the fear that neither man would be able to achieve anything great if Pompey was to return to Rome. They therefore moved quickly to ensure that Pompey received whatever he needed, and in this they were supported by the nobles (*nobilitas*). In some sense, Lucullus' career abroad would be spent waiting for Pompey and trying to keep Pompey at bay; the younger man would eventually arrive in Asia as none other than Lucullus' replacement in command.

This is the period when we first learn from Plutarch of Lucullus' resentment and bitterness. He was concerned about his own career and advancement, especially after his posting in Gaul. Lucullus was not without enemies in Rome in this period; Plutarch notes the senator Publius Cornelius Cethegus, a notoriously decadent, hedonistic former Marian whose way of life was a source of revulsion and disgust for Lucullus.[23] Lucullus openly confronted Cethegus, and the two were in a state of public estrangement and conflict. Sulla's premature, unexpected death had left a void of incalculable consequence in Roman public affairs. If the honour he had shown to Lucullus in his last will and testament was not only a token of esteem, but also an expression of the desire that Lucullus should succeed him in at least the political arena, then much was expected of the relatively young optimate in the present difficult circumstances.[24] Looming over all was the unresolved problem of Mithridates and the ultimate settlement of Roman affairs in the East. Both Pompey and Lucullus had their eyes on the great opportunities for political, military and economic glory that loomed in the realms of Asia.

Human nature being what it is, one might hesitate before thinking that Lucullus was motivated by concern for the health of the Republic in his wish to help Pompey. Certainly this would be the cynical, not to say realistic view. We can trust the reasonable enough assessment of Sallust that Lucullus was concerned about what the return of Pompey would mean for him (less likely is that he felt that Pompey would be a threat to republican government, though this is of course possible). Lucullus and his friends no doubt wanted Pompey to stay in Spain for some time. And stay he would, in large part thanks to the work of the consul Lucullus. But he could not be kept in Hispania indefinitely.

There is also the question of whether Lucullus was worried that if Pompey should fail in Spain, then Sertorius really would march against Italy, and he would need to take up his planned appointment in Cisalpine Gaul to guard against the Sertorian rebels.[25] This consideration carries with it several problems and assumptions. Was Sertorius really in a position to aspire to march into Italy? Quite possibly. Was Lucullus likely to have viewed an appointment against Sertorius as less desirable than an Asian assignment? Also quite possibly. But would Pompey have been viewed as militarily and politically finished if he returned to Italy, having been refused in his request for monetary and resource help against Sertorius? This is more problematic, one might argue, to conclude. It would have been very difficult to attack Pompey for the Sertorian mess, were indifferent senators to refuse a legitimate request for aid in prosecuting the war.

Whatever the exact reasoning, Lucullus wanted Pompey in Spain. And that is exactly what as consul he would achieve.[26]

Cyrene

We should also mention here that there has been some speculation that Lucullus *consularis* was a key player in the decision to make Cyrene a Roman province.[27] The matter is problematic in the absence of evidence, but Lucullus did have experience in the region, and Rome certainly was in need of stable additions to the imperial larder. It was a competent consulship, to be sure, neither spectacular nor particularly memorable in terms of achievement. An unremittingly negative appraisal might call it mediocre. But Lucullus was no mere server of time in office. In a difficult age, some might call it enough to have maintained both relative peace at home and much of the programme and wishes of his political mentor Sulla. Cyrene was likely made a province in 74 BC (possibly in 75). Lucullus was something of an expert on the place, having stayed there for some time on his embassy for Sulla. Cyrene was a rich place in both natural resources and especially food stuffs; in a Roman world at war, Cyrene was arguably a very nice addition to the roster of provinces. But again, we do well to remember that we lack solid evidence about the process and chronology by which Cyrene was reduced to provincial status.

Without question, Lucullus continued throughout his career and life to exhibit the virtue of *pietas* that had marked and distinguished his earliest public career. His father had perhaps not been terribly deserving of loyalty. Certainly one could be forgiven for questioning aspects of the Sullan settlement. But no one could claim that Lucullus was not loyal, both to birth father and *de facto* spiritual father. Lucullus did not falter in his resolve; he was not inconsistent in his positions. It is for this reason above all that he might well deserve the title of last of the republicans. Did Lucullus discern a threat to the Republic in the attitude of Pompey? If so, he certainly foresaw it in Caesar. There was likely no question that a man of Lucullus' pedigree would stand for and win the consulship. What remained to be seen was what he did with his term of office, and what foreign service would follow it.

Mithridates and Sertorius

Rome, meanwhile, was faced the real threat of war on two fronts, and it did not help that in 78 BC, Mithridates had made the perhaps obvious decision to seek an alliance with Sertorius in Spain.[28] Sertorius was willing to negotiate – at least, this was his public position – on the condition that he would receive significant territorial concessions in the East. Sertorius was a master diplomat as well as a capable military tactician and strategist. He was more than willing to engage in diplomatic overtures and communications with Mithridates, the Cilician pirates and even, eventually, the slaves under Spartacus in Italy. And he would come quite close to achieving a goal of erecting an independent Roman Republic in Hispania. Again, we do well to remember that anyone with a map could see the advantages to Sertorius and Mithridates joining forces – or at least agreeing to pursue a common policy.[29]

And, needless to say, Mithridates spent his time carefully mustering more forces and renewed materials for war; he knew as well as anyone that a future conflict with Rome was inevitable. If Mithridates and Sertorius needed to communicate, pirate ships were an easy and abundant source of diplomatic conveyance, for the Cilician bandits and other marauders of the sea were more than happy to ally with both against the Republic. No doubt the death of Sulla played its own part in the unfolding of international affairs; Mithridates may have felt that the time was right to strike in the aftermath of the demise of the great general who had chased him out of Greece. Indeed, if we can believe Appian's account, the death of Sulla was the major reason why the senate did not admit emissaries from Mithridates, who had come in 78 BC in the hope of ratifying the Peace of Dardanus.[30] They were simply too busy, it seems, with domestic affairs. No doubt Mithridates' representatives were incensed at the lukewarm reception. Scholars continue to debate why exactly the Romans were so curt and dismissive of the king's emissaries. It is no great surprise that Mithridates would have sought the company of Sertorius after such a rebuff – though we should be hesitant to accept the idea that the king had sincerely sought to ratify a lasting peace with Rome. The aftermath of the First Mithridatic War was simply a classic case of the problem of leaving a war unfinished. There was no serious agreement between Rome and Pontus as to where the line should be drawn between their respective spheres of influence. Appian is blunt: the preparations for what would be the Third Mithridatic War were soon fully underway, and the war would cost the king his empire and Sertorius his life.[31]

Mithridates responded to the rebuff of his emissaries by urging his son-in-law Tigranes to invade Cappadocia in modern central Turkey (Tigranes was married to the king's daughter Cleopatra). Cappadocia was an obvious theatre for war between Rome, her allies and Mithridates' empire – and in 74 BC, it happened that Lucius Octavius, the new governor of the nearby province of Cilicia, died unexpectedly.[32] For Plutarch, this was a critical moment in the life of Lucullus – he now had the chance to guarantee that no one else would be on the scene to conduct any forthcoming military affairs against Mithridates.[33] Pompey, after all, was still quite occupied with Sertorian affairs in Spain.

Eutropius' Account

The historian Eutropius has a brief, memorable account of the opening of Lucullus' consulship. He notes that in the year of the consulship of Lucullus and Cotta, King Nicomedes of Bithynia died, and that he bequeathed his kingdom to Rome. Mithridates subsequently broke his peace with Rome and invaded Bithynia, with a renewed wish to strike against Roman Asia.[34] Pompey's crisis in Spain added a major file of problems to the desks of the new consuls. If there were domestic problems to attend to in the wake of the dawn of the post-Sullan Age and the political conflicts that came in its wake, there was also the preoccupation of foreign affairs and threats. Lucullus would soon enough clearly devote himself to overseas problems; we can only speculate on how late republican history might have been different had he preferred to remain a force to be reckoned with in the capital. Times were troubled on all fronts, and the tribunes of the plebs in Rome were not about to be distracted by foreign wars – they remained committed to their pro-gramme of seeing the erosion of the Sullan constitutional changes.[35] In 75 BC, the tribune Quintus Opimius protested against Sullan constitutional initiatives that restricted the tribunes – it was also the year in which a young Julius Caesar was kidnapped by pirates, held for ransom and freed, only to return to see to the death of the Cilician brigands. Opimius would be prosecuted the following year and con-victed, and Mark Antony's father given a commission to fight the pirates of the Mediterranean. Another tribune – Lucius Quinctius – would carry on the fight against the Sullan traditionalists, directly tangling with the consul Lucullus and living to see a day when he might seek revenge over his optimate opponent.[36] The conflict between the tribunes and the optimates was a defining feature of Lucullus' political life, and one in which he was not always entirely successful in negotiat-ing.[37] In the words of one modern historian: 'In 74 BC … the consul L. Licinius Lucullus was made of sterner stuff [i.e., than Gaius Aurelius Cotta], and firmly checked the agitation of the tribune L. Quinctius for the restoration of further powers. Nevertheless the movement continued to gain momentum.'[38]

The Praecia Affair

The sixth chapter of Plutarch's life of Lucullus preserves a story that is attested nowhere else in our extant sources. Allegedly, the method by which Lucullus received his appointment to Cilicia – and, by extension, the best chance to win the command in any future war with Mithridates – was through intrigue and chi-canery with a woman of questionable reputation. There was allegedly one Praecia in Rome, a woman known for her personality as well as her stunning appearance. The senator Cethegus was absolutely infatuated with her, and would agree to no political decision unless she was in agreement that it was the right course of action. And so, simply put, Lucullus sought to flatter and impress Praecia, so that she in turn would make it known to Cethegus that she supported the appointment of Lucullus as governor in Cilicia to succeed the deceased Octavius. Plutarch admits that this course of action was in no way to Lucullus' credit; it marks, in fact, a different sort of critical moment in his life.[39] Those who would eerily trace all troubles back to a poorly made, critical choice in life might venture to say that the decision of Lucullus to employ Praecia in order to secure an Asian appointment was the morally questionable decision that began what would be a long march toward disappointment, frustration and failed aspirations.[40] Lucullus would set out for Asia to handle the Mithridates problem – but it would be resolved ultimately only by Lucullus' most feared rival, Pompey the Great.

There were those who thought that Praecia was little more than a high-priced prostitute, yet we have no way of knowing the truth of the matter in the absence of additional sources. We do know that it worked – Praecia was persuaded to support Lucullus, and she duly invoked her authority with Cethegus to win him over to Lucullus' cause. Once Lucullus had obtained what he wanted from Praecia and Cethegus, he dismissed them from his life as so many unnecessary accessories. The Roman politician and arbiter of civil affairs in Rome in the aftermath of Sulla's death would now have the chance to return to the East, to Asia – and this time, he would venture there on his own.

Chapter 4

The Third Mithridatic War

The year 74 BC was a decisive and fateful one in the life of Lucullus.[1] Not only was he in possession of the highest office in Roman political life, but he also secured the opportunity to return to the East and attain what he could hope would be the decisive victory over Mithridates. Pompey was still quite preoccupied with Sertorius in Spain, and there was no other serious contender for the command against the problematic Pontic monarch. Lucullus' consular colleague Cotta was given the province of Bithynia; his would be the task of guarding the Propontis and a key route from Asia westward.[2] Lucullus had a difficult task on many fronts. Plutarch notes that the first challenge to face the new commander was the fact that the men under his command in Asia had grown accustomed to a life of luxury and laziness. These had been the men who had been under the charge of the rebellious Fimbria, and were hardly paragons of virtue and soldierly efficiency. A fragment of Sallust's history records the action taken by Lucullus in curbing the improprieties of the army in accord with the *mos maiorum*, or 'custom of the ancestors', i.e., the traditions of Roman behaviour and practice.[3]

The First Commander

Lucullus, Plutarch informs us, was the first genuine commander these men had ever known. He refused to bribe them or engage in any sort of bargaining to earn their devotion to duty. He was willing to take decisive steps to eliminate the most problematic men of his new army, and to teach the others what it meant to be a Roman legionary. Seamlessly, it would seem, Lucullus returned to the world of the military, and now he was no emissary or legate, but the responsible overseer of the force that would finally – one might hope at least – settle the manifold problems of the Roman East.

Lucullus, it seems, could not be criticized in the early years of his new command for his insistence on discipline, rigour and military efficiency. It is possible that the war went on for too long, however, for Lucullus to be able to continue to maintain his expectation of unquestioned practice of the old virtues of the Roman Army. For the moment, however, there were pressing and unavoidable concerns. For the war began quickly, and in earnest. It would be the decisive engagement of

Lucullus' life, the principal event in a life spent in almost constant interaction with some of the greatest luminaries of the last age of the Roman Republic.

In 74 BC, Lucullus was ensconced in Cilicia, and his colleague Cotta – with a fleet – in Bithynia and the Propontis (i.e., the Sea of Marmara). These appointments were extraordinary; they were not made in accord with the usual allotment of provinces, but after a tremendous expenditure of pressure and appeal by the consuls. Within only four years, Lucullus would be in command not only of Cilicia and Bithynia, but of Asia and Pontus. The map of his power would begin to disintegrate in 69 BC, when Asia was restored to the normal senatorial provincial allotment list; that year would mark the definitive commencement of the diminishment of Lucullus' power in the Roman East. He would have something in the neighbourhood of five years to accomplish a mammoth task.

All of this would come all too soon for the optimate commander. But what of the immediate progress of the war? Mithridates took the initiative and invaded Bithynia. This he had done before, at the commencement of the First Mithridatic War. The historian Orosius is memorably succinct about this original invasion: *Bithyniam deinde pari clade corripuit*, 'then he seized Bithynia with a like slaughter' (i.e., like that he had wrought in Cappadocia).[4] Now he repeated his earlier trick. This was a perfectly plausible course of action for the king, for he might have had intelligence that indicated that Cotta would not be much of a match for a major assault. Throughout the struggle between Mithridates and Rome, the local population was left in the unenviable position of having to decide which side to favour. Fear and avarice could be equally powerful motivators; certainly the presence of either force in one's territory was a conclusive factor – even if loyalty was sometimes easier given than maintained. Lucullus could not afford to leave Bithynia undefended and bereft of help. Any plans he might have had for launching an invasion of his own against the heart of Mithridates' realm would have to be delayed until the king's offensive moves could be effectively countered. Plutarch makes clear that Mithridates had learned much from his previous experiences in war against the Romans; there was less concern with the luxurious appointments of his vessels of war (no room now for apartments for concubines and lavish baths); the army was to be concerned less with impressive display and more with effective weaponry and fighting techniques.[5]

We are unsure of exactly where Lucullus first landed in Asia; we are equally unsure of exactly whence all his forces were mustered. We do know that the situation called for rapid action. The Pontic king had a definite strategy to checkmate his Roman adversaries, and his plan had already been put into motion. Mithridates was eager not only to overrun, but also to hold Cappadocia and Bithynia – to name but two of his geographic targets.

Mithridatic Machinations

On paper, Mithridates had appreciable strengths. He was more or less closely allied with the Cilician pirates, not to mention a supporter of the Roman renegade Sertorius based in Spain. He had significant ground and naval forces of his own.

Amid these lightning fast moves of the king, Plutarch's Lucullus is once again portrayed as an effective diplomat. As he advanced into Bithynia, he had to quell the spirit of unrest among the locals, a population that was sympathetic to Mithridates, to the degree to which it was tired of Roman taxation and occupation. Unfortunately for Lucullus – and the state of Roman success in the East – Cotta was by no means ready to give up a chance at glory. Lucullus' colleague was apparently in no mood to surrender his opportunity to win some victory against Mithridates. Having withdrawn to Chalcedon – and having heard that Lucullus was on the way to relieve him and to bring much-needed assistance – he decided that he must strike now, and at once, against the king. His goal was that by the time Lucullus arrived on the scene, the battle would be over, and Cotta would have won the fame for having defeated Mithridates. As it would turn out, Cotta would become one of the more spectacular failures of the Roman engagement in the East in the waning years of the Republic – and he would face eventual disgrace for his actions in the war.

The Defeat of Cotta

We possess precious little in the way of specific details about what happened to Cotta, but what is clear is that he was decisively defeated. The battle was both ground and naval: by sea, Plutarch reports that the Romans lost some sixty vessels with no survivors; and on land, some 4,000 men were killed. Cotta was able to take refuge in Chalcedon, where at once Mithridates' forces prepared a siege. Lucullus would now arrive to help a commander who had cost the Romans thousands of deaths and the disgrace of the first defeat of the new war against Pontus. For Mithridates, the victory over Cotta served many purposes. It had immense propaganda value – the first clash in the war had resulted in a clear victory for the king. It forced Lucullus into a reactionary position. Any interest the general had in invading Pontus would have to wait until the Bithynian situation was remedied. Mithridates needed a quick win over the Romans; the pressing problem throughout the campaign, for both sides, was the question of supplying so vast an army.

Fragments of Sallust's lost history preserve some details of the defeat of Cotta. Generally speaking, the loss of Sallust's history is perhaps the greatest single loss to an appreciation of the narrative of these crucial years of the Republic. The focus of the relevant fragments is on the disorderly flight of the Romans to the walls of Chalcedon; Cotta's men were killed with disgraceful wounds in the back that they did not seek in any way to avenge.[6] Appian plainly notes that Cotta was no military man, indeed an inexperienced commander who was inadequate to the task before him. Appian reports that the Romans lost some 3,000 men in the fiasco, not to mention four ships burned in harbour and sixty more towed away by the enemy. Appian does not report the motivation of any desire on Cotta's part to seek glory ahead of the arrival of Lucullus.[7] The historian Memnon (chapter 27.7) notes that there were both naval and land clashes. In the latter, the Bastarnae – allies of Mithridates – defeated Cotta's forces; a similar disaster befell the Romans at sea. Memnon vividly records that both land and sea were covered with Roman bodies (he assigns casualty figures of 8,000 Roman dead and 4,500 prisoners from the naval clash, and 5,300 dead in the ground battle). Mithridates is said to have lost just thirty Bastarnae and 700 others. As often in ancient histories, we may wonder as to the exactitude of the figures, but there should be no doubt of the lopsided nature of the campaign.[8]

Mithridates had much to celebrate, but he had also left most of his kingdom more or less defenceless in the process. And so now Lucullus was urged – and quite strongly – to invade Pontus and avenge the loss at Chalcedon by winning a far more impressive victory in conquering Mithridates' home kingdom. One of the arguments that Plutarch records in favour of this course of action was that nobody had told Cotta to engage the enemy; his own folly had ruined his army and had subjected his men to untold privations. Why now should Lucullus be forced to abandon his best chance of ending the war for good and all? Why should Lucullus save Cotta when Pontus was open to his attack?

The Value of a Single Roman

The answer reported in Plutarch's life may be considered vintage Lucullus. One Roman, he indicated, was worth more to him than all the treasure of the enemy. To save the life of a single Roman soldier was of greater importance to him than to invade Pontus and to make Mithridates' kingdom the scene of an awesome victory. There is more than a hint here of the spirit of loyalty, that *pietas*, that marked Lucullus' early years. He was devoted to his colleague, even if his colleague had been precipitous and reckless. He was zealous to save Roman lives, even if another course of action at the moment might have ended the war sooner. Cotta was in jeopardy, and that was all that mattered to Lucullus. Episodes like this might well have led Lucullus later in life to feel that he was profoundly unappreciated, that loyalty and devoted concern for his peers and their men did not seem to count for much in the new order of affairs in Rome. Lucullus was a man of his age, and yet a throwback to an earlier time, or perhaps to a time that existed only in the dreams of republican moralists and scattered anecdotes of memorable *exempla* from earlier Roman history.

Plutarch also preserves a witty remark of Lucullus to the effect that he was at least as brave as a hunter of wild animals; he was not interested in stalking and capturing the empty lairs of his prey. The remark is alleged to have been made to Archelaüs, who had served as a commander for Mithridates in Boeotia, only to have abandoned the king's cause – the comment on courage may have been especially pointed, given the audience.

Pietas again, then, one might think, was the order of the day.[9] It was not at all unwise for Lucullus' advisors to counsel that he proceed to his Pontic invasion plans. On the other hand, to leave Bithynia at the mercy of the king would mean to jeopardize the Roman position across Asia Minor, and even into Greece and the islands. One could fairly argue that Lucullus needed to respond to the Cotta disaster, and not merely out of loyalty to his consular colleague and fellow Romans. Lucullus could scarcely afford to leave his rear undefended as he attempted to move deeper and deeper into the king's home territory. But the image of Lucullus as saviour of his fellow Romans was well deserved – and the attribution of *pietas* more than fair. Still, Mithridates' great advantage was the tremendous range of territory in which he could lose himself whenever necessary, an advantage that he would exercise again and again in his dealings with Lucullus and his subordinates.

Cyzicus

Mithridates, meanwhile, planned to move from Chalcedon to Cyzicus, scene of the famous naval engagement between Athens and Sparta in 410 BC in which the Spartan fleet under Mindarus was completely destroyed.[10] Sallust says that the king was *firmatus animi*, or firmed up, strengthened in his resolve;[11] Plutarch notes that Cyzicus had suffered the loss of 3,000 men and ten ships in the Battle of Chalcedon, and the spirits of the locals were at their nadir.[12] The decision to move from Chalcedon to Cyzicus was risky and daring, yet it was also arguably the correct strategy to pursue. There is also reason to believe that Mithridates had every intention of launching another invasion of the Aegean Sea at some point. There is no indication that he ever considered Asia, and Asia alone, as sufficient insurance against Roman assault. He wanted a foothold in Europe, and moving to Cyzicus was an important step in securing the routes to a renewed attack on Greece and the islands. Once Lucullus learned that Mithridates had proceeded from Chalcedon to Cyzicus, he prepared to shadow (not to say intercept) him, and he proceeded to the vicinity of the village of Thracia, mostly concerned with seizing control of the best routes for supply and provisioning.

Appian records that Lucullus had arrived in Asia with one legion from Rome, and that besides the two Fimbrian ones he found in Asia, he added two more for a total of 30,000 infantry and 1,600 cavalry.[13] The king was rumoured to have as many as 300,000 in his force. Plutarch confirms the Appian figure of 30,000 foot soldiers, but assigns 2,500 horse to Lucullus' army. Plutarch's Lucullus sees the tremendous size of Mithridates' force and decides wisely enough to delay an engagement (he is thus presented in marked contrast to the far less experienced, hasty Cotta). Delay and caution would become the hallmarks of Lucullus' military strategy; wisdom and prudence would serve Lucullus well in his military engagements, but would also prove to be exactly the qualities that would lead to recrimination and condemnation when the war seemed to drag on for too long, and when first one king and then another seemed to be running either away or amok in the face of a dilatory Roman pursuer. Certainly when he arrived in Asia, the Roman had significantly less manpower on which to depend than his royal rival and Asian adversary.

Celestial Omens

What happens next in the Plutarchan narrative is of particular curiosity. Mithridates had a large army, but he apparently had no interest in risking anything against an enemy he already knew all too well – the capable Lucullus – and so had prearranged to receive help from his ally Sertorius. The Sertorian commander Marius had led a force overseas to support Mithridates, and the Sertorian rebels now planned to engage the main body of Lucullus' force. At this critical juncture, some sort of meteorological phenomenon took place. Plutarch says that a large, flame-like body fell to earth between the two armies, shaped like a jar of wine, with a colour like molten silver. Whether it was a meteor or a figment of historical imagination, the point is that the two sides mutually decided to refrain from combat and drew apart, with Marius no doubt moving to support Mithridates' force. The place was Otryae in Phrygia; the event was like so many other prodigies and omens in ancient history – signs from the heavens that no dutiful, respectful and indeed scrupulous Roman would fail to ignore. In the present circumstances, the sign from the gods may well have been interpreted as a warning against pursuing what would have constituted something of a civil war. The Romans were a highly superstitious lot, very much given over to the alleged significance of heavenly portents and celestial harbingers of doom. Whatever it was that seemed to fall from the sky on that fateful night, it would keep Lucullus and the Sertorians from meeting in battle. Omens and portents fill the pages of Roman military history. One might well wonder if the story of the omen was in part embellished and exaggerated to account for what was a perfectly reasonable reluctance to avoid a major engagement at this juncture. A meteor could also serve practical purposes.

As we have seen, Mithridates may have had ten times the number of men Lucullus could muster. Plutarch reports that the Roman decided to take three captives from the enemy in sequence, and one by one to have them questioned as to the amount of provisions each man had in his tent, and the number of men with whom each one shared his store. By careful reckoning, Lucullus thus determined that Mithridates had about three or four days left before he would be in dire need of provisions. He thus decided that the wisest course of action was both to delay battle and to amass as great a supply of provisions as possible to feed his far smaller army. Lucullus was prepared for a long delay before he met his enemy, and he correctly gauged that the huge force of the king would not be able to stay in the area indefinitely without some means of support. The man who knew better than most how to provision an army properly and how to manage the logistical difficulties of supply and provisioning knew how to employ his knowledge and talents in the subversion of his enemy.

Cyzicus was on the shoreward side of the island of Arctonnesus, the modern peninsula of Kapidag. Alexander the Great was thought by some to have been responsible for connecting it to the mainland. Mithridates assumed that he could destroy it with relative ease, and decided to set out after dinner on an especially tempestuous night – hoping, after all, to escape the notice of Lucullus.[14] It did not take long for Lucullus to learn what his enemy was doing, and he moved at once to the pursuit, though being careful and prudent in refraining from falling on the rearguard of the king. Lucullus realized that the practicalities of supplies were once again a key factor; Mithridates could lay siege to Cyzicus, but both the nature of the geography of the place and the supply needs of the king's massive army meant that the Romans could relatively easily launch a blockade of their own to keep Mithridates' army from foraging and being resupplied. It was now and only now, Plutarch reports, that Lucullus announced to his men that victory was at hand, and that within a few days the Romans would win without the loss of any men.

Some scholars have asked why Mithridates was so concerned with Cyzicus, especially when he no doubt was all too aware of his supply constraints. Strategic considerations may have outweighed all others here. There were provisions of food in the city, of course, though Mithridates could not have counted on the relatively small stores of Cyzicus to help for very long, given the sheer size of his force. Most scholars agree that Mithridates was intent on capturing as much land as possible, as quickly as possible – all the better for any possible bargaining later. The king needed to be cautious and even dilatory in facing Lucullus, and lightning fast in seizing as much ground as he could.

For it is clear that Mithridates did not feel that he was in a position to force an attack on Lucullus, numerically superior forces notwithstanding – no doubt a sizeable number of the king's men were no match for the Roman legionaries. The king simply had quantity and not quality. It is also clear that Lucullus was able throughout these early operations of the war to pitch his camp in favourable locations. Roman military scientists gave great consideration to the problem of where best to pitch a camp, and how best to fortify such a locale against the enemy, and Lucullus was well versed in such practical matters.

Some of Lucullus' luck in this engagement with the king came as a result of the mysterious machinations of Lucius Magius, a Roman agent to Mithridates who convinced the king that Lucullus' Fimbrian legions were interested in defecting to the Pontic cause. We have no idea why Magius said this. There is no certain evidence that he assumed that the king would trust him, fail miserably in his endeavours, and then he would be able to defect to Lucullus.[15] Our ancient evidence is scanty on the matter, and Magius may well have been playing both sides against each other. Whatever the rationale, Mithridates listened to Magius, and Lucullus was able to seize favourable ground.

The siege of Cyzicus was another joint land and sea operation. Plutarch reports that Mithridates had ten camps of infantry assigned to the task, as well as ships ready to enforce a blockade. The citizens of Cyzicus were ready to stand firm and wait for relief from Lucullus – but they were tricked by the enemy, who insisted that the Roman camp they could see in the far distance was actually a force from Tigranes of Armenians and Medes who had come to assist Mithridates. Lucullus was aware of the desperate state of the town, and the psychological aspect of warfare. We are told that he sent a Roman soldier on a harrowing mission through enemy lines, complete with the use of a flotation device to cover some 7 miles by sea to bring news to Cyzicus that Lucullus was indeed on his way to relieve them.[16] Plutarch records other similar anecdotes related to the attitude of the citizenry: notably, a boy who escaped from captivity arrived in town and laughed when he was asked where Lucullus was; he pointed out the Roman camp to them, thereby encouraging them with the hope of imminent help. A messenger from Archelaüs was also sent, though he was less readily believed (it is possible that this man was the same as the soldier on the makeshift raft).[17]

Persephone's Intervention

The goddess Persephone is also said to have provided aid to the Roman side. Persephone was the daughter of Demeter, famous for her abduction by Hades and her status as the queen of the underworld. Her festival was at hand, and the people of Cyzicus were in such desperate straits that they lacked the black heifer proper to her sacrificial rites. They prepared nonetheless to carry out the liturgy for the goddess, and fashioned a black heifer as a sacrificial victim from dough. To their shock, the black heifer that had been raised for the dubious honour swam across the strait and presented itself for slaughter. The goddess confirmed the portent by appearing in a dream to a town official with the word that she was indeed at hand with both the victim and tidings of great joy regarding the fate of the city. Soon a mighty wind rose up, and the king's siege engines were toppled by the force of the blasts. Great expense and effort were lost in a relatively short amount of time; it seemed as if the goddess herself had acted in support of the besieged city.

The Persephone story is an even more dramatic version of the same kind of omen that was said to have kept apart the forces of Lucullus and Marius. It is certainly plausible that there was a storm that wreaked havoc on Mithridates' siege engines, and the tale of the goddess could easily have been invented *ex post facto* in light of the festival and the timing of the fortuitous tempest. Persephone was a goddess associated with death as well as rebirth; she was an infernal deity, an underworld immortal whose omens were especially frightful. In any case, the king's war machinery was apparently ruined.

Appian provides the most detailed account of the king's siege engines, and the most informative narrative of what led to the destruction of the machines.[18] Mithridates is said to have had a tower some hundred cubits high, from which there arose another tower that could fire catapult shots, stones and missiles. Two quinquereme vessels in the strait supported yet another tower, complete with a bridge that could be used by would-be attackers. Rams and other devices only added to the mighty force. There was also a human dimension to the siege, as Mithridates is said to have had 3,000 prisoners from the town who were sent to the walls and made to argue in favour of a surrender. Appian notes that the general Pisistratus told them that unfortunately they were already lost to Cyzicus as prisoners, and must therefore accept their fate with courage and bravery.

Four of Mithridates' men are said to have used the ship bridge to try to assail the walls. The defenders were taken by surprise, but fortunately for them, Mithridates' men were quite slow in following up on the attack, and the four front-line attackers were thrown over the wall. Burning pitch was hurled against the ships. Water and vinegar were used against the flames from the landward siege engines. Mithridates did manage to breach the wall with fire, but the heat of the conflagration was such that none of his men were in a hurry to rush through to invade the town, and by night the defenders were able to patch the wall successfully. This is the moment when the wind is said to have struck the siege engines.

Appian tells the same Persephone story that may be found in Plutarch, with the added information that the king was warned by his men to abandon the siege in light of the sacred status of the locale. He proceeded instead to the construction of more walls and more tunnels to seek to breach the city's defences. Appian reports that some of the king's horses were weak from lack of food – a reminder of the problem of supplies for the huge army – and were fallen upon by Lucullus as they crossed the River Rhyndacus. Some 15,000 men were said to have been captured, along with 6,000 horses and a significant amount of baggage. If we can believe Sallust (who is cited by Plutarch here), it is possible that the taking of pack animals and cavalry equipment at the Rhyndacus marked the first time that two-humped camels were seen by the Romans; Lucullus may thus be said to have introduced the animal to the Republic.[19] Plutarch is incredulous, thinking it likely that the Romans had seen the animal in previous engagements.

Plutarch's version of the military operation at the river, at any rate, is the most detailed extant account. Mithridates had decided to send away both cavalry and disabled soldiers, in the hope of reducing the supply burden on his main army. Lucullus learned of the king's plan, and set out despite stormy weather with ten cohorts of infantry and a cavalry force. It was the winter of 73–72 BC, and snow was falling; some men were overcome by frostbite and the cold, and forced to be left behind. But the victory was so great that women from the nearby town of Apollonia are said to have come out to plunder the battlefield.

Persephone was not the only goddess who was involved in the defence of Cyzicus. Plutarch relates that the goddess Athena – the pre-eminent battle goddess – appeared to the citizens of Ilium (i.e., Troy) in a dream, complete with a torn robe and perspiration on her body, and told them that she had just come from the defence of Cyzicus.[20]

Famine and Plague

The hungry horses of the king were but a symptom of the more systemic problem of hunger and want in Mithridates' camp. Lucullus was playing a delaying game that was focused on depriving the monarch of supplies. Plutarch notes that the king's generals were part of the problem, refusing to tell him just how bad the situation was (they may have been afraid for their jobs and lives if Mithridates decided that they were less than diligent stewards of his resources and affairs), but soon enough no deception or concealment could keep the problem from the king's notice, especially given the reports of cannibalism that emerged from the army. Unburied corpses are said to have spread disease and plague among the soldiery.[21] The king was incensed that a relatively minor locale was proving to be so difficult; sieges, after all, are notoriously tedious and difficult to manage, and in this case the army of Lucullus was a constant threat, always nearby and yet never willing to engage in force. Sallust reports that illnesses were also rampant on account of how the army was forced to resort to unaccustomed food (possibly herbs or grasses).[22] If we can believe the evidence of the grammarian Servius, the plague during the siege of Cyzicus was described by Sallust in a memorable style that was of great influence on Virgil in his account of the cattle plague at Noricum in his poem the *Georgics*.[23]

Memnon (chapter 28) says that Lucullus killed many thousands of the king's men at Cyzicus, and captured 13,000. Famine is mentioned as but one of Mithridates' myriad problems.[24]

The winter of 73–72 BC was not an easy one for King Mithridates, and the series of setbacks after his victory at Chalcedon seem to have induced him to decide to retreat from the scene.[25] The staggering losses at the Rhyndacus no doubt played a part in this decision, but the problem of supplying the army was the more systemic threat to his chances for victory. The people of Cyzicus could boast that they had survived one of the most massive sieges in ancient history, and they credited Lucullus as much as themselves with the achievement. And in fact the siege of Cyzicus represented a reversal of the normal pattern of siege warfare, as thanks to Lucullus, the besieger and not the besieged was afflicted with the pangs of hunger and want. Games were established in Cyzicus in honour of the Roman general, games that Appian says were still being celebrated in his day in Lucullus' name.[26]

Plutarch notes that Mithridates was interested in deterring Lucullus from pursuing him, and so he assigned his admiral, Aristonicus, the task of seeing to it that a diversion could be created on water. Mithridates had once before crossed the Aegean in the hopes of invading Greece; the hope now was that the threat of naval action against Roman interests in Greece and the islands would be sufficient to keep Lucullus busy and away from the king. The Aristonicus affair was mostly diversionary, but there was also the business of maintaining even a pretence of a threat against Greek waters, for Mithridates, we might well think, still entertained dreams and ambitions of threatening Europe.

Granicus *Redivivus*

Aristonicus was apparently carrying a sizeable sum of gold that was intended to serve as a bribe for Roman forces, but unfortunately for the king and his agent, he was betrayed to Lucullus and the money lost. Buoyed by this easy victory, Lucullus is said to have fallen on the generals of Mithridates who were busy extracting the land forces from the siege of Cyzicus. An engagement at the River Granicus resulted in the deaths of 20,000 of the king's men and a huge number of prisoners. No doubt it occurred to Lucullus that his victory was achieved at the very same river that had seen a mighty achievement of Alexander the Great against the Persian Empire in 334 BC – the first of the three major battles that the Macedonian king fought against Persia. Interestingly, Appian does not mention the Granicus engagement, but a similar loss of the king's forces at the River Aesepus. The whole effort at extraction had become a fiasco that was costing the king dearly in both lives and supplies – not to mention his reputation and honour.

Lucullus was winning victory after victory, and at relatively minor cost, yet the king, however, was as elusive as ever.

A Venusian Dream

Lucullus enjoyed a miniature triumph when he entered Cyzicus after the vanquishing of the king's forces at the Granicus. From there he proceeded to the Troad and the Hellespont with the intention of building a naval force to complement his land army (he may have been interested in settling the naval issue once and for all, and in keeping Mithridates from entertaining any dreams of regaining a foothold in the Aegean). Plutarch relates that the goddess Aphrodite appeared to him in a dream, asking why the lion was asleep while the fawns were so near for the taking. At once Lucullus rose from sleep and informed his men of the vision; soon there were messengers from Ilium who reported that the king had thirteen ships that were making their way to the island of Lemnos.[27] Lucullus moved at once to intercept the vessels, and he was successful in capturing them and killed their commander Isodorus. Lucullus knew that these units were sailing off in the hope of making a rendezvous with other elements of the king's navy; he thus set off in pursuit of these additional vessels. It turned out that the Sertorian commander Marius was with these ships. They had decided to draw up the boats on land and fight from the decks. Lucullus was forced to resort to trying to land some of his units behind them; these were able to attack from the rear and to help secure another victory. Lucullus gave strict orders to his men to kill the man with 'one eye' – that is, the commander Marius. The Sertorian was taken among the captives, and Lucullus ensured that he was slain in the aftermath as if he was a disgraced prisoner – Plutarch notes that Lucullus was especially concerned that Marius pay the price for his disloyalty. More victories followed, with Lucullus amply proving his talents both on land and sea – indeed, he stands as one of the most versatile figures in Roman military history.[28]

The other commanders of Mithridates' naval forces were Alexander the Paphlagonian and Dionysius the Eunuch. Appian reports that the three leaders were captured in a cave on Lemnos, where Dionysius took poison, while Alexander was preserved for marching in Lucullus' triumphal procession.[29] The official reason given for the killing of Marius was that a Roman senator was better off dead on the spot than kept alive for a triumph. Letters were sent in laurel leaves to Rome to announce the victory – a sorely needed bit of good news in the capital.

If we can believe Appian, Mithridates suffered another loss – and a stunning one – as he tried to escape to Pontus.[30] Another storm hit his ships, and 10,000 men were killed with a loss of sixty vessels. Plutarch does not specify the numbers of the losses, but notes that the coast was marked by wreckage for many days from the disaster. Both Appian and Plutarch preserve the detail that the king's own flagship was in such serious straits that the monarch was forced to surrender it for a light pirate craft. Plutarch once again notes the influence of the gods. He relates that Mithridates' men had plundered a shrine of Artemis and desecrated her image, and so in consequence she sent the storm that wrecked the king's fleet.[31] Orosius notes (VI.2.23) that at this same time, Lucullus invaded Apamia and took the city of Prusa. Once again, it was a time of victory upon victory. The king was in full flight, and Lucullus had further proven his mettle in the face of the Pontic threat. And yet, through it all, the situation remained frustratingly unresolved.

The Spartacus Revolt

The Roman legions were quite preoccupied with both Spain and the Third Mithridatic War in 73 BC. The outbreak of the Spartacus slave revolt in Italy came at arguably the worst of times for the Republic; when Charles Laughton's senatorial character in Stanley Kubrick's 1960 *Spartacus* film notes that the Republic was engaged in wars in both Spain and Asia, Hollywood scriptwriting reflected an all too accurate appraisal of the historical circumstances.

It is interesting to note that Lucullus was apparently advised at this juncture to give up the prosecution of the war – in other words, to pursue something of the same course of action that had marked the imperfect resolution of the First Mithridatic War, another version of the Peace of Dardanus. There may have been fear that it would be hazardous for the Romans to try to invade Pontus and to engage Mithridates in his kingdom proper. Some may have felt that it was as much by fortune as by good generalship that the Romans had done so well thus far, and that it would be tempting fate to continue. Then, too, there was the question of what exactly the end result of the war was supposed to be. Was the king to be dethroned and his kingdom in some way added to the increasingly rich Roman inheritance in the East? Was he to be reduced to the status of a client king who would pay a heavy indemnity for the war? Did political considerations in the capital warrant Lucullus' more or less swift return from Asia? If so, the pupil certainly experienced the same difficulty as the master; Sulla had a similar problem during the First Mithridatic War.

For the moment, Lucullus faced no opposition in Bithynia and Galatia. These were rich districts, and soon enough the Romans had so much plunder and abundance of supplies that there was no serious concern about provisioning the expeditionary legionary force. So bloodless, in fact, were the victories that Lucullus' soldiers began to complain that they had no chance to exercise their occupational talents as soldiers, let alone to enrich themselves on the wealth of captured cities – they had more than enough to be comfortably supplied, but none of the usual trappings of luxury that came as the reward for successfully taking towns and cities. Some were afraid that Lucullus was leading his army away from the wealthiest districts of the region, and into the arid wastelands where there would be both a lack of luxury and the army of Mithridates to face in a decisive showdown.

At the same time, Lucullus faced questioning over why exactly he was bothering to engage with every small unit of the king's forces, every nook and cranny of the region that he could scout out and occupy. Why was he allowing Mithridates to rebuild his force? Plutarch preserves a lengthy address of Lucullus to his men, in which he noted that if he allowed the king to recoup his losses and to gather together a credible fighting force, then it would be possible to face Mithridates once and for all, rather than chasing the king into remote regions where he would be assisted by new allies from the far-flung regions of his sphere of influence. Lucullus was correct in this assessment; it eerily presaged exactly what would happen in future stages of the war. Plutarch's Lucullus provides his men with an apt lesson in geography: Mithridates still had many advantages of which he could avail himself, and the Romans could still, Lucullus realized, lose the war despite their appreciable, indeed impressive victories. The territory in question was incredibly vast. Even in defeat, an enemy king could hope to recapture lost land and lead the Romans on an endless hunt. And this is exactly what would happen. Of course such a strategy could not be practised indefinitely – but it would be Pompey and not Lucullus who would benefit in the end.

Mithridates immediately sought allies in his war with Rome. He now had no hope of a quick victory, and an increased roster of friends in the neighbourhood would be ideal for prosecuting a long war of attrition. But no one of substantial resources rushed to Mithridates' aid. No doubt the feeling throughout the region was that the king had sought this fight, and it was the king's to resolve – waiting to see what would happen seemed the more cautious and prudent course of action for Scythians, Parthians and Armenians alike.

Amazons and Bees

Appian preserves a fantastic account of one of Lucullus' operations in this period. He was laying siege to Themiscyra on the River Thermodon, the legendary home of the Amazons. Lucullus' forces erected towers and dug great tunnel passageways; the tunnels were so large that significant battles were fought underground. The Themiscyrans are said to have introduced bears, other large animals and swarms of bees into the subterranean passages to assail Lucullus' men.[32] Amisus was also under siege, and the defenders charged forth and engaged the Romans in single combat. Mithridates was able to keep this locale supplied to hold out for as long as possible. There is uncertainty as to what exactly happened at Amisus.

Plutarch cites Lucullus' apparently lacklustre performance as one of the indictments brought against him by his men. In his account, the soldiers noted that it would have been easy to take the city and to enjoy its riches, had Lucullus been willing to press the matter.

There was certainly discontent – more or less significant – in Lucullus' camp during the winter of 73–72 BC. It is not clear whether or not the commander received any news from Rome in this period of the increasingly problematic situation in Italy in the wake of the Spartacus rebellion. In the early spring of 72, Lucullus was ready to move against the king. He left his subordinate, Lucius Licinius Murena, in charge of minding Amisus, and proceeded with the main body of his force deeper into Pontus. According to Plutarch, Mithridates now commanded some 40,000 infantry and 4,000 cavalry – he was consistently able to muster an impressive number of men, though not always of the highest quality or most robust and effective training.[33] The cavalry force was where Mithridates placed his courage and hope. Appian records that the Mithridatic commander Phoenix – a member of the royal family – duly warned of the approach of Lucullus by fire signal, only at once then to desert to the Roman side (an example of a sort of Eastern *pietas*, we might think). A subsequent cavalry engagement with some detachment of the king's forces did not go as well, and Lucullus' men were obliged to withdraw. Plutarch says that the skirmish occurred after Lucullus' force had crossed the River Lycus, while Appian locates it more precisely, at Cabeira. Plutarch and Appian both relate that the Roman commander Pomponius was brought to the king, in great suffering from his wounds. His life was promised him if he would be a friend of the king. Pomponius responded that he would indeed befriend the monarch – if Mithridates would come over to the Roman side. Impressed by the bravery and loyalty of the commander, Mithridates spared his life. In the display of *pietas*, we may imagine that Lucullus would have found a source of just pride in his subordinate.

Meanwhile, in terms of the larger military picture, Lucullus was cautious about becoming entangled with Mithridates on an open plain. He knew that the king was strong in cavalry units, and that he had sought out the ideal terrain for taking full advantage of his horsemen.

A Man of Chalk

Elsewhere in the Mediterranean world, not only the slave war, but the pirate war was also engrossing the attention of the Roman military machine. Marcus Antonius – the father of the more famous Roman of the same name – had been given the command against the pirate menace in 74 BC. By 73, he had moved against the marauders in Crete, an expedition that would prove disastrous. Antonius was an incompetent commander; he was forced to make a treaty with the Cretans and died on the island in 72 or 71 BC, his military commission quite unfulfilled. He was given the name *Creticus* in mockery; it could mean 'Cretan', but it also meant 'man of chalk'.

The Republic was now engaged in struggles in Spain, Asia, Italy and with the ongoing piratical menace that afflicted the life blood of the empire – the Mediterranean Sea. Lucullus was in a somewhat precarious position himself. He had achieved appreciable victories over Mithridates, but he was now facing the king in his own homeland and was increasingly distant from any reliable and safe source of provisions. There was a very real danger of Lucullus' now taking the place once held by Mithridates: besieger of cities, forever operating under the fear of starvation and lack of supplies.

Cave Dwellings

Plutarch says that Lucullus received help from some Greeks who were living in a sort of cave (no doubt in hiding from Mithridates). Artemidorus, their leader, assisted the Romans in finding their way through difficult terrain and to safer ground near Cabeira.[34] Appian has a similar account of a hunter in a cave who provided assistance to Lucullus' forces in finding their way.[35] In Cappadocia, we might note, people still live in ecologically friendly cave dwellings that remain cool in summer and warm in winter; tourists to the modern Urgup in Turkey (a reasonable drive from the city of Kayseri, an important site in ancient times for the trade between Sinope on the Black Sea and the Euphrates) are able to see examples of such dwellings, the exploration of which provides a major impetus for the local tourist industry.

A revealing story is preserved that while both Mithridates and Lucullus were avoiding a direct engagement, some Romans came upon a group of the king's men who were hunting stag. Conflict ensued, and the Romans were in full flight from the scene. When they approached the Roman camp, the men in the base urged Lucullus to let them go out and meet the enemy in full battle array. But Lucullus urged them to remain silent, even as he proceeded himself to the battlefield, there to confront the fugitive Romans. He shamed them for their cowardice in running away, and urged them to turn and face Mithridates' men in combat. The cowards-turned-soldiers were successful, but when they returned home Lucullus disgraced them by having them dig a 12ft ditch in the sight of their fellows – a reminder of how they had shamed the arms of Rome. Resolute discipline was the order of the day. Lucullus would continue to bide his time as best he could in the face of the enemy.

Assassination Plots

Both Plutarch and Appian agree that around this same time, there may have been a plot afoot to assassinate Lucullus. Our sources do not concur on the details. Plutarch records that there was a Dandarian prince named Olthacus who was exceedingly zealous for glory and honour. He conceived the idea that he might kill Lucullus after having employed the ruse of being admitted into his presence as a would-be defector from the king's cause. Olthacus would appear in the Roman camp as someone who had been disgraced by Mithridates; before long, he would aspire to be a companion of Lucullus' meals. Olthacus achieved his purpose with appreciable success, and was ready one day around noon to carry out the assassination. He had his servants prepare a horse with which he might escape – he had no intention of sacrificing his life in the pursuit of his daring quest. But Lucullus' attendant Menedemus would not admit him to the commander's tent; he noted that the commander was asleep and in dire need of rest. Olthacus became irritated at the rebuff, and noted that he had exceptionally important news for Lucullus. Nothing, Menedemus replied, could be as important as the commander's safety. And so Olthacus escaped, fearful that he had been exposed as untrustworthy.

Appian tells much the same story of the Scythian Olcaba. Once again the enemy is denied entry into the Roman's tent. Appian leaves open the possibility that Olcaba was no assassin, but merely an incensed, offended defector who fled the Roman camp in anger at having been refused admittance to Lucullus' presence, let alone having been branded a would-be assassin.[36] It is likely significant that Appian is not sure the Scythian prince was intent on murder. Something no doubt happened that involved a minor foreign potentate and the refusal of entry into Lucullus' presence, but it is not altogether certain that there was an active conspiracy.

It is not difficult to believe that Mithridates would have been interested in orchestrating or at least supporting a plot to kill Lucullus. The commander had been his most formidable Roman adversary, having eclipsed by now the work of Sulla in confronting the Pontic threat. Lucullus had also proven himself to be a dogged pursuer of the king, and was in no hurry to leave Asia. The situation with Sulla had been very different, as he had serious domestic affairs in Rome that demanded his attention sooner rather than later. The demands on Lucullus from the home front were also serious, but in a more subtle way; for now, the general had his sight focussed squarely on Mithridates.

Frontinus also mentions Mithridatic assassination plots against Lucullus, specifically the familiar story of Adathus and the attempt to gain admittance to Lucullus' presence, and then the would-be assassin's speedy escape from the Roman camp.[37]

Was Mithridates feeling desperate? Did he truly believe that he would win a victory over the Romans, were only Lucullus to be assassinated? Did he assume that with Lucullus dead, he would be able to win victories over the Romans such that he could recoup territorial losses, expand and fortify his holdings and then wait for any Roman reinforcements from a position of invincible strength? We can only speculate.

The Other Lucullus and the Resolution of the Spartacus War

Lucullus' brother Marcus, meanwhile, was enjoying his own career advancement at Rome. He was consul in 73 BC together with Gaius Cassius Longinus. He was then sent as proconsul to Macedonia, in the course of which appointment he did his part in reducing the possessions and influence of Mithridates near the Danube and the west coast of the Black Sea. In 71, Lucullus would be recalled from Macedonia prematurely to assist in the final suppression of the Spartacus slave uprising. He landed with his forces at Brundisium and was a factor in Spartacus' decision to turn and face the legions of Marcus Licinius Crassus. There was a small part, then, for the Lucullus family in the final stages of one of the most enduringly famous struggles of the period, a war that has achieved greater pop-ular fame down through the ages than the far more significant military activities of Lucius Lucullus in Asia. The Spartacus War had gone on for embarrassingly long, and across vast tracts of Italy. In some ways it was fitting that three famous Romans – Crassus, Pompey and the 'other' Lucullus – were involved in finally suppressing it.[38] Lucius Lucullus had been worried about the return of Pompey in the days of his consulship. It would be Crassus who now had his day to rue his arrival – the glory of the Spartacus War, insofar as war against mere slaves could be counted glory, would now be somewhat stolen (or at least shared). The Spartacus War ended gruesomely for the rebellious slaves, with the mass killing of some 6,000 captured fugitives.

Pompey was now finished in Spain – in something of a twist on the Lucullan expe-rience in Asia, he had never defeated Sertorius in open battle – but he had been able to see the day when his antagonist was dead, the victim of an assassination. Marcus Lucullus' involvement in the final stages of the Spartacus War shamed both Crassus and Pompey, as he was clearly the junior partner in the miniature slave war trium-virate.[39] One could note with something approaching irony that Marcus Lucullus helped to resolve a domestic upheaval that arguably helped his brother Lucius – the longer the Spartacus conflict dragged on, the less likely any powerful rival would be sent to Asia to replace Lucullus. Inexorably, from west to east, the problems of the Republic were being solved; Mithridates meanwhile remained at large.

We are not sure of the exact chronology of events in Asia in 72–71 BC. A sig-nificant part of our problem is the lack of exact correspondence between Plutarch and Appian. It appears clear enough that there were two Lucullan expeditions in search of provisions. Some would say that it is logical to assign the first to 72 BC and the second to 71, though certainty is impossible in the face of relatively scanty evidence –Lucullus' army had a serious need of provisions, and two expeditions in one year would not be outside the realm of possibility. What our main sources agree on here is that both expeditions ran into trouble from Mithridatic forces, and both acquitted themselves manfully. First the Roman commander Sornatius and then the officer Marcus Fabius Hadrianus won great victories, with Hadrianus essentially obliterating the king's force. Only the king's top commanders, Menemachus and Myron, were said to have survived the disaster.

Plutarch reports that Mithridates thought to conceal the extent of the disaster from the main body of his force, only to be caught in the sin of omission when Hadrianus marched by the Pontic camp in full battle array, complete with the spoils and plunder of the victory. The king's reputation certainly suffered from being caught in so bald-faced a lie. There was a general sense in the king's army that retreat was in order, and quickly. There was confusion and disorder – not to say resentment – when the king's attendants seemed to be the first in line to depart. The fact that some of the royal servants were caught trying to prevent the common soldiers from making their escape resulted in violence and killings at the camp exits, with the men in charge of the baggage the main casualties. A general was also slain, and a priest was trampled in the confusion at the gates. The king himself barely made his own exit, aided in the end by the timely intervention of a eunuch who provided a horse to the fugitive monarch.

Appian's version of the king's flight from his camp offers certain different details of narrative and emphasis.[40] In his account, survivors of the Hadrianus rout returned to camp and magnified the degree of the disaster, Mithridates hearing of the whole affair before Lucullus. Panic set in, and the king admitted to his closest counsellors that he thought it was time to depart. The royal advisors then immediately thought only of themselves; plans were made by each in turn to get out of the camp with as much as baggage as could be conveyed. The soldiers reacted to the servants, and the king to the general tumult. In the ensuing chaos, Mithridates was actually knocked from his horse, and had to remount and take flight to the nearby mountains with a few close followers.

What is reasonably clear from the surviving evidence of Plutarch and Appian is that Mithridates had suffered a catastrophic loss with respect to his cavalry forces. For the moment, he was quite incapable of launching any significant attacks against his Roman adversaries.

The King in Retreat

It did not take long for Lucullus to learn that the king was making his retreat, and he at once ordered an attack on the camp and pursuit of the monarch. Lucullus was clear in his instructions: the soldiers were to abstain from plunder, though they were to kill the king's men without quarter or hesitation. Appian reports that the sight of so much wealth in the Pontic camp was a greater incentive to the soldiers than the orders of their commanders, while Plutarch bluntly states that the greed and avarice of the Roman soldiers deprived Lucullus of his chance to capture or kill the king. If we can believe both sources, the Romans were literally on the verge of capturing the monarch, when a royal pack mule loaded with treasure managed to interpose itself between king and pursuers. The lure of the rich treasure the animal carried was enough to save the king to see another day. The Roman soldiers could not even be trusted to ensure the survival of a relatively minor individual, so great was their burning lust for plunder; Lucullus had ordered that one Callistratus should be brought to him alive – he was in charge of the royal papers – but the soldiers killed him when they realized he had 500 pieces of gold in his clothing.[41]

Plutarch notes in summation that Lucullus did allow the soldiers to plunder the king's camp; in all likelihood it would have been exceedingly difficult if not impossible to try to prevent them. Mithridates had escaped, and that was the main problem, some might think. Of course Lucullus had also won a tremendous victory, though his critics might say that it was as much the result of luck as careful planning and patient management of the prosecution of the war. Lucullus' persistent problem in the campaign would be that every victory he achieved was another excuse for his domestic enemies to note that the real quarry had yet again eluded capture – and Mithridates showed no interest in a negotiated settlement at this point. For the moment, time was very much on his side, and he knew it.

If the Romans were in search of treasure, treasure there was aplenty – and also a great number of Greeks who had been held prisoner by the king. The king, for his part, escaped with some 2,000 cavalry (according to Appian). He immediately made plans for the fall of his kingdom – his despair must have been as profound as at any time in his life thus far. He went so far as to give orders to the eunuch Bacchus to make his way to the royal palace and see to the deaths of the king's sisters, wives and concubines.[42] Plutarch dwells on the lurid details of the deaths of the king's Greek wife Monime the Milesian, while Appian simply notes that the women perished by stabbing, poison and hanging. The mass slaughter of the king's women in the palace at Pharnaces was too much for many of Mithridates' commanders, who defected to Lucullus at once. Lucullus for his part is said by Appian to have captured Amastris, Heraclea and some other of the king's cities, but there is little in the way of detail in Appian (or Plutarch) of these minor campaigns, and it is possible that some simply surrendered to the Romans without much of a fight, if any.[43]

Plutarch notes that when Lucullus learned of the deaths of the king's female relatives, he was seriously troubled and pained at heart; he was, after all, of a gentle and humane disposition.[44] It is another of the many details for which Plutarch's laudatory biographies are known. The contrast in the portrait of the defeat of the king is between the avaricious, greedy soldiers and their calm and collected commander, a man who is able to mourn the unnecessary loss of life of innocents, and who in the midst of war is able to recall his humanity. Plutarch notes that one of the king's sisters, Nyssa, was fortunate enough to survive precisely because she was captured by Lucullus.

Yet again, the Romans had achieved an impressive result, and once again, the king was in retreat. But as so many would-be conquerors in this region of the world came to learn, Asia is very large indeed, and the flight of the king also meant that the war would be prolonged for an uncertain additional duration – an ever more serious problem for Lucullus, especially given that events in Rome did not come to a halt while the Roman army was engaged in Asian military operations. The war in Spain was over; the slave insurrection in Italy was over – it was now only in Asia that a serious ground war was in progress, and of indefinite resolution. Yet again, it was a season of victories, of ultimately frustratingly fruitless result, some might think. Lucullus subdued the Chaldaeans and the Tibareni, and occupied Lesser Armenia. But the king was in none of those places.[45] We have no record of any serious difficulties in Lucullus' operations to subjugate these inland areas; all of them seem to have fallen without much in the way of resistance. Indeed, Lucullus' soldiers' work in subduing one Mithridatic fortress after another became the stuff of poetic legend, the Augustan poet Horace alluding to this period of tremendous victory and attainment of plunder by the soldiers of Lucullus.[46] Nobody seemed to be in any great hurry to die for Mithridates, though frustratingly, nobody seemed to be much interested in helping to secure the king as Lucullus' prisoner.

Tigranes II of Armenia

Lucullus attempted to pursue Mithridates, even in the aftermath of the mule fiasco, but the king had escaped to Tigranes, the Armenian king. Tigranes was now in a position that no doubt he did not appreciate. He was a relatively minor king, all things considered, and was in no mood for an immediate war with Rome over the fate of Mithridates. Appian notes that Tigranes would not actually admit Mithridates into his presence, but instead sent him off to stay on a royal estate, a virtual prisoner, one might think. No doubt there were significant discussions in the Armenian palace as to what to do about the Pontic problem. Plutarch provides more information.[47] Not only did Tigranes keep Mithridates away from his presence, but the region in which the king was *de facto* confined was a marshy, malarial tract of land. If Tigranes was worried at looking shameful in the matter of handing over Mithridates, he was not concerned about how he appeared in terms of his reception of his father-in-law. He appeared to be following the letter of the law of hospitality: he did not refuse Mithridates a roof, and he certainly did not surrender him to the Romans. However, there was no question that the King of Pontus had reached the nadir of his fortunes heretofore, and that he held little if any real influence over Tigranes.[48]

The Spring of 71

It was the spring of 71 BC, the year that witnessed good news from Asia, but also the settlement of the Third Servile or Spartacus War. In Spain, Sertorius had been assassinated in 72 or 73 BC by Marcus Perperna Vento, who would soon meet his own end by order of Pompey.[49] A veritable nightmare for Lucullus had indeed come true. Pompey was no longer occupied with affairs in Spain, and he had even been able to take some of the credit for the final resolution of the tedious Servile War. The year 71, in short, was good for Rome – but for Lucullus, the perils of delay were becoming more and more serious, and the hazards of staying too long in Asia were beginning to take on increasingly definable features. Throughout this, one finds evidence that his own men were a part of the tension and difficulty that the commander faced. Whether or not Lucullus was particularly skilled in dealing with the rank and file soldiers, his men would appear to have been a legitimate challenge for the tolerance and *savoir faire* of any general.

Amisus

Lucullus' work, however, was far from over, and not only because the king was still out of reach. Not every city and town in Asia was equally easy to take; indeed Amisus was still holding out against Lucullus' subordinate, Murena. Lucullus finished the task, though not without sadness and regret. Plutarch relates that the salvation of Amisus had been the mechanical defensive devices of the Greek Callimachus, who was a master at siege warfare. At exactly the time when Callimachus was inclined to let his defenders rest, Lucullus launched a fateful attack and was able to breach the walls of the city. Callimachus made his escape in part by setting fire to the doomed town. Lucullus sought at once to extinguish the flames and to spare the locale, but no one was in any mood to listen – the inhabitants of Amisus were understandably more concerned about making their escape, and the Roman soldiers were intent once again on plunder (especially after the long and frustrating siege). Lucullus thought that by allowing his men to ransack the city, he might be able to save it, the perverse logic being that the Romans would be hesitant to burn what they could steal. But the army was more mob than disciplined soldiery, and by the time Lucullus himself entered Amisus at daybreak, the city was in ruins. Plutarch reports that the commander then noted that Sulla had been blessed because he was able to save Athens;[50] for him, the gods had ordained the fate of Lucius Mummius Achaicus, who had overseen the destruction of Corinth in 146 BC.[51]

Tragic destruction gave way to redemption of some sort. Plutarch notes that a timely rain shower seemed to be the providential gift of heaven, and that Lucullus himself spent a significant amount of money on restoring Amisus. The Greeks who had been so long in hiding and prison under Mithridates were settled there, and those natives of the city who had fled were induced to return. The city was given more land and a richer provisioning than before. By all accounts, it seems that Lucullus had once again acquitted himself well in the disposition of affairs in time of war as in time of peace.[52]

Plutarch preserves yet another story that attests to the character of Lucullus. Tyrannio the grammarian was one of the 'captives' of Amisus. The commander Murena – the failed commander, some might argue – asked to have him as a war prize. This was granted, and Tyrannio was formally assigned as a slave to Murena, who then gave the man his liberty. A noble gesture, one might think – but to Lucullus, a most inappropriate action, since the man had been born free and should have had his freedom recognized from the start, and not as the result of a seemingly magnanimous gesture after Murena had enslaved him.

One reason cited by both Plutarch and Appian for Lucullus' generous treatment of Amisus was that he learned that the city had been a colony of Athens (this no doubt inspired his remark about how Sulla was blessed in being able to preserve the great Greek city). Amisus had a democratic system of government as if it were a miniature Athens; it was an oasis of Athenian culture even under Mithridratic rule (or at least the story went). Amisus had been subject to the Persians, and then liberated by Alexander the Great. Once again, Lucullus could follow in the footsteps of the Macedonian conqueror and free a Greek city from Eastern bondage. It is another anecdote to buttress the reputation of Lucullus the phihellene, of Lucullus the admirer and respectful student of Greek culture.

Sinope

Plutarch and Appian provide details of the successful taking of Sinope in (70 BC.[53] Orosius has a customarily brief account (VI.3.2–3). Here there was significant resistance; the inhabitants were doing well in defending their coastal city on water as well as land. Finally, the Sinopians burned their heavy ships and escaped on lighter vessels. Lucullus granted the city its freedom, allegedly in response to a dream in which Autolycus, the companion of Heracles in his war against the

Amazons, seemed to be calling out to him. Autolycus had been driven to Sinope by a storm, and there was a statue of the Herculean hero in the locale that was said to give oracles to the inhabitants. The Sinopians did not have time to take the statue with them, and on the day after his dream, Lucullus saw some men carrying a heavy burden wrapped in linen – needless to say, the religiously scrupulous Lucullus was careful to show some honour and respect both to statue and city. Plutarch notes that Sulla had indicated in his memoirs that nothing was so reliable as that which was foretold in dreams, and that on this occasion, Lucullus remembered the sentiment and wisdom of his mentor.

Plutarch adds the detail that the real resistance in Sinope had not come from the Sinopians themselves, but rather from the Cilicians who were in the city. Some 8,000 of these are said to have been slain when Lucullus finally entered the city. We should remember, too, that the exact chronology of events is not definitively determinable; Plutarch places the conquest of Sinope after the realization that war would be necessary against Tigranes.

The historian Memnon offers a brief account of the Sinope operation.[54] He notes that Lucullus vigorously pursued the siege, and that Mithridates' son Machares sent envoys asking for an alliance. Lucullus demanded that Machares not supply the city. In response, the would-be ally even sent materials to the Romans that had been earmarked for the king's men. This was the end of the hopes for Cleochares and his associates in Sinope; they allowed their soldiers to loot the city, even as they loaded ships with their treasure and abandoned Sinope to the flames from unneeded ships that were burned to deprive the Romans of their use.[55]

Financial Reforms

Plutarch is clear that Lucullus was a civilizing influence and indeed saviour not only over the lands once under Mithridates' sway, but also in the Roman province of Asia. If the biographer can be trusted – and there is no reason to doubt his word on this – the whole region was oppressed by financial and worse ills under occupation. Men were made virtual slaves by the system of tax collection and money lending, and the torture of debtors was common practice. Simply put, Lucullus found a brutal system of economic subjugation, and he freed the region from the vile practices that had marked the king's rule over this vast expanse of land. Part of the problem for Lucullus, however, was that every good deed that benefited the local population was almost guaranteed to stir up trouble and controversy among the tax collectors and those who made their livelihood from the *de facto* extortion of money from the locals. These men were not about to surrender their financial prerogatives without a fight, and soon enough they protested to Rome – and there were plenty of officials in Rome who were sympathetic to the complaints (and who were hardly interested in hearing about the plight of the distant inhabitants in Asia).

Lucullus, however, earned a reputation as being a model provincial administrator, a man absolutely immune to corruption and the lure of luxury. He was also obliged to work with alacrity and resolute skill on the maintenance of the financial health of the territories under his control. Ideally, the war was to pay for itself, and the local regions were to provide what was necessary for the successful prosecution of the war. The lesson of Pompey's experience in Spain, and his need to appeal for more support from Rome and the consul Lucullus, must have been very much in Lucius' mind at this time. But in his dealings with the tax collectors, Lucullus seemed determined to preserve the difference between providing support and being drowned in debt. He saw no reason to impose crippling demands for money and resources on a population that would only respond with resentment and aid that was begrudgingly given.

The *Publicani*

Lucullus was clearly willing to incur the enmity of the *publicani* and their friends and supporters in Rome.[56] Some have thought that this willingness was tied to his sense that the war was essentially over, and that Mithridates would soon be in his custody. The truth may lie in the simpler, nobler reason that Lucullus saw no reason to place undue burdens on the locals. His rationale for this thinking need not have been purely a humane one – though we should not let cynicism keep us from accepting this possibility. A practical man would realize that the benefit to Rome of keeping the conquered populations of Asia content was greater than the extra revenue that was enriching the class of tax collectors and their patrons. We do well to remember that Lucullus had significant experience in financial matters in his service under Sulla; he knew about the economic realities of the region, and the limits of forbearance of the local population. Our sources make clear that he ran foul of the professional tax-collecting class and their supporters in Rome. There is little to condemn Lucullus for in these dealings. No doubt he understood the inherent risks of his position, but his sense of honour, we may think, was such that he would not moderate his position.[57] No one, it seems, has ever tried to defend the *publicani* and their supporters in Rome for the extent of their avarice and their prosecution and harassment of those who would challenge their financial empire. They were extortionists, plain and simple – and Lucullus would have none of it.

Meanwhile, we may note that Appian records the obeisance of Machares, the son of Mithridates and ruler of the Bosporus, who sent Lucullus a golden crown (we are not told what Lucullus did with the luxurious item and symbol of regal power).[58] The exact date of when this member of the royal family turned traitor to Mithridates is uncertain, but it may have occurred after the siege of Sinope. Sufficient attention soon had to be paid to the problem of the king's survival in virtual exile in Armenia. Essentially, Lucullus had seen to the clearing of Pontus. The whole region was now under Roman control, and the king had been deprived of his kingdom – though not of his life. For Romans with a long memory, the survival of Mithridates was a mark of continuing peril. There were parallels to the situation of Hannibal and the threat that such a fierce enemy of Rome posed so long as he lived. The First Mithridatic War had ended inconclusively, and Lucullus was doubtless in no mood for the third to be concluded prematurely. Plutarch notes that when Machares sent the golden crown to Lucullus – he specifies that it was worth a thousand pieces of gold – then and only then did Lucullus consider the 'first war' to be finished. A second now loomed.[59]

For Lucullus' word to Tigranes of Armenia was simple – Mithridates needed to be surrendered to Roman justice.[60]

Chapter 5

Armenia

An Emissary's Mission

O nce again we are not sure of the exact chronology, but we do know that Lucullus sent a member of his own family to Armenia to bring the commander's demand to the Armenian royal court.[1] Appius Clodius – Lucullus' brother-in-law – was the emissary who came with word that could not have been surprising, though certainly it was unwelcome and discomfiting. Lucullus was demanding nothing less than the head of Mithridates, and Tigranes was thrust into the unenviable position of having to decide between war and peace with Rome. No doubt there were considerations other than the question of loyalty to Mithridates. The surrender of the king would make it clear that Armenia was little more than a puppet of Rome. Plutarch notes that the king's guides led Clodius on a circuitous, slow route, no doubt deliberately seeking to delay the inevitable and to buy more time for Tigranes to decide on a course of action, and to prepare for it. A Syrian freedman of Clodius soon informed his lord of a more expeditious itinerary. While waiting for the king to rendezvous with him, Clodius is said to have spent his time telling the local princes and potentates that Lucullus would soon be on the scene, and that he was looking for friends and was willing to reward those who were willing to side with him. But, for the moment, the princes were of course to remain silent about the Roman overtures.

Appian relates that by the time Lucullus crossed the Euphrates on his way to Armenia in pursuit of Mithridates, the local rulers he encountered were in no hurry to die for Tigranes – let alone his father-in-law. Lucullus was in some sense the commander of an invading force, but he carefully ensured that his only demand was what was needed to provision his troops.[2] He had two legions and 500 cavalry – and, above all, an abiding sense of mission. Plutarch assigns the figures of 12,000 infantry and 3,000 cavalry, with 6,000 left behind under Sornatius to guard Pontus. There was to be no hope of an invasion of Mithridates' homeland while Lucullus was off after Tigranes and his father-in-law. And once again, throughout his operations, Lucullus was to cultivate a reputation for his kindly treatment of local populations, a useful enough strategy – even were he not to have the humane disposition that we may believe he sincerely had – but no help, ultimately, in dealing with the fickle favour of the Roman ruling class and people. For them, two kings were now in defiance of Rome, either actual or potential. Lucullus could hold out hope that Tigranes might cooperate with his demands, but no doubt he had no serious illusions about where the king's loyalties were to be found.

Scholars have contested the behaviour of Lucullus in his diplomatic overtures to the Armenian king. It appears certain that Clodius did not leave a favourable impression on Tigranes; certainly the monarch's answer was not what Lucullus wanted to hear. The Armenians would not surrender Mithridates, and if the Romans were in consequence to launch an attack, they would defend themselves against the aggressor's invasion force. One can imagine that honour and reputation did play a role in Tigranes' reluctance to give up his father-in-law, but one can also imagine that Lucullus rued the day that his relative by marriage had created this mess for him, even if he knew on an intellectual level that Clodius had failed where no one was likely to have succeeded.

Tigranes was no stranger to aggressive tendencies. He had occupied Seleucid Syria, a troubled Hellenistic kingdom that had seen rivalries and breakdowns of loyalty in the House of Antiochus. Tigranes would in fact be forced to abandon Syria in order to defend his own kingdom in the wake of the defeat of Mithridates and the war with Lucullus.[3] He had expanded his kingdom into Parthia and Mesopotamia. He was also fond of importing citizens from abroad to populate his capital, Tigranocerta, and to try to make it a cosmopolitan centre of culture and renown. There is no reason to think that he much enjoyed the idea of sharing his backyard with a Roman occupation force, or with having his borders come up against those of a Roman province. There is, on the contrary, every reason to imagine that Tigranes was as imperialistic as his father-in-law, and that sooner or later he would have run foul of Roman interests in Asia. Lucullus had more experience by now in dealing with Asian kings than most men in the Roman Army; one can only speculate as to how others would have handled the current crisis in his situation. There is no reason to believe that Clodius deliberately tried to harm Lucullus' cause at the court of Tigranes. The situation in Armenia could likely not have been resolved satisfactorily by any emissary to the king's palace.[4]

Tigranes had been involved in a siege of Ptolemais-Ake (modern Acre in Israel) when Clodius first arrived in Antioch looking for him (and Mithridates). The hour of his great accomplishments against Hellenistic rivals was to be the commencement of his greatest crisis.[5] He would have the chance to face Lucullus in a variety of circumstances and military engagements. In some regards he would prove simultaneously both as victorious and as unsuccessful as his royal father-in-law.

It is easy in hindsight to say that the refusal of Tigranes to hand over Mithridates at once gave an easy opening to the Roman equestrians to press their case against Lucullus on behalf of the *publicani*. Lucullus no doubt thought that he could master time and solve the renegade king problem before he faced insurmountable challenges on the domestic front. But time was to work against him in this regard. The kings certainly had an easier task ahead of them.

The Significance of Salutations

But the real question about Lucullus' wisdom and diplomatic *savoir faire* at a critical moment comes from the question of salutations. It seems that the Roman addressed the Armenian with the title of 'King', while Tigranes styled himself 'King of Kings'. In the arena of monarchical vanity, the question might certainly seem to be an important one. Tigranes was incensed at what he considered to be a slight to his dignity, and noted that in return he would not accord Lucullus the title of *Imperator*.[6] Some have argued that Lucullus should have known better, and that the king's offence was easily foreseeable. Others would say that Tigranes would have sought any pretext – however slight – to rebuff the Roman demand for Mithridates. Yes, one could say in response, but this does not mean that Lucullus should have handed the Armenian king his pretext. It may simply have been the case that Lucullus was already feeling quite impatient, and that he had little if any tolerance for the salutational demands of a king who was now the sole reason he was being frustrated in his hopes to end the Eastern wars.

Arthur Keaveney does well to note that Tigranes was the ruler of an impressively expansive domain. He had land holdings that stretched over an astonishingly vast tract of territory, though with the usual problems that accompanied the maintenance of such empires: problems of communications and language, and lack of effective centralized authority.[7] Today, a statue of Tigranes II the Great stands in Yerevan, the capital of the Republic of Armenia. He would end his career and life as an ally of Rome, surviving until 55 or 54 BC. In light of the question of whether he deserved to be considered a King of Kings, we may note that some scholars have concluded that the star with a curved tail on his crown in iconography may be a depiction of Halley's Comet, which Tigranes could conceivably have seen in 87 BC. – and which he might well have taken to be an omen of his own magnificence and power. Tigranes has done well in the 'reception' he has enjoyed in the arts; there are several operas that are concerned with his story, including works by Scarlatti and Vivaldi. Armenians still speak of the vast empire that Tigranes controlled, a territory that at its height reached from the Caspian to the Mediterranean. 'Tigran' remains a popular Armenian name.[8] In any case, Tigranes had a whirlwind experience of Roman conquest. He would suffer significant defeats in 69 and 68 BC against Lucullus, while in 66, he would finally surrender to Pompey.[9] Ultimately, he would enjoy a better fate than that of his father-in-law. We do well to remember that if Tigranes was in an impossible position for the moment in terms of what to do with Mithridates, so too was Lucullus. He could not simply pick up his forces and return home with the king on the run. It would be Dardanus all over again, but after much greater expense and effort.

Eastern Kings

For the moment, however, the Armenian king was being wooed by Roman emissaries. Tigranes is said to have given Clodius an ample selection of presents as a mark of respect and homage for his embassy. Following the example of Lucullus, Clodius was willing to accept a single bowl so as not to appear to reject all overtures from the king and to shut down diplomatic avenues of rapprochement. But the rest of the gifts were sent back – there was a careful diplomatic dance to perform here, and the king was not to be given the impression that he had captivated his Roman visitor, or that Lucullus' demand was somehow to be softened.

Plutarch does little to disguise his contempt for Tigranes' reception of Clodius.[10] He notes that it must have been a quarter of a century since Tigranes had heard so free a speech – for that was the length to date of his reign, or, more accurately, his hubristic attitude. Clodius, for his part, is said not to have been cowed by the king's ostentatious displays of wealth and Eastern luxury. Tensions were already high between Roman and Armenian, and both men may have been all too well aware that a war was afoot, with Mithridates the prize.

It was perhaps inevitable that Tigranes and Mithridates would come to some sort of terms. If the Armenian king had determined to preserve Mithridates' life even at the cost of war with Rome, it served no purpose to keep the king at arm's length in virtual exile. At the very least, Mithridates might be useful to Tigranes in the matter of counsel and advice. And so the two monarchs began to hold meetings together in Tigranes' palace, and Plutarch is clear that the peace between the men came at the price of their friendships with others. One Metrodorus of Scepsis had been sent as an emissary of Mithridates to Armenia with a request for aid against the Romans. When Tigranes had asked for Metrodorus' personal advice on the matter, the ambassador had noted that in his capacity as Mithridates' delegate, he urged that the Armenians send aid to Pontus. On the other hand, if he was advising Tigranes himself, he would recommend not sending assistance. Tigranes now betrayed this confidence to Mithridates, and before long, Metrodorus was dead. Plutarch notes that Tigranes did feel remorse at the whole matter, and there is no reason to think that he intended for Metrodorus to die, though one imagines that he must have realized the great peril to which he was exposing the man who had been so honest and open with him. But the biographer concludes that Mithridates already hated Metrodorus and was merely looking for an excuse to vent his distaste.[11] Plutarch wryly observes that Tigranes ensured that Metrodorus had an extremely lavish funeral – sparing no cost in showing honour in death to the man he had betrayed in life. The clear impression one receives from the whole business is that the two kings deserved each other. Each arguably outdid the other in questionable – and most certainly non-Roman – behaviour (at least from Plutarch's perspective).

Lucullus was in Ephesus when Clodius returned with the news that Tigranes was not willing to surrender Mithridates. We cannot be certain what Lucullus expected of the embassy. Did he really imagine that the Armenian monarch would hand over his father-in-law? Was he already thinking of a war in Armenia, a renewed conflict that would bring him even greater glory and inevitable comparison to the Macedonian Alexander? Was he disturbed by the news from Clodius, or secretly heartened that there was a chance to earn renown in a struggle in which he could reasonably claim that he was in the right in the quest for the king's person and the ultimate settlement of the long and costly Mithridatic wars? The abiding problem of interpretation at this juncture in Lucullus' life is whether or not the news from Clodius surprised him. On the whole, the evidence would seem to indicate that it did not. Lucullus could read a map as well as anyone, and he knew that Mithridates had ample land in which to be lost, and that Tigranes had a sufficiently vast empire in both territory and resources so as to be able to bargain, at the very least. It may even have occurred to Tigranes that Lucullus should have come in person for any negotiation, something that Lucullus no doubt realized in advance, and likely consciously avoided. Lucullus doubtless knew exactly the sort of man he was sending to Mithridates, too: Appius Clodius was no diplomat, and there was no real chance that he would be either impressed by or impress in turn the Armenian king.

Games and Celebration at Ephesus

While at Ephesus, Lucullus did manage to enjoy some of the customary trappings of victory and triumph. Games were now instituted in more cities of Asia in his name – additional celebrations of the Lucullea. Athletic contests and gladiatorial combats were held to mark the achievements of the commander. No doubt there was a tangible sense that the work was incomplete, despite the impressive victories that had been achieved to date. This may well have been the most enjoyable time for Lucullus in his Asian sojourn, but surely he realized even now the seriousness of the challenges he faced.

For Lucullus was soon enough made aware that Tigranes and Mithridates intended to invade Roman Asia. One can appreciate Plutarch's note that Lucullus was in a state of incredulity as to why Tigranes had only now decided to participate in such a venture, after the defeat of Mithridates, when he could have been of arguably greater use to the Pontic king earlier.[12]

Plutarch notes that there were those in Rome who accused Lucullus of war-mongering.[13] As so often in military history, the question was of what exactly constituted resolution. For the moment, at least, Lucullus held to the line that the surrender of the king was the decisive factor in ending the war. But the question of Armenia could not be put off indefinitely. Was it to be relegated to the status of client kingdom? Was it to be absorbed into the Roman provincial structure? What sort of indemnity or punishment should be imposed on it for taking up arms against Rome? For the moment, these were questions that could more or less be left unanswered. But Lucullus' men were apparently less than thrilled about moving deeper into what is today central and western Turkey. They were unhappy at the prospect of a new war in unfamiliar territory and difficult terrain. It was the spring of 69 BC, and Lucullus once again had the task before him of assuaging the rebellious sentiments of his men.[14]

There is an interesting note in the fragments of Sallust's histories that when Pompey returned from the prosecution of the Sertorian War in 71 BC, he was considered to be willing to ingratiate himself with the plebeians.[15] It is possible that some of the political manoeuvring in Rome centred on the idea that Lucullus was indeed an optimate, traditionalist, Sullan politician, and his rival Pompey – now back from his long war – was willing to take up the opposite cause. The Sullan constitution, and the bad feelings that had arisen in the wake of its violent establishment, was in some sense the political prize that was being fought for in the manoeuvrings and machinations in Roman governmental life. Lucullus was increasingly easy to stereotype as the traditionalist embodiment of the old ways. If there were a new path forward, it would be the Pompeian one – at least for this hour.

Crossing the Euphrates

It was still winter, early in 69 BC. Lucullus reached the Euphrates, the dividing line between Cappadocia and Armenia.[16] Plutarch records the tradition that when the Romans arrived at the river, it was swollen from winter storms, such that a crossing seemed quite difficult – but by evening, the waters had subsided, and various islands in the channel became visible, such that the locals began to make homage to Lucullus, noting that the mighty Euphrates had voluntarily yielded to the great conqueror. Upon crossing, a heifer that was sacred to Artemis is said to have willingly presented itself to Lucullus for sacrifice to the goddess. The religiously dutiful Roman also sacrificed a bull to the Euphrates – bulls were the usual sacred animal for river gods, who were traditionally depicted as horned.[17] The local population in general is said to have received Lucullus warmly. They were in no real position to resist him, and at any rate his reputation for just and calm dealings with native peoples made it easy to acquiesce to his moderate wishes. These were more signs of great favour for the Roman conqueror. The Euphrates was one of the traditional markers of the distant East for Rome, a river associated with Persia and the conquests of Alexander, a legendary place of fame and fortune, as well as the failure of dreams and fond aspirations. We are told that Lucullus turned over the fortress of Tomisa to the king of Cappadocia – at the very least, the king was to stay out of Lucullus' way as he proceeded through the region. Lucullus made a lightning advance through the vast tracts of Cappadocian territory – he had his quarry to consider.[18]

We lack definitive knowledge about the plans of Tigranes and Mithridates in this period. As so often in military history, the real question is who fired the first shot of the new (or continuing/ongoing) war. Did the two kings intend to launch their own invasions and acts of aggression? There is certainly some ancient evidence to support this, but our sources do not permit absolute certainty. A waiting game had advantages of its own, especially when Lucullus had so much land to cross, and so many potential pitfalls to avoid in pursuit of Mithridates. Lucullus was in a position of having to make clear that his war was not so much one of aggression against Armenia and its allies, as of tracking down the fugitive Pontic king.

We do well to remember throughout that Tigranes was in a singularly difficult position. He could not eject Mithridates without running serious domestic risks. But the alternative was to risk involving himself in his father-in-law's war. Some might criticize the Armenians for not being prepared; certainly Lucullus caught them by surprise by his rapid march to the Euphrates before the usual spring campaigning season. One of the sad truths of Lucullus' life is that those who would accuse him of dilatory behaviour do so at the price of ignoring just how quickly he consistently moved when the strategic situation demanded it. This rapidity of movement put significant burdens on his soldiers, burdens that contributed to Lucullus' problems in army maintenance and affection. Lucullus' strategy was simple: the war needed to be ended quickly, and the head of Mithridates was the final goal marker. Tigranes might do better to delay, but before he knew it and could react, Lucullus was on his territory, having crossed one of the major geographical boundaries that marked his kingdom.

Mithrobarzanes

Was Tigranes a tyrant?[19] If Plutarch can be trusted, he was certainly rash and unpredictable: the first messenger who brought news to the king that Lucullus was on his way was decapitated.[20] Appian tells the same story, with hanging as the capital punishment, and the attempt at an explanation that Tigranes was trying to maintain calm in Armenia. Still, the news was important to the king's intelligence and reconnaissance information, and he prepared a reception welcome of 2,000 cavalry under the command of Mithrobarzanes (according to Appian), or perhaps 3,000.[21] Plutarch notes that Mithrobarzanes was one of the few men in the king's palace who was willing to tell him the truth – his reward would seem to be the commission of dealing with the Romans, with the orders that Lucullus was to be brought back alive, but his army destroyed. Mithrobarzenes was the king's representative in Sophene, and was to lose his life in the king's service.

For as it turned out, Mithrobarzanes would be killed in battle, and his force almost annihilated to a man. Plutarch relates that Lucullus himself saw to the organization of his camp, entrusting the task of guarding against the Armenian force to his subordinate Sextilius. Sextilius, who had some 1,600 cavalry and about as many infantry, was ordered to be cautious and to wait for the enemy – essentially to serve as a powerful sentry force to buy time for Lucullus to fortify and organize the camp for the main body of his army. Mithrobarzanes was either daring or recklessly foolish, and chose to attack – a disastrous decision. Appian relates that Lucullus met Mithrobarzanes in battle and routed him.[22] Mithrobarzanes had proven himself unable to meet the challenge Tigranes had put before him; his brave willingness to tell the king what was really happening was to be his undoing.

There may be some insight here into the workings of a despotic monarchy, one in which to tell the truth may well be fatal, but to be caught in a lie is equally deadly. The truth may well be that Tigranes was panicked; he did not expect Lucullus to be knocking at his door this quickly, and he had no road map ahead for how to settle the Roman problem that had escalated from Clodius' embassy to Lucullus' army being across the Euphrates. His only hopes now were to surrender his father-in-law – a prospect that was even more unpalatable now than before in terms of honour and saving face – or destroying the Roman force in a set battle. Merely buying time was no longer so viable a plan of action, especially against an opponent capable of rapid movement in the manner of Lucullus. It is likely that at some point in this period, Tigranes realized that the situation was more hazardous than he had initially gauged it to be. He may have felt that Lucullus would move more slowly and deliberately, either because of resistance or to allow his men to plunder at length and freely. Before he could possibly have been satisfactorily prepared, the Romans were in Armenia, having also crossed the Tigris.

Tigranocerta

The real prize in the region, however, was the great city of Tigranocerta.[23] The name of the city apparently means 'made by Tigranes', and there were four cities with the same appellation. It was located in modern south-eastern Turkey, in the region of the country that is ethnically predominately Kurdish – the exact location is elusive, in large part thanks to the action of Lucullus. Tigranes entrusted the defence of the mighty city to Mancaeus. The king meanwhile was focused on raising a large army to face any possible threat from the Romans; he was also engaged in conflict elsewhere across the vast territory of Armenia and its neighbours. One gets the impression that Tigranes was not entirely prepared for this war. Lucullus had admittedly made great use of forced marches and had appeared in Armenia quite rapidly, but in hindsight, it is reasonable to conclude that the king could have done more to ready himself for the arrival of the Roman invasion force. The fact that Tigranes needed to give the job of defence to Mancaeus is ample evidence of how caught by surprise the Armenians truly were; Lucullus was not supposed to be anywhere near Tigranocerta this early. On the other hand, the conscription of a large force would need the king's personal touch. There was simply insufficient time to do everything that was necessary to prepare for a battle with the main body of the Roman force. If we can believe the evidence of Pliny the Elder, Tigranocerta was situated – not surprisingly – on a lofty height (*in excelso*).[24]

Appian says that Tigranes raised a force of a quarter of a million men and some 50,000 cavalry, of which 6,000 were eventually sent to Tigranocerta for the sake of breaking through the Roman siege lines and rescuing the king's concubines.[25] The detail is reminiscent of Mithridates' decision to kill his female relatives and companions – Tigranes was more interested in the survival of his harem and in maintaining a lifestyle of luxury. The clear implication of the report is that the king was a decadent potentate. Tigranes was able to raise impressive numbers – his father-in-law had had the same ability – though with the problem that armies of this size were both unwieldy and difficult to train effectively. Quantity and not quality was the hallmark of the king's forces. Tigranes was able to achieve some measure of success in rescuing his apparently beloved women. There is some confusion as to the nature of the operation, but it appears that the concubines were kept in a fortress of some sort near Tigranocerta (why they would be in a separate location, outside the city, is unclear). There is also doubt as to who commanded siege operations in the vicinity of Tigranocerta in this period. Was it Lucullus himself, waiting for the advent of Tigranes, or one of his subordinates? Were there attacks on nearby towns and suburbs of the city? Our sources are not clear.[26]

Advice of an Old King

Plutarch relates that Lucullus tried his best to keep Tigranes from amassing his reinforcements. Sextilius was sent to attack an Arab contingent that was approaching to join Tigranes' main body; they were mostly slain. Lucullus was also focused on the siege of the splendid Armenian capital. He surmised correctly that Tigranes would never tolerate the siege of the crown jewel of his urban landscape, but would be goaded into joining battle as soon as possible. Appian reports that now and only now did Mithridates enter the king's presence, and that his advice was simple: harass the enemy with cavalry and choke off their supplies – in no way join battle in a set piece engagement.[27] One can understand why Tigranes might have disregarded the king's advice. He had, after all, been defeated in disgrace by Lucullus, and was perhaps not the most persuasive purveyor of wisdom about what to do in the current situation. But history would prove that Mithridates was correct. Tigranes allegedly spoke contemptuously of the size of the Roman force when first he saw it, noting that if the Romans had come as ambassadors, there were too many of them, and if as an invading army, there were too few. If Tigranes' forces had been even moderately successful in the operation to rescue the king's women, then his courage and daring may well have been supplemented.

But what are we to make of Lucullus' judgment and wisdom in dealing with Tigranes? From a military perspective, there is certainly a general acclaim for the commander's talents. But the argument that Lucullus was utterly unprepared for managing a problem like Tigranes' Armenia has been raised. Lucullus would have felt a pressing need at this time to return to Rome, were he to want to maintain his influence in political affairs. Military operations in the West had ended, and Pompey had returned home; Crassus and he were now the men of the hour. Crassus had achieved his victory over Spartacus, though Pompey had stolen some of the glory for that (with a small part reserved for Lucullus' younger brother). What was clear was that a victory over Tigranes needed to come swiftly and decisively – a rabbit hunt into Armenia would simply not do.[28]

We may explore further at this point the question of when exactly Mithridates and Tigranes were reconciled. Among our extant sources, only Appian places it so late in the course of affairs.[29] Again, Tigranes was in the difficult straits of having every action subjected to microscopic examination. On the one hand, he had the expectations of hospitality and respect for a relative. On the other, any indulgence to Mithridates might be seen as an offence against Rome and a provocation or pretext for war. It seems more logical to conclude that Appian is in error here, and that the two kings began their discussions earlier rather than later – some of which would have been relatively easy to keep concealed from a wider audience. Tigranes seems to have settled upon the idea of moving quickly in a pre-emptive strike against the Romans – he is said to have ordered an invasion of Lyaconia and Cilicia – but it is not clear exactly what his overall strategy was. It was certainly not a plan to draw the Romans deeper and deeper into hostile territory. Mithridates was sent back to Pontus to lead his own force in an attempt to recapture his kingdom, but nothing much came of this in the end, and the king without a kingdom was soon on his way back to Tigranes.

Did Lucullus catch Tigranes and Mithridates by surprise? This is likely, and may explain the significance of the stories of the near-miraculous fording of the Euphrates. If the kings expected to have more months to prepare, the speed with which Lucullus appeared before Tigranocerta would have quickly disabused them of their miscalculation. That said, one wonders what exactly Tigranes hoped to accomplish where Mithridates had failed. The Romans were in arguably a stronger position than before, and Tigranes had no navy with which to press a war on sea as well as land. And a defeated king was more a liability than anything.

The local population no doubt quickly realized that Lucullus was after one thing – the head of Mithridates. He displayed no interest in seizing and holding territory. He was not motivated by greed or infected with a spirit of hateful sadism and lust for conquering force. He had a simple mission, though the aftermath of success remained unclear and uncertain. Officially, he had no complaint against Tigranes except that the Armenian king was harbouring a fugitive from Roman justice. It is likely that Lucullus made clear to the minor rulers whose realms he traversed that he had no interest whatsoever in establishing Roman rule in these far-flung would-be outposts of empire. It is also clear that while Lucullus had legal justification for pursuing Mithridates, any complaint that he was risking a major loss to the Roman army by engaging Tigranes was also reasonable: he was now deeper and deeper into potentially hostile territory, and Rome now faced an escalating foreign crisis at exactly the time when recovery in Spain and in Italy were in full vigour. The persistence of the Asian problem was in some ways more troubling for Lucullus on the home front than on the front line of battle. Mithridates and Tigranes would prove easier opponents in some regards than Lucullus' enemies and rivals in Rome. At the same time, there is no reason to believe that the local population had any particular love for the Romans, especially as potentially long-term visitors.

Leaving aside questions of reconnaissance and intelligence, it is reasonable to conclude that the two kings expected Lucullus to aim for Tigranocerta. It was an obvious enough target, and a citadel that could not just be ceded to the Romans without a fight. The only real question was how long it would take Lucullus to arrive there, and he had already proven that he was capable of surprisingly swift movements.

The Advice of Mithridates and Taxiles

Mithridates had counselled patience and a resistance to a decisive engagement, and his one-time trusted general Taxiles was also on the scene to support his employer's wise advice. Tigranes is said to have been willing to listen, except when his Armenians and other allies began to argue that Mithridates was simply trying to deprive the king of his chance at a great victory, indeed that the deposed Pontic king was jealous of Tigranes' great opportunity to succeed where he had failed so miserably and ignominiously. Taxiles was present at a banquet where both courtiers and kings were urging Tigranes to move quickly to attack Lucullus, and Mithridates' general was nearly killed when he bravely interposed the view that caution was the best strategy. One of the best ways to defeat a delayer is with delay, but there were too many at Tigranes' court who saw the king's superiority in numbers, and the fact that the Armenians knew the terrain better, as ample reasons for striking hard and fast against what could be derided as a mere Roman expeditionary force. It is also possible that Mithridates had been tempered by multiple experiences of defeat and loss. Tigranes was relatively uneducated and inexperienced in these matters; his inclination may have been to pursue a riskier strategy than his father-in-law.

Tigranes was certainly won over by the flattering words of his allies. He is said even to have lamented that he was heading out to face only Lucullus, and not every Roman commander together and at once.[30] It is quite possible that Tigranes thought that where Mithridates had failed, he would succeed. Victory at Tigranocerta would ensure the worth of his name among even more potential allies, though a rudimentary knowledge of Roman history would have taught him that he had embarked on an exceedingly dangerous course of action, whatever the outcome of the present engagement.

Zero Hour

Plutarch respectfully notes that Tigranes had an impressively huge army of allied supporters, such that his confidence was not that of a madman. There is also the interesting detail that Lucullus duly noted the details about the opposing force in a missive to the senate. A politically cautious and expedient man might have cautioned the commander that by revealing the size of the enemy units before the battle had been joined, there may have been consternation in Rome at the idea that Lucullus was leading the Roman military into a dangerous and unnecessarily risky venture deep in enemy territory. No one could claim, at any rate, that Lucullus was dishonest.

Plutarch records that Tigranes commanded 20,000 archers and slingers, 55,000 cavalry (of which 17,000 were armoured, the so-called cataphracts) and 150,000 infantry.[31] The army appeared even larger than it actually was, given that Tigranes deliberately placed his engineers and other workers in the rear to augment the massive force. When the inhabitants of Tigranocerta saw the mighty army of the king massed for battle, they cheered and celebrated at the hour of their deliverance – and at once the Romans faced a difficult decision. We do well to remember that sources can be prone to exaggeration in the matter of the numbers of enemy forces. Plutarch's figures are given the support of Lucullus' actual senatorial dispatches, though one might wonder if the commander himself rounded the numbers up to embellish his achievement, or if he estimated incorrectly because of the misleadingly huge appearance of the enemy host. There is a fragment of the second-century AD historian Phlegon of Tralles, who was a freedman of the Emperor Hadrian. Phlegon composed a so-called *Olympiads* in sixteen books, of which only fragments survive. He asserts that the Armenians had 40,000 infantry and 30,000 cavalry – smaller numbers than Plutarch, to be sure, and perhaps closer to the truth. But Phlegon's numbers still point to a seriously imbalanced competition.

Some urged that Lucullus should at once take to the field and face the army of the king in set battle. Others noted that the city was dangerous, and that to abandon the siege was to expose the main Roman body to harassment and worse from the rear. Lucullus decided to leave Murena behind to maintain the siege of the Armenian capital, with a force of some 6,000 men, while he himself would lead twenty-four cohorts, with a total of some 10,000 heavy infantry, against the king. In addition, he would bring about 1,000 cavalry, archers and slingers.

The appearance of the Roman army brought down mockery from Tigranes' men on the weak impression Lucullus' force made. Soon, we are told, the king's commanders were arguing for the honour of moving forward alone to destroy such a seemingly insignificant force. Those who had argued against Taxiles and Mithridates now seemed to have had their position amply vindicated; it was believed the Romans simply had too few troops to pose any real threat to the ranks of Armenians and their countless allies.

The Sixth of October 69 BC

It was 6 October 69 B.C. – a day that was destined to enter the annals of the great victories of the Roman military machine. The exact date was noted in the sources, in part because on that same day in 105 BC, the Romans had lost a major engagement against Germanic tribesman at Arausio (the modern Orange).[32] Some of Lucullus' officers noted to him the unlucky status of the day – always a matter of serious concern to superstitious, nervous and anxious Romans. For once, Lucullus was bold in the face of omen and portent. He simply noted that he would convert 6 October into a day of good fortune and luck for the Romans – he intended to defeat Tigranes. Arthur Keaveney notes that no extant source offers a reason as to why Lucullus chose to give battle on this day. It is possible that he was deliberately recalling the Roman defeat that had marred the reputation of the day; it is also possible that the difficult business of the siege, and the overwhelming size of the king's force that would have taxed his sentinel abilities and surprise manoeuvrability were decisive factors in his taking immediate action.[33] The loss of Quintus Servilius Caepio, at any rate, would be avenged.

Appian's account of what happened is short and dramatically effective.[34] Lucullus is said to have taken a hill in the rear of Tigranes' force, and to have used his cavalry to coax the enemy into attacking them. Once successful in the provocation, the cavalry would continue to retreat, all in the hope of tempting the enemy to break ranks and follow in disorganized pursuit. This is exactly what the king's undisciplined force did. When Lucullus saw the Armenians chase after his men and dissolve their formations, he announced to those near him that they had won the battle. The Romans immediately attacked the king's baggage train, causing a chain reaction as these fled and fell upon the infantry, and then the infantry upon the cavalry in turn. A complete rout ensued. Part of Tigranes' problem was the fact that so much of his army consisted of draftees and conscripts from his subject territories; the confusion of the rout would have been increased appreciably by the difficulties of communication.

Plutarch offers a longer version of the events of the dramatic day. At first, we are told, the manoeuvres of the Roman army led some – not least the king – to imagine that Lucullus was retreating. Taxiles once again showed his wisdom in appraising the situation, and warned the king that such a stroke of good fortune was not to be believed. The king was quickly disabused of such notions, and he arranged his force with his own royal command to be in the centre, the left entrusted to the king of the Adiabeni and the right to the king of the Medes. On the right, the bulk of the armoured cavalry were arranged as a protective screen. The disposition of forces was a more or less textbook arrangement.

Lucullus, for his part, drew his sword and noted to his men that the enemy's reliance on archery and missile weapons could only be countered by a rapid advance across both the nearby river and the open plain beyond. The precise identification of the river is uncertain since we do not know for sure where Tigranocerta once stood. After crossing the river, Lucullus caught sight of the armoured cavalry of the enemy, and ordered his own Thracian and Gallic cavalry to engage the king's equestrian force. Plutarch notes that the armoured horsemen were equipped with long spears, against which the short swords of the Roman allies would be more effective. Lucullus himself took two cohorts to seize the aforementioned hill, then ordered an attack on the enemy's armoured horse, giving specific instructions to strike at the exposed legs and thighs of the horsemen.

But there would be no need for such an attack: for the enemy horse took flight and fell upon the infantry, and the infantry in turn on their rear, such that there was a confusion and great slaughter with nary a wound or the shedding of blood.[35] The Battle of Tigranocerta would seem to have been a marvellous example of disorganization and poor planning on the one side, and careful attention to disciplined order and awareness of the critical moments of a campaign on the other. A superior smaller force had once again dislodged and routed an army that was impressive only in size and number. For the rout, once again the casualty numbers are disputed; Plutarch would have us believe that as many as 100,000 were slain, while Phlegon is once again more sober, with just 5,000 dead. Philip Matyszak notes that the numbers are not necessarily incompatible: many of Tigranes' men may simple have deserted, and were marked down as lost.[36] Again, whatever the truth in terms of numbers, the Romans had won a dramatic victory, with a lopsided count in terms of dead and wounded.

Frontinus cites Lucullus' conduct of the Battle of Tigranocerta as an example of excellent appraisal of when to take best advantage of a given situation, noting that the Romans did not have above 15,000 men in arms, and yet they were able to achieve a decisive victory, since Lucullus knew that a large, unwieldy army must be struck just when it was most unprepared for battle.[37]

We do not know, then, the exact course of events on the fateful day – the day that Lucullus would turn into a red letter day for Rome. But all of our evidence concurs on how Lucullus managed to win his victory by a timely application of cavalry power at exactly the right spot to secure panic in the ranks of the king's forces. And it is certainly possible that Tigranes panicked and fled too quickly. A more collected and calm commander might have stayed to try to salvage the day. However, we have the benefit of hindsight in this regard.[38]

Was Tigranocerta truly the greatest victory the sun had ever seen, as Plutarch would have us believe? It was certainly the most dramatic achievement of Lucullus' eastern career, and the most glorious day heretofore in the Roman engagement with Mithridates' new protector. It would not be enough, however, to win the day for Lucullus and his optimate cause.

Chemical Warfare

An important epilogue note may be added here. Tigranocerta is notable in the history of military engagements for what may qualify as one of the first instances of the use of a sort of chemical weaponry in recorded history. The walls of Tigranocerta were defended by impressive towers, but the more terrifying weapon that faced the Roman besiegers was naphtha.[39] Our source for the Armenian use of naphtha is Dio (or at least Xiphilinus' eleventh-century epitome thereof);[40] he notes that the success of the weapon against the Romans fortified the courage and confidence of Tigranes as he moved the main body of his force against Lucullus. Naphtha was also mentioned in Sallust's histories, in a detail about how the substance was used by the Persians to ignite fires; the context may well have been Lucullus' exposure to the fiery peril.[41] Dio also speaks of the use of arrows that may well have been dipped in naphtha. Tigranocerta therefore may well have posed the most serious risk to Lucullus' force in the annals of Roman siege warfare in the Mithridatic campaigns, and in no small part due to chemical weapons. But neither these novel weapons nor the king's tremendous advantage in numbers and quantity of equipment would secure his victory.

The Aftermath

Tigranes' subordinate, Mancaeus, beheld the disastrous routing of his king's army from the walls of Tigranocerta. He had a significant force of Greek mercenaries in the city, and he at once suspected that they would turn traitor and go over to the Roman side, with concomitant betrayal of the city to Lucullus. The mercenaries immediately realized that they would be suspected of treachery and were in danger for their lives, so they took steps to defend themselves. Sure enough, Mancaeus ordered his forces to attack them, and in the ensuing engagement within the city, the mercenaries acquitted themselves more than adequately and won the day. They duly admitted the Romans to the city. Our source, Appian, does not record whether or not the Greeks had always intended to side with Lucullus, but whatever the case, the city was handed over with surprising ease in the wake of the great victory on the battlefield.[42] Nobody in Tigranocerta was in any hurry to die for Tigranes. Lucullus was now in possession of not only the capital of Tigranes' burgeoning empire, but also an immense amount of wealth and treasure. The fall of Tigranocerta was a blow of incalculable significance to the king's war plans. Unfortunately for Lucullus, it would not translate into sufficient success to silence the increasingly vocal opposition to his work in the East.

Plutarch is more explicit about the behaviour of the Greek mercenaries in Tigranocerta. He notes that they rose up in the wake of Lucullus' victory and made clear that they were ready to hand over the city to the Romans.[43] Dio Cassius asserts that most of the population of Tigranocerta was Cilician, and that these foreigners revolted against the Armenians and opened the city to Lucullus. In consequence, the Romans plundered everything except what belonged to the Cilicians.[44] Tigranocerta was essentially to fade from the map of history; there would never be any serious attempt by Roman or foreigner to rebuild it to a place of any significance. It is perhaps not entirely surprising that the city was so easily handed over, as the inhabitants had no good reason to endure a siege for a king whose defeat had been so total, and for whom they had no motivation to risk hardship and loss of life. Lucullus would enjoy the opportunity to plunder one of the richest prizes he could have hoped for on the map of his opponents' holdings. Tigranocerta was wealthy and economically healthy; its capture was a devastating loss for Tigranes, and it is a testimony to the resilience of Mithridates in particular that the Armenian king was able to be roused to continued military action in the wake of the defeat.

Plutarch notes that Tigranes fled in horror from the scene of his great defeat. His despair was so profound that he even handed over his royal diadem to his son, and urged his would-be successor to save himself by another escape route.[45] The prince, however, handed over the crown to a slave, and the slave was captured by Lucullus' men – so the Romans could literally say that they had captured the royal crown of Armenia.[46] Plutarch claims that the king lost 100,000 infantry and most of his cavalry, while Lucullus suffered about 100 casualties, with only five dead – an astonishingly lopsided victory, the numbers of which may be exaggerated. There is no reason, however, to distrust the summation that Lucullus won an enormous victory, and that 6 October had indeed been converted into one of the luckier and more fortunate days in the Roman calendar. Lucullus did permit his men to plunder the city, though he prudently took the royal treasury into his own custody. Plutarch is ever concerned to note that Lucullus was a man of literature, culture and the arts; he records that Lucullus took advantage of the fact that the city had so many artists, with the result that the victory celebrations and triumphal affairs were of an especially fine quality.

Tigranes' reputation had suffered grievously, and he would lose territory beyond his treasure city. The Armenian king would lose significant quantities of both money and land as a result of the decisive defeat on that dread October day. Most of the king's holdings south of the Taurus mountain range would swiftly be lost. Tigranocerta was one of those battles that mattered – but it would not matter enough to secure Lucullus' ultimate victory.

Plutarch offers a concluding comment on the Battle of Tigranocerta that cites lost sources of commentary. The unanimous evidence the biographer references attests to Lucullus' deserved fame for the enterprise. The general was credited with how he showed the ability and discernment to destroy Mithridates by careful and slow delay, and Tigranes by swift and sudden action.[47] The fact that the Romans were so ridiculously outnumbered was also noted to the commander's fame, favour and glory. We are told that in the aftermath of the battle, the Romans laughed at each other, noting that they really had no need of arms and weapons against such an army of slaves. This particular detail may refer both to the large number of conscripts in the king's army, and to the recently concluded Servile War in Italy. The battle had been preceded by mockery of the seemingly insignificant Roman forces by the Armenians; it was followed by self-deprecation on the Roman side, as they enjoyed their own joke at the expense of Tigranes' ruined and disconsolate army.

Diplomatic Dexterity

As a manager of peaceful settlements of conquered cities, once again Lucullus showed himself a master. Not only the Greeks, but also all the barbarians who had been forced to resettle in Tigranes' showpiece city were not only sent home, but were sent with funding for the journey. Plutarch makes clear that all the essentially reborn cities hailed Lucullus as their founder and saviour. The reputation of the Roman conqueror continued to grow in fame and glory. The biographer is careful to note that Lucullus was not interested in military renown, but in a reputation for honest dealings and responsible behaviour. Client kings were the desired goal of the day; there would be no Roman province of Armenia, but instead a network of kings who were loyal to Rome because of respect for Lucullus. Every gesture was calculated to help to achieve this end. If the wife of a king could be saved from assault, her husband would be all the more inclined to support the Roman position. And so it happened.

The Hope of Surrender

But Lucullus could not expect that Tigranes – let alone Mithridates – would simply now enter into negotiations to end the war. Both kings had everything to lose from an immediate surrender; they could have no serious expectation of surviving such a gesture with their heads intact. There was also the advantage of the season of the year. Winter was coming, and the Romans were quite deep in foreign territory. A fruitless hunt in search of the fugitive monarchs could easily put a blemish on Lucullus' record. His time in Asia had already been long; his men were no doubt ready to go home, and in no mood for continued operations in Armenia, especially after the capture of a city so rich in plunder and wealth. And yet the lesson of the First Mithridatic War no doubt haunted Lucullus as he now faced the prospect of not one but two renegade kings on the loose, and the war could not be considered definitively and conclusively settled until both men were killed or captured. How exactly to go about achieving that reasonable enough goal was the problem that confronted Lucullus on the evening of his astonishing victory.

Plutarch gives some insight into Mithridates' thoughts and character in the critical period before Tigranocerta. He notes that the king was in no particular hurry to show up at Tigranes' capital. He assumed that Lucullus would do what Lucullus had seemingly always done up to this point – exercise supreme caution and move slowly. No doubt he was shocked to learn that the Roman commander was also capable of dramatic military gestures. Plutarch says that on his way to Tigranocerta, he encountered Armenians in flight, and immediately realized what must have happened in his absence. He finally managed to meet Tigranes, and was responsible for shoring up the courage of the defeated monarch. Plutarch tellingly reveals that Tigranes was insolent in his behaviour to his father-in-law (did he upbraid him for not showing up to the scene of the battle in a timely fashion?), but that Mithridates did not return jibe for jibe and insult for insult; rather he shared his own royal insignia with his son-in-law, and began to encourage him to face the next stage of the ongoing struggle against Lucullus.[48]

Orosius has very little to say about the course of operations at Tigranocerta. He notes simply that Lucullus crossed the Euphrates and the Tigris, and then fought a successful battle against both monarchs at Tigranocerta, a battle in which he overcame his two opponents despite an appreciable imbalance in size of force. The casualty figure for the enemy is fixed at 20,000 dead, Tigranes is said to have escaped with barely 150 cavalry, and the detail about the surrender of his diadem and insignia of royal power is noted. Orosius associates the victory at Tigranocerta with the coming to Lucullus of almost all of the East in the position of suppliants, as legate after legate arrives seeking peace.[49] Eutropius does not give casualty figures, but does detail the size of Tigranes' force, and notes that Lucullus' victory at Tigranocerta was so great that Lucullus destroyed a great part of the Armenian population in one battle.[50]

It is clear that Lucullus' overall strategy remained diplomatic more than military. He wanted to create a network of pro-Roman client states, not to establish a permanent Roman presence in the form of provincial government apparatus and the potential for endless wars with new neighbours. And Tigranes – let alone Mithridates – had not done very much to earn the loyalty of the local potentates. Lucullus' reasonable, humane behaviour had an appeal all its own, and his overtures mostly met with success. The strategy was both reasonable and respectable – but it also opened Lucullus to the charge that he was seeking to ingratiate wealthy microstates to his own cause and enrichment. His enemies and rivals in Rome could easily offer a negative interpretation for his cordial, even warm relationships with eastern kings. And the heads of now both Mithridates and Tigranes remained frustratingly out of reach. The war could not end until the problem of both kings was resolved.[51] In the meantime, the charges being levelled against Lucullus became more and more bizarre: there were even accusations that he had invaded Armenia not for the sake of finding Mithridates, but to raid a sacred temple precinct for his own financial gain.[52] Lucullus was likely aware of the risks to his reputation that were occasioned by the continued ability of the enemy kings to slip through his fingers. But his options may well have been quite limited. While 69 BC would be the year of a great victory, and there would be another victory (though not as dramatic) in 68, Lucullus would be home in 67, the ultimate victory having eluded him.[53]

Renewed Preparations

In the immediate aftermath of Tigranocerta, whatever despair had enveloped Tigranes soon gave way to the realization that new plans were necessary, and quickly. And so the king opened negotiations with the Parthian Empire, asking them to help in his quest to destroy Lucullus' force. A new army would need to be drafted, but this time, Appian reports, Mithridates was to command the force. Appian notes that Tigranes thought that his disasters must have taught him something; we are not certain of the details of the negotiations and discussions between the two kings, but there is almost an air that Tigranes had been disgraced at Tigranocerta, and so he was now in lower repute than the Pontic king who had been defeated first. And, no doubt, there was the memory of how Mithridates and Taxiles had urged exactly the course of action that had been disregarded. In any case, one political development in the shadow of the battle was that Mithridates' star was again in something of the ascendant; he was now once more the commander of an army in the field. It no doubt helped the king's reputation that he had avoided actually being present for the disaster at Tigranocerta. In some ways his timely arrival must have seemed like a note of salvation from on high at a time of deep malaise and depression in the Armenian camp. Mithridates, to his credit, seems to have been aware that the time for tears must be brief, because plans were needed, and expeditiously, in order to win the war in the aftermath of the loss of the battle. The presence of two kings on the same side, too, allowed Mithridates and Tigranes to pursue a two-pronged strategy. Indeed, Lucullus would end up chasing Tigranes into northern Armenia, even as Mithridates prepared to invade his old kingdom by moving into eastern Pontus.

One could argue that Lucullus did the best that he could at Tigranocerta, and indeed that he deserves high praise for his victory. But there was one unfortunate consequence of his success: Mithridates was now the senior partner in the anti-Roman coalition. Tigranocerta seems to have revivified his spirits. It is possible that now he was, perversely, on equal terms with Tigranes – both men had suffered major defeats at the hands of Lucullus, and his son-in-law Tigranes could no longer maintain a certain *hauteur* as being his saviour and protector. Tigranes had lost his magnificent city, and his despondency was understandably profound. At this juncture, Mithridates was able to take heart and guide plans of renewed vigour against the Romans. Mithridates was also never a man to be content with just a little when he could aspire to have everything. He may well have seen a way at this juncture to dominance over not only an expanded Pontic kingdom, but also Armenia. Mithridates may have had his eye on greater power than he had ever known – and Lucullus was now left with two rabbits to hunt instead of one.

The surviving narrative of Dio Cassius (Book XXXVI) picks up just as Mithridates assumes command of the renewed prosecution of the Armenian war. Dio notes that there was an atmosphere of new beginnings, as if the war was only now commencing. Dio indicates that after the defeat at Tigranocerta, Tigranes' camp immediately made overtures to the Parthian Empire for potential help and alliance against Rome. The initiative was difficult, given that the Parthians were not exactly friends of the Armenians – there had been territorial disputes and border disagreements that threatened to escalate to open war – but the Armenian argument now was essentially that the two sides faced a common enemy.[54]

Parthia

Lucullus was aware that Parthia was a potential player in the war, especially as the Romans moved ever eastward. He sent his own emissaries on the difficult mission of securing either assistance to the Romans or neutrality. The Parthian response was a classic example of diplomatic caution. Appian says that the Parthians made arrangements with both sides, but that privately they were interested in staying out of the conflict. Indeed, the Parthian attitude may have been similar to what Tigranes would have felt had his marriage relative Mithridates not decided to take refuge in his kingdom. We have no knowledge of what the Parthian opinion of Tigranes was, but it is possible that he was no particular friend of theirs, at least not a friend for whom they were willing to risk a war with Rome. Plutarch specifies that the Parthians actually offered Lucullus an alliance, but that the Romans discovered that the Parthians were also telling the Armenians what they wanted to hear – specifically, in fact, that they would be interested in helping Tigranes if he would guarantee that they could take over Mesopotamia in the wake of victory. If we can believe Plutarch, Lucullus thought, for a moment at least, that it might actually be possible to defeat not one, nor two, but three kings in quick succession. Parthia would be a major thorn in the side of Rome for years to come, and the events of the next stage of the Armenian conflict led to an interesting set of circumstances in which to ponder alternate histories. For the moment, it seems that Lucullus was thoroughly unimpressed by the Parthians' willingness to play both sides against the other, and that he was likely asking his general staff to at least consider the possibility of war against the next great empire in the neighbourhood.

Dio observes, as we have noted, that the Parthians had territorial disputes with Tigranes, which the king was ostensibly willing to resolve. The Armenians also told King Arsaces (also known as Phraates) of Parthia that if the Romans were to defeat Tigranes and Mithridates, then Arsaces would be next – a reasonable enough summation, though a question complicated by the willingness of the Romans to continue the eastern wars indefinitely.[55] Dio further observes that at first the Parthians had no reason to suspect the Romans of any hostile intent, and were willing to consider an alliance and friendship – but then became suspicious that one of Lucullus' emissaries was really in Parthia to spy on the kingdom and to plan for future action against Arsaces.[56] And so he refused to give any assistance to Lucullus, but he did maintain his neutrality. Dio notes that the king's point in this was to see both Lucullus and Tigranes in a state of potential risk and hazard. The Parthians could remain safe and secure, while the Romans and the Armenians would expend men and material in their mutual destruction (or at least weakening). The Armenian struggle offered one of the first major opportunities for the Romans to negotiate with the Parthians; the great kingdom in the East would soon enough be the principal threat and source of strategic balance in Asia for Roman interests. Of the other great men of Lucullus' day, Crassus would lose his life in the pursuit of military glory against the Parthians, while Caesar would be assassinated on the cusp of his own planned departure in a great expedition against them. Mark Antony would face a disastrous campaign against Parthia that would do much to wreck his reputation at Rome. Parthia would be a significant counterbalance to Rome for years; it would be for Augustus to 'settle' the Parthian question essentially by agreeing not to prosecute a war against the empire. Propaganda, of course, could always be served by the return of the standards that Lucullus' contemporary Crassus had lost in his disastrous engagement at Carrhae.[57] For the present, no Roman could definitively decide what Parthia was thinking. There was certainly no clear avenue of advantage to Phraates' siding with Rome against Armenia – or *vice versa*. Lucullus was certainly under no illusions about Parthian trustworthiness.

One interesting surviving source for the dealings with the Parthians is the letter of Mithridates to Arsaces that is reported in Sallust's histories.[58] The purported speech – which may owe something to the example of the Greek historian Thucydides – is a masterpiece of rhetorical innuendo and counterpoint. The Romans are presented as bloodthirsty, insatiable conquerors. First they are said to have attacked Philip V of Macedonia, then Antiochus III of the Seleucid Empire. Mithridates paints himself as a victim of Roman greed and avarice; he was wealthy and not willing to submit to slavery, and so he was a target of Roman aggression. He highlights his successful attack on Cotta at Chalcedon, and notes that the siege of Cyzicus went badly precisely because he was not assisted by any of the locals in the matter of supplies. For Mithridates, the Romans are interested principally in the overthrow of all monarchies. Arsaces would be next, and if he were to ally with Mithridates and Tigranes, the war could be won far from the homes and hearths of Parthia. The survival of Sallust's attributed speech offers a valuable insight into one aspect of the ongoing diplomatic games that were a key part of the progress of the Armenian conflict.[59]

It is telling that Appian records that Mithridates conscripted another exceptionally large force, of which he selected 70,000 of the best infantry and about half as many cavalry. Clearly, in the aftermath of Tigranocerta, the King of Pontus decided that huge armies of incompetent draftees would not work against Lucullus' disciplined and highly trained force. The rest of the recruits were simply dismissed – Mithridates wanted to build a cohesive and reliable army. He also handed the men over to his own officers, as he no doubt had little confidence in his son-in-law's general staff. The elite army was divided into cohorts in imitation of the Roman system. Mithridates had undoubtedly developed respect for Roman military practice in the course of the long progress of the Asian wars.

Many of those kings who had been inclined to support Tigranes and Mithridates now lined up in favour of Lucullus. Plutarch makes clear that the reason for this was mostly Lucullus' generous and kind treatment of foreigners. We are told that Zarbienus, the king of the Gordyeni, had applied for an alliance with the Romans, but had been discovered by Tigranes – who had the king, his wives and his children all killed. When Lucullus entered the kingdom of the Gordyeni, he ordered a solemn requiem and lavish funeral rites for the murdered king, and declared that he was a friend and ally of Rome – he burned various trappings of Tigranes on the pyre as an immolation in Zarbienus' honour. He ordered an impressive monument to be built in the king's memory, and insisted that the payment for the memorial honour should come at no expense to the local population.[60] Gestures of this sort endeared Lucullus to the native contingents who might otherwise have been persuaded to join Tigranes. No doubt the Armenian king's own insolent behaviour did not help his cause. In the battle to win over the hearts and minds of the diverse peoples of the region, Lucullus was achieving handsome dividends. But all the while, his home-front enemies – the *publicani* and their supporters – were all the more emboldened to strike out against him. Every day the war remained unresolved was a gift to their cause.[61]

Meanwhile, Lucullus' subordinate commander Sornatius had been left behind in Pontus. He was now ordered to bring his army to Lucullus, so that with a sufficiently larger force a decisive move could be made against the fugitive kings – such a force was needed for any operations deeper into Armenia. Unfortunately, the Roman defenders of Pontus were apparently quite happy to be doing very little of a military nature, living a decadent life of luxury and in no mood to proceed to Lucullus and risk the hazard of a new war. When the Lucullan forces heard of the reluctance of their fellows to join them, they too began to ask why they should have to engage in another perilous enterprise. The Romans in Pontus were of course not aware of Mithridates' plans to strike fast and hard against the invaders of his former kingdom, should circumstances prove favourable for such an assault, which soon enough they would.

Plutarch attributes the decision to abandon any designs against Parthia to the near mutiny of the soldiers. Lucullus would spend the winter of 69–68 BC in preparation for the still elusive 'final' settlement of the war, and it was increasingly clear that there would be no realistic chance of adding Parthia to his list of conquests. There was something of the spirit of Alexander's age afoot here; just as the Macedonian conqueror's men had finally had enough of their seemingly endless eastward march, so here there was a definite limit to what the Roman soldiery was willing to endure.[62] The argument that the two kings needed to be dealt with was easy enough to make and defend. Pursuing dreams of glory against a third empire was another matter entirely.

As for the Parthians, for the moment they had nothing to gain from involvement in the Roman-Armenian War. There would be time aplenty for entanglement with the western empire that seemed increasingly to encroach on their sphere of influence. Negotiations, at any rate, were time-consuming – and time was something Lucullus did not have in abundance.

We should note here that Dio preserves the detail that Lucullus was thought by some to have essentially let Tigranes escape at leisure, in the hope of prolonging the already seemingly endless war still further.[63] And indeed, political machinations in Rome were well underway to deal with the question on some minds of when exactly Lucullus intended to return home. The province of Asia was handed over to the praetors, and later, Lucullus was relieved. A fragment of Sallust seems to indicate the commonplace judgment that Lucullus was outstanding in all respects, except in the matter of his great desire to extend his command.[64]

And yet the kings *were* still at large, and the pretext for the continuation of war was more than just, one might well assert. Arguably, the most valid charge that could be placed at Lucullus' door was that he was dilatory in his prosecution of the war. His slow progress, however, was balanced by ample proof of the ability to strike quickly and decisively – and by and large, his men had been safe and sound in their distant, dangerous enterprise. There may have been more than five dead at Tigranocerta, but nobody could claim that Lucullus was not cautious and careful with his men's safety. And every day in a war of the sort that confronted Lucullus in Asia was an opportunity for his men to complain and to harbour resentment; every day offered another occasion for the general to experience the anxiety of holding ultimate responsibility for what happened and the outcome of decisions major and minor. And all the while, Lucullus had to deal with local potentates. In the aftermath of Tigranocerta, for instance, Dio records that Lucullus met with Antiochus, the king of Commagene in Syria, and Alchaudonius, a chieftain of the Arabs.[65]

Xerxes in a Toga

In several important regards, Lucullus would lose the long and bitter battle for an enduringly positive reputation. It is possible that no man would have been capable to meet the challenge. The question ultimately hinges on whether or not Lucullus could have brought the war to a hastier conclusion. So long as Tigranes and Mithridates had eastward territory in which to run, the answer may well be no. But Lucullus' enemies – and in the viper's nest of the late Republic, he had his fair share and more – were determined to paint a picture of a man who was intent on wealth and plunder, on conquest for the sake of renewed warfare. The famous appraisal cited by scholars is that of the Tiberian era historian Velleius Paterculus, who in his histories relates that Lucullus did indeed accomplish much of note and worth in Asia, but with the inability to bring the war to a satisfactory conclusion, not for want of capability, but for want of inclination – to end the war would mean to end his chance to acquire still more treasure. And so Pompey would be appointed to replace him in the matter of Asian military affairs, and it would be Pompey who could aspire to the mantle of the Roman Alexander.[66] Velleius' judgment has found many modern supporters; the ancient historian notes that Pompey had criticized Lucullus for his greed, and Lucullus disapproved of Pompey for his insatiable lust for military power – and in the conclusion of Velleius, both men were right. And so Pompey is said to have referred to Lucullus as *Xerxes togatus*, 'Xerxes in a toga'. Lucullus, after all, was said to have let the sea in on the land by digging channels through mountains and to have built great piles at sea, much as Xerxes had attempted to bridge the Hellespont and to have constructed a canal through the isthmus at Mount Athos.[67]

Velleius' summation is simple: *summus alioqui vir* – he was otherwise the greatest/loftiest of men, but his weakness was luxury.[68] We may well wonder if the politically charged judgment of Pompey had won the day in the matter of Lucullus' reputation. The record as preserved in our sources does not justify such a claim, at least by the time Lucullus found himself deep in Tigranes' territory, in the spring of 68 BC.[69] And yet today, Lucullus remains most renowned for exactly the sort of charge that Pompey and others levelled against him, a charge that only seemed to increase in validity the longer Lucullus stayed in the East (a region that for 'traditionalist' Romans was itself a byword for luxury and decadence).

Artaxata, 68 BC

The year 68 BC was one of victories and frustrations for Lucullus. Armenia had many villages and locales that were easily taken; if Tigranes wanted to deprive the Romans of supplies, his strategy would fail. The kings offered no real resistance to Rome. They were undoubtedly preoccupied with rebuilding the main body of their army, and with preparing for another decisive engagement, and both Armenians and Romans realized that such a battle would likely be waged near Tigranes' ultimate capital, the city of Artaxata.

Artaxata is south of modern Artashat in Ararat Province in Armenia. Artashat is on the Araks River, a little over 18½ miles south-east of the capital Yerevan. The modern Artashat is a relatively recent foundation that dates from Soviet times (1945), and is some 5 miles north-west of the ancient site. Allegedly, the ancient city was developed on the recommendation, advice and supervision of none other than Hannibal, who had fled to King Artaxas of Armenia and served as a counsellor to the monarch.[70] The Roman army had marched something in the vicinity of 930 miles, so it is small wonder that some men were eager to see the sight of home.

It is clear from our sources that Lucullus intended to strike at Tigranes' capital, while Mithridates' strategy was to avoid any direct engagement, wearing down the Romans by unrelenting harassment deep in enemy territory. Both men were correct in their appraisal of the situation. Artaxata was the 'old' capital of Armenia; it appears that Tigranocerta was to be the new jewel of the king's empire – now he had fallen back on the original centre of his imperial realm, and here his wives and the bulk of his treasure awaited siege and defence. There was no question that Tigranes would need to defend his city. Mithridates' strategy of attrition may have been wise and correct, but it would only work if the Romans could be kept busy now with a prolonged siege of the Armenian capital.

Plutarch notes that in the summer of 68 BC, Lucullus was disappointed to find that the crops were still unripe on account of the relatively cool climate of far eastern Turkey and western Armenia.[71] Some scholars have blamed him for his lack of knowledge and realization about the climactic conditions, but in his defence we may note that weather reports were not easily forthcoming, and the Romans had limited knowledge about this distant corner of their known world. The villages that Lucullus plundered for food and supplies made up for some of the problem. All indications, however, pointed to a need to bring the war to a conclusion as soon as possible – Lucullus had every reason to believe that his men would not easily tolerate spending the winter of 68–67 BC in Armenia, and that his own political survival at Rome depended on him making a return sooner rather than later to his own capital. Appian reports that Tigranes' forces harassed Roman foragers. The Armenians were beaten off, and eventually the Romans were even willing to dare to expand their foraging operations into the territory Mithridates held.[72] Plutarch reports that there were some two or three occasions when the Armenians were routed in these minor operations. Lucullus was eventually ravaging enemy territory in open view, but the demoralized Armenians decided not to engage in further skirmishes.

It is clear that the verdict of Mithridates won the day in Tigranes' camp: there would be no major engagement, at least not until Lucullus was in a position to threaten Artaxata. Dio notes that Lucullus tried to draw the enemy into a major battle by attacking here and there, hoping to coax Tigranes' forces into an engagement in defence of native soil and resources. But the Armenians did not take the bait. The enemy cavalry was willing to clash now and again with the Roman horse, but whenever the Roman infantry appeared, the Armenian horsemen prudently withdrew – to the increasing frustration of the Romans.[73] Roman infantry were picked off and slain by the 'Parthian' tactic of archery and missile fire from the retreating cavalry, who often used poison arrows. The kings were clearly not interested in a major, pitched battle – they rightly feared they would be defeated – and so Lucullus may well have considered that his only option was to strike at Artaxata in the hope of provoking the 'final' engagement.

There was a 'Battle of Artaxata', but it was not, in the end, a battle for the capital. The details of what happened on the road to the great city are relatively scanty, and there are significant problems of interpretation, in part because it is not clear that either Dio or Appian even describe the engagement.[74] Plutarch notes that Tigranes was ready for the approach of the Romans, and that Lucullus – once again an exemplar of religious *pietas* – made sacrifice to the gods and then prepared to engage the enemy in a pitched battle. The Armenian force consisted of a significant cavalry and infantry array (the latter especially well trained), protected by mounted archers and Iberian lance-men. There was an initial skirmish between these Iberians and the Roman horse, and soon the Iberians were in full retreat. It appears the flight was the result of fright more than deliberate intent, and the Roman cavalry pursued. Tigranes now appeared at the head of his cavalry contingent, and Lucullus is said to have been frightened by the number of the force and their resplendent array. He thus ordered a halt to his own pursuit of the enemy and proceeded to march against the Atropateni who were massed opposite him. These were routed, and soon enough there was a general flight. Plutarch is careful to note that Mithridates was the most cowardly of the three kings who ran for their lives on that day.[75]

Our sources agree that considerations of weather played a significant part in the interruption of continuing military operations. Appian says that the onset of winter halted manoeuvres on both sides; Plutarch notes that an unusually early winter struck the region, so that September would already have been inhospitable.[76] The two authors are probably describing successive winters and not the same season. We face a difficulty of chronological analysis in the later stages of Lucullus' Armenian campaign because of the vague nature of Appian's account in particular, and the generally intractable differences between his narrative and that of Plutarch. Plutarch says that there was already ice and frost, snow and generally damp and unhealthy, difficult conditions at the time of the autumnal equinox. The pursuit of the enemy was a major problem for Lucullus' force, and once again the escape of the kings must have been a source of tremendous frustration to the Roman commander, who was living, after all, on borrowed time both in terms of the tolerance of his men and the political situation in Rome. Now he faced the problem of every military adventurer in autumn: winter was coming. Artaxata represented all too real challenges of terrain and weather – conditions that only made worse the constant difficulty of keeping an army resupplied in the field, especially so deep in potentially hostile territory.

What is reasonably clear is that in the aftermath of the Artaxata engagement, the two kings once again separated. Tigranes headed deeper into Armenia and Mithridates returned to what was once the heartland of his Pontic kingdom. The reason for the division is unclear, but it may reflect a strategy of seeking to divide the Roman force and either draw it off in two directions, or at least prolong what the kings must have realized was an increasingly favourable situation for them in terms of calendar and attrition. Appian says that Mithridates had 4,000 of his own soldiers, with an additional 4,000 whom he was supplied with by Tigranes. Lucullus eventually resolved to follow Mithridates, in part because he was already facing his own provisioning and supply problems and needed to return to the richer real estate in Pontus that he had left relatively lightly defended. Mithridates' strategy was to wear Lucullus down, and in this he was reasonably successful. Artaxata was to be another Tigranocerta; it was to be another major engagement, this one definitive. Lucullus' hopes in this regard would be dashed. Victory at Nisibis would still await him, but it would prove to be a poor consolation prize.[77]

Nisibis

We have observed that Lucullus' men had been eager for a return home almost immediately after the engagement – such as it was – at Artaxata. The situation was critical. Plutarch notes that not long after Artaxata, the tribunes had come to Lucullus to beg him to give up the pursuit of Tigranes and Mithridates. There was shouting in the soldiers' tents at night, which the biographer says is a mark of mutiny and incipient rebellion.[78] Lucullus sought to counsel patience and renewed tolerance for the hardships of the campaign, but his words must have been ringing increasingly hollow. He tried to argue that Artaxata was the 'Armenian Carthage', the city of Hannibal, but his men were in no mood for history lessons about the Second Punic War. In the end, Lucullus had to agree not to pursue Tigranes at least – the Roman army had moved as far east as it seemed willing to proceed.

Nisibis was under the control of Tigranes' brother Gouras, and it also benefited from the technology expertise of Callimachus, the Greek who had been such a threat to Roman safety at Amisus. Nisibis was apparently not to be one of the more difficult or challenging tests of Lucullus' ingenuity; the city fell without much of a siege process. Plutarch gives no details of the campaign, and focuses instead on how Lucullus was willing to treat Gouras with kindness, while Callimachus was brought to him in chains because, by his actions at Amisus in particular, he had robbed Lucullus of the chance to treat Greeks with respect and clemency.[79] His death would follow shortly.

Appian adds the detail that Nisibis was a treasure city of Tigranes, a city he had seized from the Parthians. It was a strongly fortified city, with two walls of brick with an intervenient moat. Appian provides more details of the actual siege than Plutarch. He notes that Lucullus prosecuted the siege with vigour, but that between the walls and the moat there was little that he could do – the city was so secure that even Tigranes did not see any need to come to assist in its defence, treasures notwithstanding. But then winter came, and on a moonless night there was another terrible storm – and the defenders of the city relaxed their guard. At just the most unexpected and infelicitous time given the weather, Lucullus struck. The few guards who had been left to man the walls were killed; archery and fire were utterly useless, given the torrential rain. Nisibis was captured because of the ability of Lucullus to judge exactly the right moment to launch an assault that could not be countered. If Tigranes really did conclude that Nisibis could defend itself, he had woefully miscalculated. Yet once again, the loss of a city would not mean the end of the war, and would arguably add another charge to the indictment of avarice composed by Lucullus' enemies. Nisibis could easily (if rather unfairly) be claimed to be more treasure-laden than strategically significant.

Dio makes clear that Tigranes thought that Nisibis could withstand a siege, and that the king headed for Armenia and the regions around the border with Pontus. We are told that Lucius Fannius opposed him, and that the king launched his own siege – an operation that was foiled when Lucullus sent aid to Fannius.[80] Fannius had served in Fimbria's army; his career between desertion and rescue by Lucullus is not entirely clear.[81] Tigranes and Mithridates had clearly mastered the strategy of dividing their forces and compelling Lucullus to chase first one, then the other. Artaxata had not been taken; Nisibis was a very real prize, though less significant than Tigranocerta, and equally pointless in terms of the critical question of the capture of the kings. And Pontus was weakly defended by understaffed Roman legions, with a population that was more than willing to welcome back Mithridates.

Eutropius has a brief comment here on the Nisibis operation: *Inde Nisibin profectus eam quoque civitatem cum regis fratre cepit*[82] (Lucullus advanced to Nisibis, and captured the city and the brother of the king). Another victory for the roster of conquests – and a royal captive, but not the king who mattered, and not the end of the war. Success at Nisibis would soon enough be followed by serious disaster elsewhere for the Romans.

Nisibis is the modern Nusaybin in south-east Turkey, not far from the Syrian border. It would be captured by the Emperor Trajan in AD 115, and later by Septimius Severus. It would be the general locale of the final engagement between

Rome and Parthia in AD 217, but hardly the last time the Romans would fight near its walls.

If someone wanted to be cleverly critical of Lucullus, they could say that he had abandoned the road of difficulty and taken the path to luxury and decadence. Nisibis represented the latter, while Artaxata may well have symbolized the former. But in a fair appraisal of the situation, and given the army he was blessed or cursed to have, Lucullus arguably did the best he could – yet the best was to prove simply not good enough in the current constraints.

Roman Disasters and Recovery; Zela

Mithridates, for his part, of course knew where he was heading, while Lucullus needed to wait for reconnaissance and intelligence reports in the aftermath of the Nisibis siege – not to mention tend to the rescue of Fannius' forces. Before Lucullus could hope to catch the fugitive monarch, Mithridates was able to launch a surprise attack on the defensive forces in Pontus under the command of Fabius Hadrianus. Both fugitive kings were fully occupied with surgical strikes behind enemy lines, as it were, hitting hard at Roman forces which might be considered easy prey – and diversionary bait for Lucullus. The Romans now suffered a serious blow, with some 500 slain. Hadrianus was in such desperate straits that he even resorted to freeing the slaves in his custody so that they could supplement his embattled force. A total disaster may well have been averted by the timely wounding of the king himself, who was struck by a stone in the knee and a missile weapon under the eye. The wounds were serious enough that Mithridates' army was concerned that the king might die then and there. The Romans, for their part, were unable to do much in the immediate aftermath of the king's injuries because of how badly they had been mauled in the engagement.[83] Dio tells us that the local population in Lesser Armenia and Pontus was willing to welcome back Mithridates, given that he was, after all, their king of long standing and that they had been mistreated by the Romans.[84] These Romans, who had been left behind by Lucullus to secure the captured territory of the king, clearly lacked Lucullus' gentle touch in dealing with local populations. Hadrianus was now essentially trapped in Cabeira, and Mithridates – wounded or not – had won back some of his lost glory. His victorious mood would not last for long, though for now things were not going badly for the kings, relatively speaking. There had been victories over smaller Roman forces not under the command of Lucullus in 68 BC, and 67 BC would see an even greater Roman defeat. And this was the worst possible time for the Romans to incur significant losses.

The king's battle wounds were perhaps cured by the Agari, a Scythian tribe noted for the use of snake venom (they may have been involved in the curing of his wounds after the Battle of Zela; we cannot be sure). Plutarch does not engage in such memorable accounts, simply noting that word reached Lucullus that Hadrianus had been defeated by the king, such that the Romans in his camp felt shame at the loss.[85] Hadrianus had suffered the defection of Thracian mercenaries and slaves in his camp who decided to join Mithridates. The whole affair might have been catastrophic for the Roman position, had fortune not intervened. The wounding of Mithridates bought the Romans sufficient time to send help to Hadrianus, who was in danger of a critical siege. The general Gaius Valerius Triarius was sent with a relief force. Once again, nature and the forces of storm or tempest played a part in the unfolding of military history. Triarius relieved Hadrianus and took command of the Roman soldiery, moving to engage with Mithridates' force, but a terrific storm rose up and destroyed tents and animals on both sides of the battlefield. For a while, waiting out the weather was the order of the day.

Once again, the quest for glory and the desire for an ambitious undertaking were to be the undoing of a would-be hero – at least in the view of Plutarch and Appian.[86] Triarius learned that Lucullus was indeed on his way, and that before long his superior would be on the scene and ready to settle affairs with Mithridates. He decided, then, that this was his hour to strike; he wanted desperately to have a victory to his credit before Lucullus could snatch the glory. Triarius ordered an attack on the Pontic camp. The fight is reported to have been long and brutal, but Mithridates was finally able to decide the day, and the Roman infantry were driven back to a muddy ditch and slaughtered in frightful numbers. It was another chaotic defeat for Rome, until fortune intervened to favour the children of Romulus. Mithridates had destroyed the Roman infantry, and was now in pursuit of the cavalry. A Roman centurion then managed to come close to the monarch in the chaos of battle, apparently in the guise of one of his attendants. He moved to strike the king in the thigh with a sword – he was aiming for an exposed part of the body, and hoping to assassinate Mithridates and thus save the day for his comrades.

A Failed Assassination

It was an incredibly brave and foolhardy action; the Roman soldier was immediately slain by Mithridates' men. But the king was in dire straits once again, or at least so went the story in swift rumour among his men. Appian says that the king's doctor, Timotheus, immediately moved to staunch the bleeding, and, perhaps more importantly, to show the king to his army – to literally lift up the monarch and encourage his men that all was well. Mithridates' main concern at this point was to chastise his men for having abandoned the pursuit of the Roman cavalry because of their fear for his life. Once treated, the king moved to lead an attack on what was left of the Roman camp.

The Romans had abandoned the site of their fortified base. Appian says that after the clash, twenty-four tribunes and 150 centurions were found while the king's men were stripping the dead – one of the heaviest death tolls in the officer corps for one's day action in the annals of Roman military history, indeed, possibly the worst ever.[87] Dio notes that Triarius had feared Mithridates' overwhelming numbers; he was waiting for Lucullus, but the king's attack on the Roman baggage at Dadasa had frightened them into action.

Plutarch offers additional details of the disastrous encounter between Triarius and Mithridates. He says that some 7,000 Romans were killed (he reports the same officer casualty figures as Appian), and notes that when Lucullus finally arrived on the scene, he prudently hid Triarius to save his life from the angry action of his infuriated soldiers.[88] Not surprisingly, we learn that Mithridates was in no mood to engage with Lucullus in battle – his attrition strategy was working wonders for his cause, and delay was the order of the day for the Pontic monarch. The so-called Battle of Zela of 67 BC was fought somewhere near the modern central Turkish city of Sivas. Triarius suffered what may well have been his first defeat; it was certainly his worst. Some twenty years later, Zela would be the scene of another battle, with a very different outcome, when Julius Caesar defeated Pharnaces II of Pontus, the occasion for the celebrated *veni, vidi, vici* report.

Taking Stock of the Disaster at Zela: 67 BC

The Zela engagement of 67 BC was a Roman military disaster, details for which are frustratingly elusive. Triarius was clearly the responsible party for the loss – and Lucullus the ultimate winner in that he successfully relieved the Roman position and drove off Mithridates. The Pontic king was not willing to stay and face a man who had defeated him before; the story of Lucullus' military career in Asia would not change – the king was perfectly happy to run away yet again. Especially in light of Caesar's later victory in the same vicinity over a Pontic king, we may conclude that the First Battle of Zela had an eerie outcome. This would be Lucullus' last real chance to destroy Mithridates, and the king would once again refuse to take any unnecessary risk. Before long, Mithridates would be seeing to the restoration of his rule over huge swaths of Pontic land. He was soon busying himself with the rebuilding and rehabilitation of his kingdom in what was increasingly clearly the waning period of Lucullus' military life.

One might well wonder if Lucullus had given premature hopes to his Roman audience that the business with the two kings was finished. In any case, the disaster at Zela would have been a godsend for his enemies in the capital. In 67 BC, the Romans could celebrate Quintus Metellus' subjugation of Crete and the island's reduction into a province. But Mithridates had defeated a Roman force at Zela and

Tigranes had moved to recover Armenia. Much had changed in five long years. In 72, Lucullus had defeated Mithridates at Cabeira (the year the pirates had done well against Marcus Antonius off Crete). Mithridates had fled to Tigranes, and Lucullus had spent 71–70 BC engaged in pursuit and further (albeit relatively minor) victories. In 70, Metellus began his pirate campaign in Cretan waters. In 69, Lucullus reached the apex of his power with the astonishing victory at Tigranocerta. But already in 68, the decline was in full vigour, and 67 was a year of bad news for the opponents of both Mithridates and Tigranes. Zela would prove to be Mithridates' one truly impressive achievement over a Roman army, though he would not profit much from the victory in the long-term. If Appian is a reliable source, the king's victory was in part achieved because he was able to pin down the Romans in a muddy trench that impeded their movement; the Romans were caught by Mithridates and slaughtered in the ditch.[89] Mithridates was about 67 years old in 67 BC – and he now had a present to celebrate the year. Zela was the high point of his career of animosity against Rome. All Mithridates and Tigranes had to do for the moment was to run amok through Pontus and Cappadocia.[90]

Mithridates was unwilling to engage Lucullus the way he had engaged Triarius – but Dio records that another Mithridates, the son-in-law of Tigranes from Media, did attack some Roman units and win another victory over Lucullus' force.[91] There was also news that Tigranes himself was on the way, with another large force. The epitome of Livy sums up the whole affair succinctly and with understated, litotic restraint: *C. Triarius legatus Luculli adversus Mithridaten parum prospere pugnavit.*[92] History has not been kind to Triarius, and the definitive truth about what led to the Zela disaster may be forever lost; whether Triarius was hastily seeking to forestall Lucullus' arrival and victory or not, he had performed disastrously against an admittedly formidable opponent – and he would be remembered for his loss.

Lucullus, for his part, had moved against Nisibis – great prize as it was – and Mithridates had moved back into Pontus and inflicted appreciable defeats on Roman garrisons there. Deservedly or not, Lucullus' reputation was at a low point. The fact that Lucullus arrived in time to prevent total destruction did not do much to restore it. But Mithridates was smart enough not to engage Lucullus directly. He knew that time was very much on his side, not his Roman adversary's. Cities and towns that did not expect an attack, however, were a tempting target for the renewed strength of the king. A fragment of Sallust's histories may reflect how Pontus was once again at Mithridates' mercy: *Simul inmanis hominum vis multis e locis invasere patentis tum et pacis modo effusas <urbis>.*[93] Cities that were living a peaceful existence in the aftermath of war were once again prizes; Mithridates was restoring his lost empire, and Lucullus could do little to halt the Pontic resurgence. We do well to remember that many of the local inhabitants would likely have been happier under Mithridates' authority than Roman rule. Lucullus may have been a benevolent conqueror, but there was little affection for Rome in these distant outposts. In the end, Mithridates would have a free hand for some time in Cappadocia because Lucullus did nothing to stop him in the aftermath of the forthcoming revolt of his men, and because Glabrio was not yet on the scene to take the lead against the king.[94]

The decision had been taken in Rome to relieve Lucullus, it would seem, even before the news of the Zela disaster reached Italy. Matters had already gone on for far too long in the prosecution of the war against Mithridates.[95]

The Character of the Commander

Plutarch gives a summation of Lucullus' character and mindset in the aftermath of Nisibis that is revealing in part for how markedly different it seems to be from the biographer's previous appraisals of the man.[96] This is the point in time whence Plutarch records a failure in Lucullus' ability to achieve his ambitions, and indeed the moment when the general found it increasingly difficult even to maintain what he had amassed. Plutarch is clear that Lucullus was still brave and patient – indeed patience had been one of the hallmarks of his generalship, and one of his most enduringly successful and praiseworthy qualities. But these positive notes of character no longer availed him, and in Plutarch's estimation the responsibility was not only that of fortune or luck, but also of Lucullus himself. He was not willing to try to curry favour with the common soldier, and was equally unwilling to come to terms with his social and military equals.[97] He is said to have despised his colleagues, as if he was acutely aware that he was more talented than they. The picture that emerges of Lucullus is of a man who was supremely frustrated at the abilities of those around him, a man deeply troubled and anxious because his associates in the prosecution of the war – and his colleagues at home in Rome – seemed so utterly inferior to the task. Plutarch is careful, and almost apologetic; these were the bad qualities of Lucullus, but only these. It is telling that luxury and decadence – the later watchwords for which 'lucullan' would enter our vocabulary – are not among the alleged vices for which the biographer is willing to indict the general. The summation concludes with a note that Lucullus was tall and of pleasing appearance, and an excellent orator – indeed, one equally suited for the Roman forum and the world of forensic oratory and for the field of battle.

Plutarch's judgment of Lucullus is followed at once by more evidence of how both the army and the commander's enemies at Rome were quick to condemn the man. The soldiers had the more legitimate complaint, one might argue. They had spent two winters in camp; they had not enjoyed the solace and recreational comforts of Greek cities. Lucullus was condemned at home for maintaining sole command over a vast swath of land, and for having ransacked the Armenian king's

palaces and treasure cities for what appeared to be his own enrichment. The praetor Lucius Quinctius was one of the leading voices in attack against Lucullus.
The measures Quinctius was recommending included replacing Lucullus in his
province, and freeing many of his soldiers from the burden and expectation of continued fighting in foreign wars. It was clear that no rhetorical ability would be able
to save Lucullus for much longer from the increasingly solemn toll of the bell. He
would soon be forced to make a return to Rome, fugitive kings notwithstanding.
As one modern histiorian has noted, 'People deplored the fact that poor Italian
lads seemed to be condemned to wander endlessly through the wastes of Asia.'[98]
Quinctius, we may remember, had cause to be annoyed with Lucullus and to be in
search of personal revenge; he had come up short in oratorical debate, and now,
he correctly assessed, was his chance to strike back. Provinces needed to be taken
away from Lucullus: first Asia, then Cilicia. Little by little, Lucullus' power would
be diminished. If Tigranocerta had been a great victory, it was not great enough
to give Lucullus a free hand in the East. There were clear signs of ongoing war
against both fugitive kings, and possibly the peril of involving Rome in a war with
Parthia. No doubt Lucullus' enemies found ready audiences for their complaints.
We do well to remember that Lucullus was fighting two wars - one in the East and
one in Rome – and he was at a distinct disadvantage in being unable to respond to
the challenges of the domestic struggle, given his remote removal from the capital.

Assessment

Dio offers his own extended appraisal of Lucullus.[99] He credits Lucullus with
the supreme title of confidence among Roman generals. He cites him as the first
Roman military commander to have crossed the Taurus with an army in time of
war, and as the conqueror of two powerful and dangerous kings. He does note
that Lucullus seemed in no hurry to end the war, but that his final 'defeat' in
the manner of the revolt of his men was occasioned by how he expected so very
much of his soldiery, was strict and unforgiving in his camp discipline and the
imposition of punishments to maintain order, and was hardly one ready to admit
common soldiers into his presence. For Dio, he was a man incapable of winning
over an army by persuasion or mildness; the soldiers were thus willing to obey
him when plunder and wealth were in abundance, but equally ready to abandon him at the first sign of trouble or hardship. Dio concludes that the ultimate
proof of Lucullus' problem is that the very same men who revolted against him
were willing to serve Pompey – a perhaps somewhat unfair assessment, given that
many of Lucullus' men were apparently discharged at the same time as their commander, and that (as we shall see) significant changes of circumstances attended
the transfer of command.[100]

Clodius' Machinations

Publius Clodius Pulcher – Lucullus' brother-in-law – was no help in the matter. It seems that he felt that in no way had he received his due of honour and benefaction for having aided Lucullus (we may recall his embassy to Tigranes). And so now he played his own role in the undermining of Lucullus, mostly by working on the frustrations and anger of the soldiers, and by noting that although they had more or less defeated two great foreign kings, they were still living abroad in relatively wretched conditions, while Pompey's men were enjoying the comforts of family, home and hearth in Rome, merely for having fought against exiles in the Sertorian War in Spain, and the mopping up operations of the Spartacus War in Italy. To Lucullus' men was owed far more honour than their general seemed interested in bestowing upon them; they were literally carrying the gold and treasure that was meant to further Lucullus' career, while their counterparts in Pompeian service enjoyed their own treasure.

It was no doubt a powerful argument, made all the more so because it was not novel. The soldiers in Asia had been complaining for some time; indeed it could be said that Lucullus was a general in search of a better army in terms of patient acquiescence and loyal support of a commander. The Fimbrian contingent in particular had always been something of a weak link in Lucullus' military array; Clodius knew exactly which soldiers would be most receptive to his efforts.

Dio makes clear that Clodius was a lover of revolution.[101] His sister's marriage to Lucullus was no impediment to his seeking a revolt against the optimate commander. The passage of Dio XXXVI.14.4 that speaks of Clodius' alleged love for upheaval and turmoil is of uncertain date; scholars argue even about exactly how many mutinies there were in Lucullus' camp. What is clear is that Lucullus' brother-in-law was now acting against his interests, and that if there was any struggle politically between pro-Pompeian and pro-Lucullan factions in Rome, the former side was winning the day.

It is unlikely that Mithridates and Tigranes knew much about these political and personal machinations on the Roman side. And yet in an important sense, they had no need to know. All they needed – at least *versus* Lucullus – was to drag out the proceedings in a war of attrition.

Final Stages

It could be said that Clodius succeeded in his plans, though he was hardly working alone to his own, solitary purpose – or even to that of Pompey. Lucullus' men were in no mood to pursue either Tigranes in Armenia or Mithridates in Pontus. In fairness to the soldiers, it may be noted that it is exceedingly easy to run, and that the kings had plenty of land and territory in which to exercise their flight. It is true that the desperate situation of Fabius and Triarius was enough to spark some light of valour against the enemies of Rome in this distant land. Mithridates might be unwilling to face the Romans in a direct engagement, but Tigranes was rumoured to be on his way, and Lucullus had hopes of engaging the Armenian monarch as he approached his Pontic ally. Such a potentially decisive engagement was simply not to be. The Fimbrians were not willing to fight, and to a man they were more than happy to inform Lucullus that by order of the senate and the people of Rome, they were discharged from further service to him. It was a rebellion, one could argue, but one that Lucullus had no effective means to suppress. Appian says that word had arrived from heralds of the proconsul of Asia that Lucullus had been accused of unnecessarily prolonging the war, and that in consequence the soldiers were disbanded, with the penalty of confiscation of property to be imposed on anyone who resisted the edict.[102] Indeed, Appian notes that there were some poor individuals in the army who stayed loyal to Lucullus; they had nothing to lose, of course, and arguably a chance to gain something from continued fidelity to their wealthy commander. Appian's narrative is less condemnatory to the Roman army; his account makes the whole matter seem like an orderly and legal proceeding, and not some mutinous revolt against Lucullus. No doubt the truth exists somewhere on the nebulous, misty border between the two.

The aftermath of the Zela disaster was clearly the last opportunity for Lucullus to win the day. It was a perhaps impossible task for any man. The fugitive kings may not have been aware of all the particulars of the Roman political situation, but Lucullus' men were well aware that the days of their commander's rule were in a sense already finished. Every day of paralysis on Lucullus' side was another day the kings could work to re-establish their control over the vast territory of Cappadocia and Pontus. While 67 BC may well have been the worst year of Lucullus' life, it was certainly the year in which he either learned or was reminded definitively of the fact that not everyone in Rome shared his sense of *pietas* and loyalty.

A War Ends Inconclusively

The Third Mithridatic War was thus inconclusively ended, rather in the manner of the first. Appian notes that the Romans were in no mood to prosecute the war aggressively, given the continuing peril of the pirate menace, *inter alia* (among other things). Mithridates was more than willing to take advantage of the Romans' lackadaisical attitude, and soon enough, he had his sights set on invading Cappadocia and beginning to reconstitute his imperial holdings. He correctly surmised that the Romans would do nothing about it, at least for the moment. Lucullus had not even made his way from Asia before Tigranes was joining in the plundering of Cappadocia; no provocation seemed great enough to persuade the Romans to renew fighting. The territories in question were vast, and the ability of the enemy to run away from any chance of direct engagement with the main body of Lucullus' force was practised and well honed. Lucullus could do little other than watch the virtual dismemberment of the gains he had achieved in Pontus and Lesser Armenia. Arthur Keaveney does not mince words; in his appraisal, the Third Mithridatic War ended 'disastrously' for Lucullus.[103] Failure in the field against Mithridates and Tigranes was compounded by problems at home, where Sullan supporters would be increasingly unhappy with the constitutional reforms and initiatives that were now in play. Lucullus had needed a stopwatch in Asia; he had needed sufficient time to fulfill his military mission and to return to a Rome that was firmly ruled under the Sullan provisions. Inexorable time had been Lucullus' undoing, at least in part. It is no surprise that he might have found hours in his libraries in the company of philosophers and men of letters to have been more appealing and engaging than hours in the senate and forum.

Cherry Trees

Pliny the Elder (*Naturalis Historia* XV.102) records one bit of information about Lucullus' dealings with Mithridates that has contributed to the general's reputation as a gastronome. Cherry trees (*cerasia*) were unknown in Italy, Pliny notes in his botanical writings, until Lucullus won his victory over Mithridates; that is, Pliny specifies, 74 BC. Lucullus is said to have brought them to Italy from Pontus, and a century and twenty years later they made their way even to Britain, though there was no success at cultivating them in Egypt.[104]

Plutarch reports an interesting and even sad detail about this period. Lucullus had written to the senate that Mithridates was all but dead, and that the prosecution of the war had gone very well. But now, visitors from Rome who had come to oversee the process of transition saw a king who was on a renewed path of destruction against Roman interests, and a Roman commander who had lost the respect of a large number of his men. Lucullus looked like a failure, and even a liar; mendacity was in fact not a charge that could fairly be imputed to him, but the timing of the arrival of the Roman overseers and commissioners could not have been worse. Mithridates was more than skilled at taking advantage of just the right moment. He had proven this talent over and over in the course of the complicated events of three separate and yet continuous wars, and he would have the chance to show once again his acumen for being a master in judging the demands of the hour.

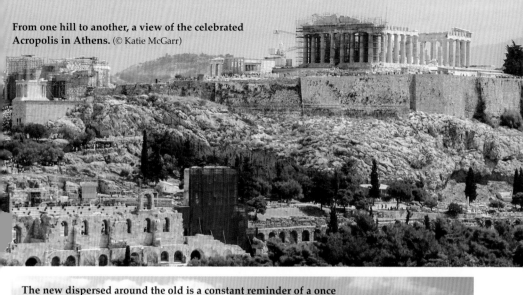

From one hill to another, a view of the celebrated Acropolis in Athens. (© Katie McGarr)

The new dispersed around the old is a constant reminder of a once glorious empire centred in Athens. (© Katie McGarr)

The traditional gateway to the underworld: the lair of Hades at Eleusis. (© Katie McGarr)

Vis, Croatia, a key island for viticulture and wine production in the Mediterranean. (© Katie McGarr)

A view of the countryside of the island of Naxos, where Theseus was said to have abandoned Ariadne.
(© Katie McGarr)

The famous temple of the goddess Demeter on Naxos.
(© Katie McGarr)

Sunset in Naxos, one of the many fiery skies seen by Lucullus and his Roman sailors as they pursued their military campaigns in the eastern Mediterranean. (© Katie McGarr)

Night-time in Larnaca: A Cypriot sunset on the island of the goddess Venus. (© Katie McGarr)

Paphos, Cyprus: A stroll down the beach that once witnessed the birth of the goddess Venus. (© Katie McGarr)

Salamis, Northern Cyprus. (© Katie McGarr)

The agora at Salamis, Northern Cyprus. (© Katie McGarr)

The amphitheatre at Salamis, Northern Cyprus. (© Katie McGarr)

Olympos, Turkey.
(© Katie McGarr)

A view of the sea from the top of the castle in Kekova, Turkey. (© Katie McGarr)

A turquoise getaway on the island of Solta, Croatia, once a staging ground for Roman naval manoeuvres. (© Katie McGarr)

Stone cold Medusa supports
the structure of a basilica
cistern in Istanbul, Turkey.
(© Katie McGarr)

A crisp walk through one of
the canyons in Cappadocia,
Turkey.
(© Katie McGarr)

Cave dwellings, known for being cool in the summer and warm in the winter, are still used for housing today by Cappadocians.
(© Katie McGarr)

A crisp, autumn stroll through Goreme National Park in Cappadoccia.
(© Katie McGarr)

A sunrise view from a hot air balloon - the best way to get an aerial view of the famous tent rocks in Cappadocia.
(© Katie McGarr)

A traditional dish of lamb and cabbage, cooked by the peka method that is native to Vis, Croatia. The dish cooks for three hours over the fire, which marries the flavours. (© Katie McGarr)

Lucullus Taverna on Naxos, which claims to be the oldest restaurant on the island. (© Katie McGarr)

Wine and restaurant view at the taverna on Naxos that was named after Lucullus himself. (© Katie McGarr)

Contempt

The arrogance of the Roman soldiers is well illustrated by the anecdote in Plutarch that, at the close of summer, the men assumed their armour, went out of camp with brandished weapons and shouted in challenge to an enemy already long departed. When no soldier of Mithridates or Tigranes replied, they solemnly announced that the time had now passed in which they were obliged to obey Lucullus – in other words, they had clearly discharged their duty to him if there were no enemies willing to respond to their call to action. The sorry, shabby treatment of Lucullus in some quarters had already begun to evoke feelings of sympathy and regret; when Pompey was eventually put in charge of finishing operations against Mithridates and Tigranes, there were those who noted that Lucullus had done all the real work, and that Pompey was merely being summoned to earn a triumph for an easy victory.[105] In an important sense, the seemingly hollow gesture of the soldiers had a significant point: under the command of Lucullus, they had achieved much, indeed the bulk of the labour of the defeat of the king. What would follow could be considered a mere postscript to Lucullus' achievements.

Quintus Marcius Rex – consul in 68 BC – was Lucullus' replacement as Cilician governor. A fragment of Sallust notes that he was unwilling to come to Lucullus' aid in Cappadocia, citing the *voluntas* or will of his soldiers.[106] Manius Acilius Glabrio was his successor as consul in 67; like Rex, he would never make it into the field against Mithridates.[107] Pompey would receive command over the Mithridatic problem in 66 BC as a result of the so-called *Lex Manilia*, or 'Manilian Law'; the law would pass in large part because of Pompey's tremendous success in ending the pirate menace in the Mediterranean. Neither Rex nor Glabrio would do anything of note in their time in command in the East; the stage was being set – and deliberately – for the advent of Pompey. Glabrio's appointment was largely due to the political machinations of the tribune Aulus Gabinius, a devoted Pompeian who would later be known as the commanding officer of a young Mark Antony in Egypt (55 BC). Glabrio had already tangled with Lucullus in the aforementioned episode of the breaking of the chair when Lucullus allegedly slighted Glabrio by not standing in respect. Glabrio would now be in charge of fighting Mithridates, while Pompey would tackle the pirate problem. It is reasonable to wonder about Pompey's attitude in this period. He likely realized that where Lucullus had failed, Glabrio could never hope to succeed. Glabrio could never aspire to be more successful against the king than his accomplished predecessor. Pompey may well have realized from an early date that he could handle the pirate menace and then move to solve the Mithridates problem.

Glabrio, then, was merely a useful expedient, an intervenient commander whose likely incompetence would make it all the more understandable that a man of Pompey's ability would need to be sent to the front.[108] Politically, it was far more advantageous for Pompey to succeed Glabrio and not Lucullus. The *Lex Gabinia* would give Pompey a pirate command; the *Lax Manilia* would secure for him his real desired prize – command against the elusive Pontic king. We may note that Pompey's eventual antagonist Caesar was a supporter of the bill to award Pompey the command against Mithridates, and of the earlier bill for the pirate command. For the time, Caesar was on Pompey's side, and that was probably the safest and most politically expedient role for him to play. Caesar need not have been a political strategist of any great note to realize that Pompey was in the ascendant. Given his own history in the days of Sullan power, it was no surprise at all that the young patrician would side against Lucullus. Whatever the future held, Lucullus would not be a major player upon his return to Rome. While politically active, it was perhaps no surprise given his temperament that he would shy away from overt action in the manner of a Pompey or, soon enough, a Caesar.

Replacements and Departures

Quintus Marcius Rex had received Cilicia in 68 BC, but had not arrived in the East until 67. Manius Acilius Glabrio was assigned to replace Lucullus sometime in 67, it would appear – command of the Mithridatic War would thus definitively pass to another. This was the year of the Triarius disaster at Zela, which may well have been the final bit of bad news that would be tolerated in the matter of Lucullus' pursuit of Mithridates. The situation was, however, a bit hollow: admittedly, Mithridates had had a very good spring of 67, but he was also a spent and largely exhausted force, and Pompey would soon enough not have to do very much to put him to flight.

The Fimbrians were the first Romans to depart from Lucullus' command – and they certainly had the force of law behind them, if not *pietas*. Neither Rex nor Glabrio was in any hurry to tell Lucullus what to do, but Pompey would be a different matter entirely.[109] Lucullus was even to suffer the ignominy of not being able to distribute rewards or punishments among those who had served under his command.[110] If he had powerful friends and supporters in Rome, they had not been able to win the day so far against the Pompeians – but there was that increasing sense that Lucullus had been treated poorly. The idea that Lucullus and Pompey should have a joint meeting, a chance to clear the air, as it were, was appealing to some. For the moment, Lucullus had retreated into Galatia, an altogether inconvenient presence for Pompey. The man who would one day lose to Caesar was, for the moment, the man of the hour. He had triumphed in Spain, had won his share of glory for the ending of the slave war and had made short work of the pirates. When he would meet Lucullus, in some sense it would be an eerie foreshadowing of the fate that would one day await him with Caesar.

Chapter 6

Early Retirement?

U ltimately, Lucullus would be replaced by Pompey. Gnaeus Pompeius had been born in 106 BC, and in some sense by the time he took full command in Asia in 66 BC at the age of 40, the situation there was much as it had been in 74 when Lucullus had first arrived. One of our most valuable surviving sources for the takeover of Pompey is the speech that Marcus Tullius Cicero gave in support of the bill that was designed to give the general unlimited time, resources and freedom of place in prosecuting the war against Rome's eastern enemies. The speech *de imperio Gnaei Pompei* – better known as the *pro lege Manilia* – is a masterpiece of Ciceronian oratory.

Cicero is complimentary to Lucullus, whom he refers to as a *summus vir* – literally, 'the highest man'.[1] Lucullus' prosecution of the war against both Mithridates and Tigranes is spoken of in praiseworthy terms; Lucullus is lauded for his *virtus*, or courage and bravery, rather than his *felicitas*, or fortune. If Cicero's speech was intended to placate the nobles as much as to support the side of popular opinion, then Lucullus would need to be treated with reserve and respect. The silent undercurrent of the speech, however, is that Lucullus failed to secure a lasting solution to Rome's eastern problem, and that Pompey is the new man of the hour, the commander who would be able finally to put to rest the threats to Roman economic life in Asia.

Cicero begins his appraisal of Lucullus' résumé by noting that the general entered a situation that was exceedingly challenging.[2] Mithridates had enormous forces and was prosecuting the siege of Cyzicus with vigour. Lucullus lifted the siege by his *virtus*, his *assiduitas*, or constant perseverance, and his *consilium*, or plan/skill. The Sertorian rebel fleet was also destroyed, great numbers of the enemy were killed as the Romans advanced into Pontus, and Sinope and Amisus were taken. The king himself was finally forced to go as a suppliant in search of allies. All of this was accomplished without threat, either to Rome's allies or her revenue stream. Cicero notes that none of the opponents of the Manilian law had ever praised Lucullus to the extent uttered by Cicero; Cicero sets himself up as the greatest celebrant of Lucullus' enduring reputation and fame.[3]

Mithridates as Medea

Cicero famously compares Mithridates in flight to the mythological Medea, who escaped from her native Colchis with the Greek hero Jason by means of dismembering and scattering the limbs of her brother (she correctly assumed that the pursuing vessels of her father's ministers would stop to retrieve each and every body part of her poor brother). Mithridates escaped by scattering treasure, as it were, tempting riches and gold, that was promptly seized by pursuing Roman armies. Mithridates successfully arrived at the court of Tigranes in Armenia, and by the time of Lucullus' arrival, Rome had new and powerful foes – enemies Rome had never expected to have. The impression had been given to the kingdoms of the East that Rome was interested in total conquest and plunder. Even after the armies of Lucullus seized Tigranocerta, there was a general sense among the soldiery that they were far too removed from home for their liking and comfort. Mithridates rallied more and more men to his cause by pity and the arousal of sympathy for his plight; the idea that the Romans were a danger to all was part of his ability to raise increasing numbers of supporters and allies. Before long, Mithridates was able to recoup his losses and achieve more in defeat than he had ever hoped to win in happier times. And Rome suffered startling setbacks and defeats. Allegedly, there was a story that the Romans had come to sack a sacred temple, and before long, Lucullus had embroiled Rome in a far more complicated war than the Mithridatic one. Cicero is cagey throughout. He does not blame Lucullus for these events in so many words, but the portrait – even when complimentary – is designed to point the way to Pompey as the saviour of the hour. The longer Mithridates was on the defensive against Lucullus, Cicero notes, the more sympathetic he appeared to his neighbours, and one by one the king found new allies who were willing to shield and support him in his time of crisis.

Soon enough, there was disaster. Lucullus heard about Mithridates' resurgence and attack on Roman forces, not from any messenger from the battlefield, but from the rumours that emanated from the countryside.[4] The disaster of which Cicero speaks more or less vaguely is that of Zela; all the emphasis of the oration is on how the king was on the rise, even after the defeat at Tigranocerta.

Lucullus was forced to hand over his command to Glabrio at precisely this hour of crisis, because precedent and custom demanded that he give up his generalship.[5] *Multa praetereo consulto*, says Cicero – there is much that I leave out on purpose. An effective rhetorical device is thus employed to pass over controversial topics and the real heart of the matter – how exactly was it that Lucullus was removed from his office? But the rest of the speech – its bulk – is taken up with praise of Pompey as the present and ready saviour of Rome in her hour of eastern crisis. As one critic of the speech has noted, 'The superseding of Lucullus was merely the result of jealousies and intrigues at home.'[6] The *pro lege Manilia* is a rhetorical masterpiece on many levels, but if it has one stunning quality in terms of Lucullan studies, it is the manner in which it scrupulously avoids condemning Lucullus, even while implicitly proposing him as a *deterior* commander to Pompey. The Lucullus that emerges from the lines of the speech is past his prime, while Pompey is the versatile general whose experience in a wide range of conflicts is what the crisis demands.

Danala

We have noted that a meeting was eventually arranged between Lucullus and Pompey, apparently by the friends of both. We can only imagine the awkwardness of the arrangements and the plan. Pompey had made it known that he wanted no one to visit Lucullus, and he had taken steps to countermand his orders by his own decrees and edicts. The two men finally met in a Galatian village, Danala, the exact location of which is not known. Plutarch indicates that the meeting opened in a friendly manner, each man warmly congratulating the other on his victories and achievements.[7] Both commanders were honoured with laurel that adorned the so-called *fasces* (the bundle of rods with axe blade that served as a symbol of Roman magisterial authority); Pompey's is said to have been dry and waterless because of the desolate tracts of land through which he had travelled. When Lucullus' lictors saw this, they gave some of Lucullus' green sprigs to Pompey as a sign of respect. Pompey's men took this as a good omen, since the victories of Lucullus did arguably adorn those of Pompey and provide an ornament.

Nothing good was achieved at the meeting, however – or at subsequent ones.[8] No agreement was ratified. On the contrary, the two men are said to have left the meeting in a worse state than they had arrived. Lucullus was to be left with 1,600 soldiers, and not a man more; all his orders were nullified. The 1,600 men left with him were there mostly to adorn his triumph, and Plutarch reports that they were not happy with the assignment. Dio offers the note that Lucullus initially told Pompey that there was no need for a new military expedition, since the war was over; when he failed with this argument, he turned to abuse, arguing that Pompey was greedy for war, for public office, and so forth. Pompey essentially ignored Lucullus – he knew, after all, that the page of history was now his. He simply instructed his subordinates to ignore any of Lucullus' orders – the 'old man' was now to be treated as a curious irrelevancy.[9]

It is perhaps unsurprising that the first detail Dio preserves about Mithridates in the wake of the Galatia conference was that he continued to flee. He had had great success with leading Romans on chases, and saw no reason not to employ the same strategy against Pompey as he had against his predecessor. Lucullus could not have had any serious trust in the efficacy of the argument that the war was over. If anything, his point must have been that he had done all the real work, and that his replacement was on the scene merely to do something akin to what he had done with Crassus in the closing movements of the Spartacus War. If Pompey was incensed at the argument, he merely had to bide his time until Lucullus was safely on his way back to Rome. The memory of how Pompey had treated him at Galatia would leave Lucullus rankled for some time; he would have his chance to repay the favour, at least in some small sense, when the day came that he would demand that the senate examine and approve each of Pompey's measures individually and in turn.[10] For the present, however, Lucullus and his retinue of would-be triumphal soldiers faced a long journey back to Rome. The days of Lucullus' foreign adventuring were over at long last. The man who could arguably lay hold to the title of the last of the Sullans – if not the last of the republicans – was coming home to an uncertain future.[11]

At this point in his narrative, Plutarch makes another general assessment of Lucullus the military leader. Lucullus' main problem was that he could not retain the affection of his men. If he had, Plutarch is certain that the Romans would not have marked the border of their empire at the Euphrates, but by the very limits of Asia and the Hyrcanian (i.e., the Caspian) Sea. Tigranes had already conquered so much, and the Parthians were not that powerful, and so by defeating the Armenian king, Lucullus would have truly been the Roman Alexander. In implicit contrast to Lucullus' failure to win over the hearts and minds of his soldiers is the popularity for which both Pompey and Caesar would be celebrated (especially the latter). The verdict of many modern scholars on Lucullus is that his excellence and ability in the field were not remotely matched by the warmth and affection that his rivals and peers enjoyed from their men. It is all too easy to label Lucullus more or less crudely as 'old-fashioned', even something of a martinet. The truth, however, may be that Lucullus was quite effectively stereotyped, especially in his absence, and that any commander would have had significant problems in keeping his men from mutiny in identical circumstances.

Plutarch has another comment on Lucullus, specifically on the Parthian problem. For Plutarch, Lucullus did great harm to Rome, greater indeed than the good he did for Rome, for by his very achievements in distant Asia, he tempted Crassus to seek his own fortune against Parthia. Crassus would suffer defeat and death in 53 BC; Plutarch notes that Crassus would learn that Lucullus' enemies had been defeated not because they were cowards, but because of how competent and bold Lucullus really was. Lucullus had known better than to stir the Parthian bear, but his successors in the East would not all share such wisdom.

Were Lucullus' men simply fickle? Did they have legitimate grievances against their commander of so many years? Did many of them, indeed a majority, harbour a strong desire to return to Italy, trading in the life of a military adventurer for that of a gentleman (at best) farmer? Certainly many of Lucullus' men stayed with Pompey. When the time came for decisions and debate, it may well have been that many of the army's men had attachments in Asia – women and the prospect of immediate reward in the form of plunder – and the idea of returning to an Italy that held little for them personally may have been a factor in persuading many soldiers to remain under arms in Asia. They were professional soldiers now, and not some militia that was ready to return to civilian life. Claims that one desired to return 'home' to Italy and Rome, of course, were always poignant laments for soldiers who had spent so long in the field. Perhaps the prospect of a new commander filled some with the hope of increased rewards, donatives and special favours as a general's insurance for the challenges that lay ahead.[12]

Home Again

Lucullus did not have a pleasant homecoming to Italy. He may not have recognized some aspects of its daily governmental processes and senatorial order, for much had changed in the years since he had embarked on his Asian mission. He learned soon after his arrival that his brother Marcus was under investigation and prosecution by Gaius Memmius for the conduct of his quaestorship under Sulla.[13] And Lucius himself was soon under the microscope, with the usual accusations that he had appropriated the property and plunder of the state for his own use and had needlessly stretched out the war in Asia to further his own financial and military/political ambitions. There was even the denial of the triumph that many would have felt had been justly earned – though of course Mithridates was still on the loose.

It may well have seemed that life was coming full circle. The brothers had needed to defend their family honour in their youth, and now one after the other the brothers were being attacked by a man who could arguably claim no accomplishment that came anywhere near matching what the Luculli had achieved. For Lucullus to have a triumph would only encourage credence to the view that he had done all the 'real' work, and that Pompey was merely putting the finishing touches on a project that was mostly to the credit of Lucullus. One may well wonder if the Memmian prosecution and attacks on the brothers was the decisive factor in Lucullus' decision not to be the standard bearer of the optimates against the power of Pompey – again, in some sense he may well not have recognized the Rome he had re-entered. Marcus had enjoyed a triumph for his part in the resolution of the Spartacus mess; it was not nearly enough, however, to free him from the threat of an ambitious prosecutor – and his brother would fare no better. If someone was inclined to conclude that the prosecutions were political in nature, they would not be unreasonable in the analysis.

Lucullus defended himself. He did have friends, after all, and those who no doubt continued to feel sorry for the treatment of the man in the wake of his manifold victories and deeds of valour. Eventually, the decision about the triumph was rescinded; 66 BC would be the year of his hour in the spotlight, his chance to be honoured for his Asian achievements. Plutarch notes that the triumph was not quite of the ostentatious magnitude of some; Mithridates, of course, would have been the only trophy that mattered in the procession. There were many captured arms and royal siege engines, with tokens aplenty to commemorate the most impressive of Lucullus' achievements. One might well imagine, however, that it was a triumph with a certain forlorn, hollow quality. For no one knew better than Lucullus how abortive the whole enterprise had been. The general had been cheated, some might say, of the ultimate prize.

Cataphracts were present, and scythe-bearing chariots, along with an appreciable enough assembly of some sixty of the king's generals and friends.[14] Perhaps most remarkably, we are told that Lucullus brought back 110 bronze-beaked ships and a 6ft tall golden statue of Mithridates – an incredibly valuable substitute for the living monarch, though again a perhaps all too painful reminder that the king himself was still at large, indeed running amok. Interestingly from a political point of view, there were tablets that had the figures and sums that Lucullus had paid to Pompey for the prosecution of the pirate war – a perhaps overly subtle reminder that Lucullus had financed the spectacular achievements of Pompey at sea, and a class-laden rebuke of the charge that Lucullus had profited personally from his conquests in Asia.[15] Each of Lucullus' men had received 950 drachmas – a possible reminder that complaints were inappropriate from his soldiery – and in a detail that is of some special interest given Lucullus' culinary connections, we are told that the general provided a magnificent feast for the Romans, a true celebration to mark his special day.[16]

Memmius had failed in his efforts to deny Lucullus a triumph, but he had managed to sour the day of glory by his political machinations. It was one thing to celebrate a triumph – another thing entirely to have to wait to observe the day of honour. No one may have been much convinced that Lucullus' war against Tigranes was unjust, but there was ample room for manoeuvring in the matter of delaying the commander's rewards.

Divorce

At this juncture of his biographical treatment, Plutarch notes the divorce of Clodia. Lucullus was no doubt more than exhausted from his dealings with her family, and the dissolution of their union could not have been unexpected.[17] Lucullus promptly married Servilia, a niece of Marcus Porcius Cato, but unfortunately for Lucullus, Plutarch notes that the marriage was just as bad, with the sole redeeming feature that there was no incest with the wife's brothers! Servilia is condemned as being just as wicked and vile as Clodia in all other regards. Lucullus is said to have tolerated her for a while for the sake of Cato, only to divorce her, too, in the end. The divorce of Clodia is attributed to the incest of the wife with her brother. We have no idea when Clodia began to be unfaithful to Lucullus; her indiscretions may well have started quite early in the marriage. Any involvement with her brother may have had a quite long duration, one that preceded her nuptial union with Lucullus.[18] We may be certain that no one in Rome was particularly critical of Lucullus' decision to sever ties with his spouse.[19]

There was another facet to the relationship between Memmius and the Luculli. Memmius was married to Fausta Sulla, the daughter of Sulla and Caecilia Metella. She was divorced in 54 BC, and would eventually marry Titus Annius Milo, the rival of Publius Clodius Pulcher for the consulship of 52 BC. Milo's men would be responsible for Clodius' death in the infamous encounter between the rival political gangs at Bovillae in January of that year.[20] We have no record of what Lucullus' thoughts were on the marriage of his ward to Memmius. All we can be certain of is that the nuptials were a casualty of the deteriorating relationship between the two men.

Memmius and Lucretius

We may say a word here about the Gaius Memmius who is cited as having been an opponent and prosecutor of both the Lucullus brothers. Memmius is perhaps best known to history as the patron of the poet Titus Lucretius Carus, the author of that Epicurean verse evangel, the epic *De Rerum Natura*, or 'On the Nature of Things'. Memmius makes appearances, too, in the surviving poetry of Gaius Valerius Catullus; he was originally a supporter of Pompey, but later defected to the cause of Julius Caesar. His antagonism toward the Luculli no doubt stemmed simply from his partisanship for Pompey. Memmius' own reputation was checkered. He was hardly a paragon of moral virtue and upright behaviour. His attack on Lucullus (not to mention the younger brother) was a chance to ingratiate himself in certain circles, perhaps even to have some of the worst of his sins overlooked. Memmius was certainly more than engaged in exactly the sort of activities that Lucretius warned against and condemned in his philosophical, didactic epic.

Famously, we know very little about the life of the poet Lucretius. A passage at the end of a letter of Cicero to his brother Quintus from February of 54 BC is often cited among the *testimonia* of the poet's work.[21] The detail there about Cicero's appraisal of Lucretius' work has been taken by many to imply that the poet was dead by the spring of 54, but in fact we cannot be certain of this or much else in Lucretius' biography. What we do know is that his epic is infused with anxiety about the state of political life in Rome. Would a literary man like Lucullus have been ignorant of Lucretius and his work? While there is no definitive evidence to support the conclusion that Lucullus was an Epicurean, there is good reason to think that he knew of Lucretius' work – indeed, one may well wonder if Lucretius was a visitor to his gardens and libraries. We cannot be certain of the chronology of composition of the books of the *De Rerum Natura*, though scholars have long observed that Memmius is a more prominent figure early in the poem. Is it fanciful to think that something of the poet's admonition to Memmius is rooted in the circumstances of the patron's treatment of the Lucullus brothers? Ultimately, are the warnings of the poet's epic aimed both at Memmius and Lucullus (and Pompey after him), who went to the East presumably at least in part in search of riches, financial boon and military glory? Whether card-carrying Epicurean or not, did the Lucullus who returned to Rome in the wake of his replacement by Pompey find that he sympathized with the message of the Roman epic poet?[22] And if Lucullus knew Lucretius, to what extent did the poet's relationship with Memmius make for awkward tension? On these and similar issues we can only muse.

Lucullus' Children

We know that Lucullus and Clodia had one child, a daughter Licinia.[23] From Servilia, a son would be born – another Lucius Lucullus. We are not sure of his birth year, but we do know that he never achieved anything of note in the worlds of politics and the military – an obscurity that may of course have saved his life in the waning years of the Republic.[24] We can be reasonably certain that the period from 64-c. 60 BC was not a particularly happy time for Lucullus in terms of family life. Servilia may well have been having an affair with Memmius, and Lucullus would in no way be blessed with domestic harmony and tranquil peace.[25] Again, we may think of Lucretius, in particular the fourth book of his epic and its condemnation of passion and discourse on the dangers of love. Given his experience of both Clodia and Servilia, one might well conclude that Lucullus would have appreciated Lucretius' sentiments. Again, we can only speculate – but so much of Lucullus' life allows for a reading of Lucretius as a virtual commentary on his career, both domestic and foreign. This may be thought to be true of any number of eminent Romans of the Republic, but Lucullus holds a special place in this regard, given his literary tendencies and emphasis on *pietas*, a theme that takes on special prominence in the closing movements of Lucretius' epic,[26] and most of all given the fact that after so much in the way of accomplishment, Lucullus was ultimately cheated of his prize.

The consulship of Marcus Tullius Cicero, the *novus homo* or 'new man' who had risen to the highest office in Rome, and who would soon enough distinguish himself in the matter of the famous 'conspiracy' of Lucius Sergius Catilina (the notorious Catiline), was in 63 BC. Cicero's major dealing with Lucullus up to the time of his consular service had been as the author of the speech in defence of the

Lex Manilia; if anything, one might have thought that Lucullus had just cause to view Cicero as an enemy. There is no evidence that such animosity existed on either side. As we have seen, Cicero's speech did speak in eminently respectful terms of Lucullus, and we have no reason to think that the two men were ever hostile to each other. Indeed, Plutarch reports that they were on friendly terms even after the controversy over Pompey's appointment and Cicero's role in securing the command for Lucullus' rival. They were frequently in touch and in friendly conversation and interaction.[27]

Cicero had done a number of services for the Lucullan cause. He was one of the defenders of Lucullus' *quondam* subordinate, Lucius Licinius Murena, for whom he wrote the celebrated oration, the *Pro Murena*.[28] In the autumn of 63, Murena faced a charge of electoral corruption that would have prevented him from taking office as consul in 62. Murena was in the end acquitted, and entered into his consulship; we can be certain that Cicero's speech was the key factor in Murena's salvation – although scholars generally conclude that he was guilty. Cicero was probably interested at this political juncture in balancing the power of the rival factions in Rome, and it is possible that he was trying to engage in a particularly favourable deed for the 'Lucullan' side. It was increasingly unclear, however, what exactly that 'side' constituted in terms of leadership and direction.

For Lucullus was to be no hero of his optimate cause in these latter years of his life. If anyone in Rome wanted Lucullus to be a counterweight to Pompey, they would soon be sorely disappointed. It seems that Lucullus showed no interest whatsoever in re-entering the maelstrom of republican political life. This is the point in Lucullus' life at which Plutarch notes the entry of the former commander into a life of luxury. The biographer is quite specific in his analysis of the man and his decisions. Plutarch offers a weighted alternative of sorts, we might think: either Lucullus thought that the political situation in Rome was too far gone – and thus beyond his abilities or perhaps anyone's to resolve – or he thought that he had had enough of glory and honour, and that now he more than deserved to retreat into enjoyment and luxury. Plutarch notes that many praised Lucullus for his decision – whatever the rationale behind it – noting that men like Marius and Cicero would have done better if they had known the proper time to retire from public life. Crassus and Pompey were not among Lucullus' admirers in this regard; they observed that hedonism and luxurious, decadent behaviour was even more questionable in an older man than participation in public and military affairs. More of the same, then, from the usual suspects. Lucullus needed to be removed as an effective force in political life, and it appears that for whatever reason, he was quite unwilling to do very much to fight against his opposition.

There was also the suicide of Mithridates in 63 BC. Pompey had done what Lucullus had failed to achieve – he had put an end to the war against the Pontic king. Mithridates would emulate Hannibal by committing suicide; there was a certain defiance in the deed, as if Rome was being deprived of the chance either to exact punishment or offer clemency. Pompey would return to Rome in 62, ready to see to senatorial approbation of all his dispositions for the East in the wake of his victory – all along he had political as well as military goals to pursue. Lucullus would be ready to repay something of the favour for the treatment he had received in Galatia.

The Archias Affair

In 62 BC there was the celebrated court case that considered the question of whether the poet Archias was a Roman citizen.[29] We do not know the exact disposition of the case, and we can only speculate as to whether or not Cicero's famous defence of Archias was successful. We can be sure, however, that the Archias affair was really nothing less than a political attack on Archias' patron, Lucullus, the man whose deeds the poet was said to have celebrated in epic verse (a *Luculliad*, one might say).[30] Almost all we know of Archias is derived from Cicero's speech; there are thirty-seven epigrams in the so-called *Greek Anthology* that have been transmitted under the name 'Archias', though there is scholarly question as to how much of this corpus can be safely attributed to the 'Ciceronian' Archias.[31] Cicero gives some insight into the details of Archias' epic work on the war with Mithridates. He refers to the glory not only of Lucullus, but also of the Roman people (who were made famous by the deeds of the outstanding general). Pontus was opened up for Rome with Lucullus as *imperator*; with not so very many men, Lucullus subdued the nations of Armenia. Lucullus is credited with responsibility for the salvation of Cyzicus in its hour of crisis. Under Lucullus' charge, an enemy fleet was destroyed off Tenedos, and the king's naval threats quelled. Again, all that we know of the epic is due to Cicero. We know that it was written in Greek (Cicero proceeds, in fact, to a spirited defence of Greek literature just after his reference to Archias' epic), but have no idea how long the poem was, if it was ever finished, and indeed how familiar Cicero himself was with its contents. We certainly have no sense of when it was lost to the mists of time.

Cicero notes in his speech that the house of the Luculli sheltered not only the early youth of the poet, but also his declining years.[32] Cicero notes in his defence of Archias' Roman citizenship that his client's absence from census rolls was due in large part to his tenure with Lucullus in Asia.[33] While Cicero's brief speech in defence of Archias does not add any information to our knowledge of Lucullus' campaigns in Asia and Armenia, it does make clear that the commander was accompanied abroad by his own Homer, as it were – his own epic poet who could record the history of the campaign for poetic posterity. It is one of the tragedies of Lucullus' life that such verse glorification of his work – especially given his philhellene tendencies – exists today as little more than a footnote in the long history of Roman involvement with Mithridates and Tigranes. Of course, Archias' celebration of Lucullus' life and work would have made him the perfect target for political attacks orchestrated by Lucullus' enemies in Rome. Archias' loyalty to his patron could not be questioned, and the Greek poet was an ideal focal point for any harassment of the optimate politician.[34]

The Bona Dea Scandal

December 62 BC witnessed a celebrated scandal that centred on the behaviour of the notorious Clodius, into which Lucullus was perhaps inevitably drawn. The basic story is simple. The rites of the so-called 'Bona Dea' or 'Good Goddess' – a divinity of women's chastity and fertility – were the preserve of women alone. But Clodius had been discovered in women's clothing, hiding as it were in plain sight among the devotees of the goddess. He was seeking nothing less than the most opportune chance to have a romantic assignation with one Pompeia, the grand-daughter of Sulla himself (her mother had been Sulla's daughter Cornelia). Caesar would end up divorcing Pompeia over this drama – but for the moment, the question was one of sacrilege and profanation of sacred rites, and Clodius faced trial and condemnation.

In the end, Clodius would be acquitted, despite the vigorous attempts of Lucullus to see him successfully prosecuted. Clodius' very life was at stake; the alleged crime of desecration of the goddess' rites was a capital offence. This was the hour, to be sure, for Lucullus to seek revenge for the mutiny of his army after the capture of Nisibis; this was time to charge Clodius with incest and myriad other offences and delicts.[35] In the end, Lucullus would expend what political capital he had on a difficult and ultimately unsuccessful effort. Caesar, for his part, was now in a most embarrassing situation as a result of the shenanigans of his wife with Clodius – whether genuine or merely rumoured and insinuated.[36]

We can speculate with some confidence that Lucullus was personally shocked and offended by the scandal. No doubt he agreed with Cicero that Clodius was indeed guilty, and this episode far surpassed any 'immortality' that might have been found in the Praecia affair. Lucullus no doubt knew Clodius better than most, and was shocked by the sacrilege, even as he was not surprised by the culprit. If Lucullus wanted to embarrass Caesar, the scandal was also a ready-made opportunity for that target shooting. Caesar would have wanted the whole matter closed as quickly as possible, probably without the publicity of a (very) public trial.[37]

Clodius managed to escape condemnation – juries could, after all, be success-fully bribed. He would remember the part played by Cicero in the prosecution as a star witness – in three short years, Cicero would be exiled, largely at the instigation of the vengeful Pulcher. Clodius would ultimately meet a violent death in a clash of their rival entourages (not to say gangs) with Titus Annius Milo on the Via Appia near Bovillae in 52 BC. In the meantime, he would not likely have forgotten how Lucullus was a prosecution witness against him.[38]

An Ancient Comedy

Plutarch compares the life of Lucullus to an ancient comedy.[39] The first part of his life was replete with the glories of military and political life, and the latter part with revelry, the frivolous nonsense of luxury and the pursuit of pleasure as an end in itself. If Lucullus had been noted as a praiseworthy patron of the arts and literature, now he was open to the criticism that his love for 'Greek' life was the source of disrepute and indulgence in folly; rivers of money were poured forth not on the betterment of the state, but on the improved living conditions of the man. The gardens of Lucullus are cited as being the most expensive of imperial botanical retreats, and the money expended on all of this luxury was of course derived from the general's expeditions in Asia. Plutarch even takes care to note that the money spent by Lucullus was excessive in light of the increased luxury costs of his own day; Lucullus could rival the spending of the later emperors.

The gardens of Lucullus – the celebrated *Horti Luculliani* – were located on the Pincian Hill. The Villa Borghese gardens occupy some of the same land on which Lucullus' property once stood.[40] The gardens would later be associated with Claudius' notorious young wife Messalina; she would be killed there in AD 48 after her disastrous affair with Gaius Silius.[41]

Plutarch details the extravagances that were attributed to Lucullus. Pompey is said to have criticized Lucullus for arranging one of his properties in the best possible way for summer, but not for winter. Lucullus retorted that he had more sense than cranes and storks, and was thus capable of changing residences with the season. A praetor asked about purple cloaks for a spectacle; when Lucullus asked how many cloaks were needed, he doubled the cited number from 100 to 200.[42] Plutarch cites the aforementioned comment about Lucullus being nothing less than 'Xerxes in a toga', though with the attribution of the remark not to Pompey but to the Stoic philosopher Tubero.[43] Whoever made the remark – and no doubt it became all too popular in Roman gossip and waggish commentary on the now retired commander – no one could question the immense building projects that Lucullus commenced. Tunnels were built through mountains, moats were constructed around his properties for all manner of ichthyological embellishment and vast structures were built out to sea on piers and piles.

Gastronomic Indulgence

It was now that the lifestyle of rich indulgence in exotic food and lavish dining ware began in earnest. Another anecdote preserved in Plutarch reveals something of the interaction of Lucullus and Pompey. Pompey was ill, and the physicians had prescribed a certain thrush that was apparently only available in the summer season on one of Lucullus' estates. Pompey argued that something else would need to be prepared for his medical repast, since one such as Pompey should not have to die because Lucullus was not excessively indulgent in luxurious gastronomical choices. Cato – Lucullus' father-in-law – was predictably censorious of his son-in-law's habits. A senator was allegedly once delivering a very boring speech on the virtues of temperance and frugality, when Cato objected that the individual made money like Crassus, lived like Lucullus and talked like Cato.[44]

Plutarch goes so far as to say that Lucullus affected the lifestyle of a *nouveau riche*. The indictment of anecdotes continues in the biography – anecdotes that Plutarch notes point not only to a love of pleasure, but to an absolute pride in the pursuit thereof. Some Greeks were being entertained by Lucullus, and they eventually expressed concern at the high costs that were being incurred every day on their account. When they finally voiced their worries, Lucullus assured them that while some of the money was being spent on the Greek guests, the majority was being spent to entertain the host Lucullus himself. Similarly, a servant once put forth a rather humble dinner on a night when Lucullus was dining alone. When criticized and upbraided by Lucullus for the apparent slight, the servant noted that he simply had taken note of the fact that there were no guests on the agenda today. Did the slave not realize, Lucullus retorted, that tonight Lucullus was dining with Lucullus?[45] A clever quip, to be sure – and the sort of comment that often finds a way to be remembered for centuries in the biographical and anecdotal tradition.

The Descent into Luxury

We are to believe, then, that the frustration of his military and political career after 66 BC is what accounted for the more or less sudden descent into a life of virtual hedonism for which Lucullus is indicted in the closing chapters of Plutarch's biography, and in the lasting appraisal of so many of those who have essayed to pass judgment on the man's life and career.[46] Certainly it is possible – indeed, arguably likely – that Lucullus felt supremely unappreciated by the political and military leaders of the late Republic; it is more than plausible that he felt that he deserved better for his many years of service.

His early career had been founded on principles of loyalty and *pietas*, qualities he felt were utterly lacking in the treatment that he received from so many in the waning years of his career and in his period of retirement from public life. He had been accused unjustly of having indulged his own pleasures, so perhaps in a passively aggressive fit of reaction, he decided to give in to the indulgence of that for which he had been maligned for so long. The fact that his detractors would then argue that he had always been a libertine was of no real account; Lucullus was finished and done with caring much about his reputation among men he may well have come to despise as intellectual and moral inferiors. As for Pompey, he likely felt that if his great rival was to accomplish anything of note in the East, it would be because Lucullus had made it possible – and anyone with reason and unprejudiced, sober judgment would recognize this salient truth. Lucullus' father had had a poor reputation, and his mentor Sulla had occasioned far more controversy than most – Lucullus had been scrupulously loyal to both men, and no doubt felt tremendous resentment that his *pietas* and devotion to his 'fathers' was not rewarded or even much appreciated. The Roman world had changed significantly, even in the time that Lucullus had been away in the East, and it would soon see the downfall of Crassus, Pompey and Caesar in turn, as the Republic lurched towards its imperial demise.[47]

In some ways, the most brutal indictment of Lucullus' alleged decadent living is found in Plutarch's *Moralia*, in his essay on the work of older men in public affairs.[48] There, Plutarch notes that Lucullus was among the very best of the generals in Roman military history, a man noted both for thought and action. But later, he became like a wasted skeleton, a sponge in a calm sea (which will soon enough rot away). Plutarch also notes in his *Moralia* that Lucullus indulged in inappropriately hedonistic behaviour.[49]

Cicero indicted Lucullus, too, in his *De Legibus*.[50] He noted that Lucullus was once criticized for the luxurious state of his villa at Tusculum. Lucullus is alleged to have replied that he had a Roman equestrian living above him, and a freedman below; their villas were quite luxurious, and so surely Lucullus' should be as well. Cicero apostrophizes Lucullus and notes that the wastrel ways of the equestrian and the freedman are, in fact, the fault of Lucullus. Lucullus was the one responsible for setting the good example, indeed for pursuing the passage of sumptuary laws, so he should have seen to it that villas were not stuffed to the rafters with statues and paintings, especially those that were public property or the property of the gods. For Cicero, it is less a vice that men of high station pursue luxury, than that they set an example that lesser men follow. The state is corrupted when the aristocracy is corrupted.

Cicero was working on the *De Legibus* in the final years of life, when Lucullus had already been dead for some time. No doubt the condition of life in the Republic in the mid-40s BC contributed to some of the antagonism that Cicero seems to have felt toward his old friend, on whom he seems to lay the blame for so much of the excess and hedonistic pursuits of his own day. Seneca the Elder also indicts Lucullus for *luxuria*;[51] the context is how much the Romans tolerate in their generals, the vices that they endure in their military leaders.

The idea that Lucullus not only practised luxurious living, but actually was to blame for introducing it, also appears in the late second-century AD work of Athenaeus, the *Deipnosophistae*, or 'Scholars at Dinner'.[52] Lucullus is said to have defeated Mithridates and Tigranes, and to have returned home to celebrate a triumph. At that point, he was given over to luxury by an exploitation of the wealth of the two defeated kings. In fact he introduced Rome to such decadent living. The source cited for the charge is Nicolaus of Damascus, the Greek historian and philosopher of the Augustan Age who is perhaps best known today for his biography of Augustus, of which two substantial sections remain, one dealing with the youth of Octavian, and the other with the assassination of Caesar (a valuable source for the latter).

Marcus Terentius Varro also references Lucullus' alleged luxury in his books *De Agricultura*, where there are mentions of his painting collection (I.2.10), estates that were built to the financial detriment of the Republic (I.13.7), his famous fish ponds (III.3.10), his aviary (III.4.3) and his work in cutting through a mountain near Naples to let sea water into his fisheries (III.17.9). There is no allusion whatsoever to Lucullus' political and military accomplishments; every last note of the man is a record of extravagance and indulgence.

The anonymous author of the brief biography of Lucullus in the *De Viris Illustribus* sums up the matter, but with special focus on the arts: *Nimius in habitu, maxime signorum et tabularum amore flagravit*. Lucullus was a connoisseur of the arts, of statues and paintings – and to an excessive degree. His love for them was burning and consuming; he was luxurious in his pursuit of *objets d'art*. There is no mention in the admittedly short account of any other aspects of his decadence.[53]

Literary Pursuits and Libraries

But even in this seemingly easily criticized last stage of his life, Plutarch finds grounds to praise Lucullus. A library was established, and Plutarch notes that Lucullus was not merely some collector of rare manuscripts – he actually read his books and used his libraries, and indulged an intellectual curiosity about literature and history.[54] His libraries were also open to all, and the Greeks in particular were invited to make full use of the resources that Lucullus had gathered together. Lucullus was a regular visitor to his own library, and more than happy to indulge in intellectual conversation and pursuits with his associates. His home became an intellectual sanctuary and preserve for the Greek community in Rome; he was a passionate lover of philosophy, interested in the study and pursuit of inquiry into all schools of intellectual thought. Lucullus no doubt engaged in lengthy philo-sophical discussions with his friend and sometime dinner companion Cicero.

Many philosophers and great thinkers counselled that a man of intellect and means should not shirk the duties of public life, and for Lucullus, 'retirement' was not absolute. Plutarch notes that even now, Lucullus continued to try to help his friends and the general cause of the senatorial faction. If Pompey had aligned himself firmly with popular support, then Lucullus would continue to aid the sen-atorial or optimate cause, even if Crassus and Cato were to be the *de facto* leaders of the movement. Lucullus was not willing to be a leader in any attack on Pompey, but he could be counted on for support and assistance in the initiatives of others.[55] What emerges from the Plutarchan biography is a complex array of seemingly con-flicting lifestyle endeavours. Lucullus is willing to indulge in lavish dinners and ridiculously extravagant building projects, even as he finances libraries and studies philosophy and literature with genuine zeal and ardour, all the while finding time to enter the public arena now and again to defend his friends and their common cause.

In fact, it is not at all easy to say with any definitive certainty when exactly Lucullus may fairly be said to have retired from public life.[56] It is possible that there was no one date to which retirement may be ascribed, but rather a sequential withdrawal from public life, a process by which he slowly yet certainly made his withdrawal from political affairs. Military command may have ended in 66 BC, but political influence and action continued for years thereafter.

Revenge

Lucullus did not entirely remove himself from public life. In his continued partic-ipation in the political life of the state, he managed to accomplish much. Plutarch's narrative is brisk and informative, though it raises as many questions as it answers. Lucullus is said to have made certain that the dispositions that Pompey made after the final defeat of the Eastern kings were nullified. Together with Cato, Lucullus is said to have taken care that Pompey's wishes for land distribution for his men were also to come to naught. The result of all this was that Pompey sided with Crassus and Caesar. Soon enough, the city was filled with Pompey's men under arms, and the partisans of Cato and Lucullus were expelled from the forum. Pompey's mea-sures were soon ratified.

One might almost think from this cursory narrative that the formation of what would come to be known as the First Triumvirate – the alliance between Pompey, Crassus and Caesar – could be credited to the machinations of Cato and Lucullus. Plutarch's brief version may be compared profitably with the more extended account in Dio Cassius.[57] On his return to Italy in 60 BC, Pompey hoped to have all he wanted ratified by the consuls Lucius Afranius and Metellus Celer. His main objectives were indeed the land distribution proposal, and, more generally, his various arrangements and acts with respect to the East. Needless to say, the optimates were not pleased with him. The consul Metellus was annoyed with Pompey because the war hero had also distinguished himself in the official's eyes by having divorced his sister, despite having had children with her.

And there was Lucius Lucullus. Dio notes that Pompey had treated Lucullus with contempt in Galatia, and now Lucullus repaid the favour. He insisted that every proposal of Pompey should be subjected to minute and careful scrutiny. There should be no question, Lucullus argued, of a single vote; Rome was a Republic and not a monarchy, and the actions of a commander needed to be reviewed one by one. And there was a personal note. Since Pompey had set aside some of Lucullus' own arrangements in the East, now the senators should review both sets of plans side by side and make individual decisions on each item. Metellus is said to have agreed with Lucullus, and also Cato. The tribune proposed the land distribution scheme, but the consul Metellus opposed him so violently that the tribune finally resorted to having Metellus imprisoned. Metellus called for a senate meeting in the prison; the argument of the optimates was clearly that the populist Pompey was acting like a tyrant.

Pompey was afraid that he and his supporters might appear to be acting in too heavy-handed a fashion. He soon also made clear, however, that he thought that Metellus and the rest were jealous of him, and that he would make this case to the plebeians. We may reasonably surmise that Pompey argued at this juncture that Lucullus was simply bitter and resentful that Pompey had finished what he had failed to resolve.

In the end, however, Pompey gave up his demands, allegedly out of fear that the *plebs* would not support him. Pompey was immediately regretful that he had seemingly overplayed his hand.

To make matters worse for an optimate politician – an old and unreconstructed Sullan like Lucullus – 60 BC was the year of the formation of the so-called 'First Triumvirate', the agreement of convenience and mutual benefit between Crassus, Pompey and Caesar. The three men knew that for the moment they had more to gain by unity than division, and that there were ample opportunities afoot for them to help each other in achieving at least some immediate goals – all while paving the way individually for uncertain futures.

At this point we may compare the information provided by Plutarch in his life of Pompey.[58] Plutarch notes that Lucullus was treated outrageously by Pompey in Asia. The senate was ready to honour Lucullus in every way, and was eager for Lucullus to take his part in public life as a counterweight to Pompey's increasing power. Lucullus was allegedly already beginning to succumb to luxury, but he launched a vigorous attack on Pompey – and with the help of Cato, he succeeded in his initiatives of revenge. Pompey had no real support then, he felt, except from the tribunes; Clodius was first among these to help him. Soon enough, Pompey entered his alliance with Caesar and Crassus; Pompey filled the city with his soldiers. One day the consul Marcus Calpurnius Bibulus was going to the forum with Lucullus and Cato when a crowd set upon him and broke the *fasces* of his lictors, and there were insults and mockery. Pompey quickly won the ratification of that which Lucullus had contested.[59] Lucullus had once again played a significant role in Roman public affairs, only in the end to be thwarted in the attainment of his ultimate goals.

Chapter 7

Twilight Time

The Vettius Plot

The equestrian Lucius Vettius met his death mysteriously in 59 BC. He is a significant figure in one of the last 'public' incidents in the life of Lucullus – an incident that we may call the Vettius Affair, which took place perhaps in the late summer of 59.[1]

In brief, Vettius was allegedly caught in a plot to assassinate Pompey. When confronted and questioned, he cast aspersions and imputed culpability on some younger Romans (including the Brutus who would one day kill Caesar). Soon enough the story expanded, and he blamed Lucullus in part for the scheme; Lucullus' name was invoked as one of the forces behind the planned murder.[2] First the young people had been named, then the older members of the optimate faction. No one seems to have believed Vettius, however, and a few days later he was found dead in prison. Some said that he died of natural causes, but his body had marks of violence, and so the story spread that the very men who had commissioned the assassination had now taken care that Vettius would be eliminated.

Plutarch notes that this episode was the cause of Lucullus withdrawing even more from public life. Dio, as often, offers more information.[3] He claims that Cicero and Lucullus conceived of the idea to have both Caesar and Pompey killed, and that Lucius Vettius was recruited to assist in carrying out the plan. All three failed, and all three were in mortal danger. Vettius was caught, and he immediately implicated Cicero and Lucullus; fortunately for them, he also named Bibulus. The accusations against all three men seemed baseless, and merely the attempt of Vettius to improve his own desperate situation. Dio carefully notes that many stories were *au courant* about the whole episode, precisely since nothing was ever definitely proven – and in this he may well be absolutely correct. Vettius was thrown into prison and later murdered. Cicero was held in suspicion ever after by both Caesar and Pompey. Lucullus rather fades away in Dio's account of the episode. The definitive facts about the Vettius affair remain elusive. Was Caesar behind the plot? Was the whole matter a fiction of Pompey's to arouse sympathy and shore up his support base? Was Lucullus really involved in what would have seemed to some to be an act of just revenge for the treatment he had received in Asia? We simply cannot know.[4]

Vettius already had a dark reputation in Rome as an *index*, or informer. He was not among the more reputable or honoured men of his age, even if his skills had been used on behalf of Cicero in the days of the Catilinarian conspiracy. He had approached Gaius Scribonius Curio the Younger with his plan to assassinate Pompey, and the Younger Curio had told his homonymous father of the plot. It would appear that Vettius was seeking to discredit Curio by hoping for Curio to join eagerly in Vettius' 'plot'; Vettius never expected that Curio would tell his father of the whole matter. If the story seems especially byzantine, we may rest assured that it appeared quite the same to Vettius' contemporaries. The 'guilty' kept changing, and nobody knew exactly what was afoot. What mattered most in the end, perhaps, was that Vettius was found dead – his usefulness had no doubt run its course, and perhaps he was annoying the wrong people with his ever-expanding, ever-changing tales of conspiracy. Brutus – one day famous as a tyrannicide – was plausibly enough named among the culpable, and Lucullus was no friend of Pompey, most might think – but there is no good reason to believe that there ever was a serious assassination plot, and even less to believe that Lucullus was somehow involved. If Lucullus really was involved, so, it would seem, were several other men of different ages and temperaments. In the end, the only casualty of the affair was Vettius himself. There were those who thought that Caesar himself was responsible for silencing Vettius permanently; again, we have no way of knowing for sure. Given the sensational nature of the proceedings, it was perhaps inevitable that Lucullus' name would be thrown in with other would-be killers of Pompey.[5] The fact that the First Triumvirate was by now in full swing no doubt added to the climate of conspiracy and tales thereof. Caesar himself had nearly died in the days of the Sullan proscriptions; no doubt he felt some pride in being a part of the dismantling of the Sullan regime, of which Lucullus was an increasingly aged, insignificant relic.

A letter of Cicero to Atticus, perhaps from August of 59 BC, preserves some commentary on the Vettius scandal (II.24). Cicero expresses little concern about how the whole matter will unfold, though he notes that he is sick of life (II.24.4 *sed prorsus vitae taedet*) – and he writes that Pompey assured him not to be concerned about Clodius.[6]

Diminished Capacity

In any case, from this juncture in his life, Plutarch dates the alleged diminution of Lucullus' mental abilities.[7] Plutarch cites Cornelius Nepos for the story that Lucullus' descent into senility was not the result of either old age or disease, but rather of drugs that were administered to him by his freedman Callisthenes. The drugs were allegedly given in order that Lucullus might be more pliable to the Greek's wishes; in fact they ruined his mind, so much so that eventually his younger brother had to take over his affairs. Lucullus eventually died, and the people are said to have mourned for him just as much as they might have been expected to grieve had he died at the very height of his military and political exploits. There was a clamour and outcry for him to be buried in the Campus Martius, where Sulla had also been buried. Plutarch vaguely notes that no one had expected this request, and the preparations for it were not easy (he does not explain why this would be so) – and finally Lucullus' brother was able to convince the people by prayer and supplication that Lucullus should be buried where he had planned to be buried, namely at his Tusculan villa.

Plutarch closes his biography by noting that Lucullus' brother followed him in death not long after – a truly affectionate brother, who had followed Lucius in both age and reputation. We are not sure of the exact date of Lucullus' death; it appears to have fallen either very late in 57 BC or very early in 56 (his near contemporary in age Crassus – himself also a commander under Sulla – would be dead in the East in some three years' time). One wonders what Lucullus' funeral oration emphasized; likely it dwelled on the role he played in confronting Mithridates, but his signal quality of *pietas* may also have proven an irresistible topic for praise. It was some two years since the Vettius affair. There is no reason to doubt the story of mental decline, or to imagine that Lucullus was somehow faking certain problems in order to protect himself. It is likely, too, that he had had more than enough of the New Republic. We have noted the theory subscribed to by some that Lucullus suffered from Alzheimer's disease. While we have no way of confirming the legitimacy of the diagnosis, our ancient evidence does point to a decline in mental abilities and certainly public appearances; Lucullus' end was not sudden in the manner of his mentor Sulla.

In his *Moralia*, Plutarch offers a few more details about Lucullus' dotage.[8] He notes that Callisthenes tended to Lucullus much in the manner of a quack or a fake doctor; Marcus Lucullus eventually drove the fraud out of his brother's house and proceeded to nurse Lucius – now essentially childlike in mind – for what little remained of his life. The *De Viris Illustribus* closes its account of Lucullus' life with the note that Lucullus lost his mind in his later years, and that he became essentially a ward of his brother Marcus. In his *Naturalis Historia*, Pliny alludes to the story that Lucullus was driven mad by an *amatorium*, or love potion.[9] Neither Pliny nor Plutarch gives much in the way of detail as to why the drug was administered. Pliny does not mention Callisthenes, while Plutarch speaks vaguely about the whole affair. Lucretius was said to have been poisoned in much the same way; it is possible that there is more than mere coincidence here, and that those who ascribed to Lucullus certain seemingly Epicurean tendencies may have appreciated the idea that both men were driven mad by a similar method.[10] In short, we do not know for sure if there was a drug. If there was one, we have no idea of what it was composed; but we do know that such potions existed and were brewed, bought and sold, and that the tale – shared as it is by Lucretius, not to mention Caligula (though not fatally) – may well be true.[11] If a fabricated romance, we may speculate as to the reason for the invention of the fiction. It may point to Lucullus' reputation as a decadent *bon vivant*.[12] At the very least, the similar stories offer another connection between commander and poet.[13] Did the story of the love potion that led to Lucretius' suicide originate in tales of the death of Lucullus?[14]

Plutarch's Summation

It could be argued that Lucullus left the stage of Roman history at a particularly opportune moment. This is the sentiment with which Plutarch opens his comparison of Lucullus and Cimon – the most extended ancient appraisal we have of the character of the Roman general and man of letters.

For Plutarch, Lucullus was blessed precisely because he died at a time when Rome was still free. On the other hand, while Cimon died in the field, and at the head of an army, Lucullus met his end amid feasts and revels, and with disordered mind. Plutarch condemns Lucullus as one who pursued pleasure as an end in itself; for him, Lucullus behaved more like an Epicurean than a follower of the Academy. While Cimon was disreputable in his youth and changed for the better, Lucullus was disciplined and possessed of a noble sobriety in his youth, only to age in an ever more pronounced fashion into a life of luxury and questionable leisure.

Both men were wealthy, but Lucullus squandered his money in Eastern fashion; if Cimon had a democratic and charitable dinner table, Lucullus was known for sumptuous luxury and excess. Plutarch admits that Cimon might have become just as decadent as Lucullus, had he lived as long, and, conversely, that Lucullus might have avoided all censure had he died in Asia. This last sentiment is seemingly at odds with the notion that Lucullus died fortunate in that he was a casualty of the Republic and not the Empire – but the two views are not really mutually incompatible. Lucullus might have been better off had he died in battle in Asia, if one were to judge that his later life had no real successes that made up for his descent into a life of what some would call indolence. Lucullus could thus be said both to have spent too much time in Asia, and not to have spent enough; he was cheated of final victory, though arguably he had had plenty of time in which to attain it.

Plutarch proceeds to the question of the relative merits of each man's military skill and reputation, with particular reference to the question of each man's relationship with his national sponsor. Here, in general appraisal, Cimon comes out the better –the main complaint lodged against Lucullus is that he was despised by his soldiers (while Cimon was loved). Lucullus' failure to make his Asian victories complete is attributed to his lack of attention to the grievances of his soldiers, for which Plutarch blames him even if the question was one of ignorance of their demands and complaints. Plutarch has an explanation for the problem: aristocratic temperaments are little suited to dealing with the problems of the crowd. The aristocrat tends to annoy the commoner, even when his positions are correct and sound; he is like the bandage of the physician, which does so much to reorder the broken, but which brings irritation and annoyance to the patient – a medical metaphor that describes memorably how Plutarch viewed the social clashes and struggles between Lucullus and his men.

Despite these negative assessments, Plutarch has much to say in praise of Lucullus' military ability. He is credited with crossing the Taurus with an army; mastering the Tigris and capturing Tigranocerta, Nisibis and elsewhere; with expansion to the Phasis, Media and the Red Sea; annihilation of the armies of Mithridates and Tigranes; and a failure only to capture their persons – for like wild animals, Plutarch says, they escaped his grasp by flight into the forests. Plutarch notes that after Lucullus, Mithridates and Tigranes achieved nothing of real note – and Tigranes in his moment of abject surrender to Pompey flattered his Roman conqueror with the achievements of Lucullus. Lucullus is compared to an athlete who hands over a weaker antagonist to his successor.[15] We do well to remember that age and battle injuries had taken their toll on Mithridates; the king Pompey would face would be significantly enervated compared to the king of the days of Lucullus and Sulla.

Beyond all this, Plutarch notes that Tigranes had never been defeated when he faced Lucullus (whereas Cimon fought against Persia at a time when Persian power had been seriously weakened). In the final analysis, Plutarch refuses to say which man was the greater, observing that a decision is exceedingly difficult. Divine power seems to have pointed the one to what he must do, and the other to what he must avoid – an enigmatic remark of much psychological insight. But both men, Plutarch concludes, were noble and indeed godlike in nature. And both, we might note, were masters of military versatility. Cimon was present for the dramatic naval engagement at Salamis in 480 BC, but it was perhaps at the Battle of the Eurymedon where the Athenian statesman most decisively demonstrated his talent for war on both land and sea. In his work on behalf of the Delian League, Cimon more than proved his abilities in both types of warfare, while his diplomatic abilities were also exercised throughout his long career. He offered, in short, a natural pairing with Lucullus – not least in the circumstances of his difficulties at Athens and eventual exile, the somewhat unresolved and unfulfilled undertakings of his life and his eventual honourable burial in his native soil.

Arthur Keaveney makes the reasonable argument that Lucullus was happier in Asia, under the service of military life, than he ever was in Rome.[16] Keaveney concludes too that Lucullus never intended to make himself master of the Roman state, in contrast to Pompey (at least in some regards), and especially to Caesar. Keaveney's own final summation is balanced, one might think: 'A cultured and humane man, possessed of many talents, he did much good in his own lifetime and if he failed of greatness it may very well be because he lacked what was needed to achieve it in that age: ruthlessness.'[17] By any measuring stick, Lucullus was certainly less ruthless than his mentor Sulla, his rival Pompey or the great Caesar. One might well add Crassus to the list. It may be that Lucullus alone of the lot was not interested in *de facto* monarchical rule, that even in time of great constitutional crisis, he did not have the will or desire to serve as dictator. He was thus an exceedingly noble champion of the senatorial cause, and the obvious choice to defend the rights of traditional republican government in the face of those who would turn the Republic into the possession of a military adventurer with the legions to make novel laws legal. One wonders to what extent he appreciated the inherent challenges of being a republican optimate in the guise of a new would-be Alexander – or *vice versa*, depending on analysis and point of view.

A Lucullan Life

We began our investigation into the life of Lucius Licinius Lucullus by noting that he could be considered the consummate man of his age, at least in some ways. Arthur Keaveney's biography of Lucullus' mentor Sulla offers the subtitle 'the last Republican' as a verdict on its subject. One could argue that Lucullus is more deserving of the title. Unlike Sulla, Lucullus was never possessed of a great urgency to return to Italy and Rome, being content to stay in the East until his task was completed. Avoidance of the Italian peninsula brought a long list of positive and negative results for Lucullus' career. He certainly managed to be spared the reputation for involvement in the worst aspects of the civil strife in Italy that marked the turmoil of the Sullan years – though in the end his close relationship with his master and mentor may have been enough to condemn him in the eyes of many (Pompey was better in this regard in amassing items on his résumé that obscured, at least for some, his own formative experience under Sulla). At the risk of indulging speculative psychological analysis, it seems that Lucullus' main problem upon his return to Italy was a feeling that he was supremely unappreciated by his colleagues and peers in Rome, while being unwilling to circumvent republican principles in the defence of the Republic. His interest in and patronage of the arts and literature made him an easy enough target for those who would dismiss him as an aesthete with greater concern for libraries and gardens than the life of the forum and the law courts. Age and illness also played their part in ensuring that Lucullus would commence his departure from the Roman republican stage at exactly the time when Pompey and Caesar were in the ascendant.

If meeting a peaceful end is a blessing, Lucullus triumphed over his contemporaries. Crassus, Pompey and Caesar would all meet their ends by violence, Crassus deeply entangled in Parthia, and with a record of failure – and Caesar with *post mortem* deification as perhaps his most lasting consolation for a daring political and military life. Pompey would face the most shameful end, treacherously murdered in Egypt in the wake of his defeat at Pharsalus in the great civil war against Caesar. It is perhaps interesting to note that Lucullus' demise had more in common with the final days of his mentor Sulla than with any of his great rivals for military fame and political glory.

Lucullus was an optimate politician who quickly came into his own as a conservative, indeed traditionalist supporter of a mode of government and manner of statesmanship that was under increasing threat from the pressures in a system some would call inherently unstable. What distinguished him from certain others of his generation were the long sojourns that he spent in the East at two critical points in his life – foreign sojourns that invited him to walk in the steps of not only Achilles, but also Alexander. Hauntingly, a *de facto* revolt or mutiny of the army would doom the ambitions of both Alexander and Lucullus. Lucullus' manner of life was deeply rooted in his conception of the traditions of the Roman Republic; his mission in the East was in several important regards profoundly at odds with that vision of Rome. It was a harbinger of an imperial Roman world that Lucullus may well have been happy not to have seen, with his demise a blessing that spared him the grim sight.

And when he finally met his death – whatever the exact pathology of his illness, or the state of his mental faculties and intellectual power – Lucullus died as one of the supremely successful Romans of his day, a man who had made possible what was achieved in the Roman East for a generation and more after his death, and a man whose record survived largely unblemished in an age when it was all too easy for men in public life to succumb to all manner of crime and morally questionable action. His failures, such as they were, reflected in part the hazards and structural problems of the very Republic he so dearly loved and cherished. That his name is affectionately remembered today by the hospitable owners of highly regarded, quality restaurants throughout the eastern Mediterranean may in some ways be a more complimentary and praiseworthy legacy than that enjoyed by several of his great rivals and antagonists, both foreign and domestic.[18]

He was also a testament to the wisdom of the teachings of the man who may have been his acquaintance, if not his friend – the poet Lucretius.

Endnotes

Chapter 1: From the Dawn of an Optimate Life

1. At the time of writing, the internet address is www.lucullus-naxos.com. One imagines that Lucius might be pleased to know about his legacy in the virtual Hellenic world, well over two millennia since he visited Naxos. The 'Lucullus' tavern in Chora, Naxos, boasts itself as being the oldest restaurant on the island (founded in 1908).

2. Cf. the 'Loukoulos' Restaurant in the very heart of Heraklion on Crete, housed in a lovely neoclassical edifice with courtyard; also the winter season Lucullus Restaurant in a beach hotel in Ayia Napa on Cyprus. The Pontic monarch Mithridates – who had so devastatingly swept across the Aegean and invaded Europe – does not seem to have inspired so fervent a devotional cult among the restaurant owners of the eastern Mediterranean. There is also a 'Lucullus' restaurant on the Dalmatian island of Hvar in Croatia; the establishment has been noted for some eccentricities of its staff that have included serving fish with a snorkel mask and filleting the fish while dressed in surgical garb – and opening wine with a sword. It is not clear what the gastronome Lucullus would have thought of the theatrical wonders of his namesake establishment. The so-called Lucullus Circle was founded in New York City in 1951 at the Waldorf-Astoria Hotel; dinners were lavishly arranged, with such novelties as, e.g., on one occasion serving food only on golden plates and with golden knives and forks.

3. Lucullus is also known to students of German theatre and opera for Bertolt Brecht's radio drama on Lucullus, *Das Verhör des Lukullus*, in which the Roman general is tried *post mortem* to decide whether he should enter Hades or Elysium. The drama was originally conceived as an opera; it had a complicated production and composition history, and was eventually premiered in 1951 as *Die Verurteilung des Lukullus*.

4. The name Lucullus may well be a diminutive version of Lucius; both words are likely to be derived ultimately from *lux, lucis* – the Latin word for 'light'. The name 'Licinius' has been derived from an Etruscan word for 'curving' or 'slanted'; why this adjective would have been applied to a family name is uncertain.

5. 'Lucullus was a strategist and tactician of truly exceptional talent' A. Goldsworthy, *In the Name of Rome: The Men Who Won the Roman Empire* (London: Phoenix, 2003), p.191.

6. Cf. here C. Edwards, *The Politics of Immorality in Ancient Rome* (Cambridge, 1993), pp.146–47, 153.

7. On this see especially A. Keavaney, *Lucullus, A Life* (Piscataway, New Jersey: Gorgias Press LLC, 2009), second edition with a new postscript of the 1992 Routledge original. There is also a French language monograph by J. Van Ooteghem, *Lucius Licinius Lucullus* (Bruxelles: Palais des Academies, 1959), with illustrations and maps; these are the two 'standard' scholarly overviews of Lucullus' life. Antonelli 1989 may be added to the 'basic' Lucullan bibliography, though his treatment is more popular than Keaveney's or van Ooteghem's. There is a helpful, concise and informative account of the world in which Lucullus lived in the essay of Jürgen von Ungern-Sternberg in the 2004 *Cambridge Companion to the Roman Republic* (translated by the editor, Harriet Flower), pp.89–109. This is one of the best synopses of the difficult problems of 'The Crisis of the Republic'. Lucullus' name receives extensive commentary from van Ooteghem, 1959, pp.5 ff.

8. And on how Caesar allegedly treated Lucullus with insolent contempt, see R. Syme, *The Roman Revolution* (Oxford, 1939), p.56 (after Suetonius, *Divus Iulius* 20.4; cf. Plutarch, *Vita Luculli* 42.6); also A. Goldsworthy, *Caesar: Life of a Colossus* (New Haven/London: Yale University Press, 2006), p.173. The episode is reminiscent of the story we shall soon enough consider of Lucullus' encounter with Glabrio and the voluntary humiliation of Lucullus; the difference between the two encounters is telling for how much Rome had changed in just a few years of Lucullus' adult life. For a possible reconstruction of what really happened between Caesar and Lucullus, see Keaveney, 2009, pp.217 ff.; cf. Gelzer, 1968, p.75. 59 BC was, in any case, an exceedingly difficult year for Lucullus; his health may have already entered an irreversible decline, and the future – however finite – belonged to such as Pompey and Caesar.

9. In the case of Clodius, it was apparently to enable himself to serve as tribune of the *plebs*, so as more easily to seek revenge on Cicero for the latter's machinations against him on the occasion of the Bona Dea scandal of December 62 BC – a subject to which we shall return.

10. For general introductory commentary on Plutarch's life, see G.B. Lavery, 'Plutarch's Lucullus and the Living Bond of Biography', in *The Classical Journal* 89.3 (1994), pp.261–73. Lavery considers the problem of what exactly Plutarch thinks of his biographical subject; the problem of whether Plutarch liked, admired and respected his Roman subject. 'Plutarch undertook a formidable business in composing a biography of Lucullus, more than most Romans a man of paradoxes and contradictions, a man who opened himself to conflicting verdicts by his behaviour at different points in his career' (p.262). A comprehensive account of certain themes of the biography is the work of M. Tröster, *Themes, Character, and Politics in Plutarch's Life of Lucullus, The Construction of a Roman Aristocrat* (*Historia* Einzelschriften 201) (Stuttgart: Franz Steiner Verlag, 2008). The standard Greek

text of the life is the Bibliotheca Teubneriana (Teubner) edition of Hans Gärtner, *Plutarchus: Vitae Parallelae, Volumen I, Fasciculus I*, (K.G. Saur Verlag, 2000) (fifth revised edition). The life is also found in Volume II of the Loeb Classical Library edition (1914), with English translation by Bernadotte Perrin. There is also an excellent introduction to the life (with translation, including the comparison to Cimon) in the 'Penguin Classics' volume *Rome in Crisis*, edited by Ian Scott-Kilvert and Christopher Pelling (2010). Dryden's translation of Plutarch's lives has remained regularly in print as a part of the Modern Library series of editions of the classics.

11. Ancient sources for Lucullus' life also include historians and other writers interested in the general's military exploits: we shall return to the evidence of the Latin writers Florus, Eutropius and Orosius (*inter al.*), and Book XXXVI of the monumental Roman history in Greek of Dio Cassius. But the major sources are Plutarch and Appian. Sallust's histories (Books III and IV in particular) also provide valuable evidence, though they survive only in fragments. There is a particularly valuable Loeb Classical Library edition of the fragments (edited by John T. Ramsey); the Loeb offers a generously annotated text of the fragments with translation and detailed introduction (2015). There is also a commentary by Patrick McGushin in two volumes, for the Oxford Clarendon Ancient History series (1992; 1994). The first volume is concerned with Books I-II; the second with III-V. McGushin has exceptionally detailed notes on the historical problems of the remains of Sallust's work.

12. The nine essays of Brunt, 1988, offer a good starting point for exploration of a well-documented period and set of problems.

13. On the difficult question of Plutarch's methodology in chronicling the fall of the Republic, see C.B.R. Pelling, 'Plutarch's Method of Work in the Roman Lives', in *The Journal of Hellenic Studies* 99 (1979), pp.74–96.

14. Lucullus' uncle was no friend of Gaius Marius – a fact that may have added to the youth's attractiveness to Sulla. The cognomen *Numidicus* was earned for his achievements in the Jugurthan War; he was exiled in 100 BC but returned within two years. Lucullus himself never received an *agnomen* or special title; he was not, for instance, ever referred to as Ponticus (unlike his colleague Cotta).

15. Cf. Cicero, *De Officiis* 2.50, where the prosecution of Servilius by the Luculli is considered a matter of *ulcisci*, or the seeking of vengeance. The enmity between the families is noted also by Cicero at *De Provinciis Consularibus* 22.

16. Diodorus Siculus XXXVI.8–9 is the principal surviving source. Diodorus is most conveniently available in the Loeb Classical Library edition.

17. Lucullus Senior had already distinguished himself – at least in some fashion – for having put down a servile uprising in southern Italy; for the so-called Vettius Affair, see Keaveney, 2009, pp.4–5 (another affair involving a very different Vettius would involve Lucullus Junior); Diodorus Siculus XXXVI.2. Diodorus relates that an

equestrian fell in love with another man's slave girl; he bought her at a high price, but was unable to pay the debt by the agreed date. When he felt that he could no longer delay, he conceived the mad plot of raising an army of hundreds from his own slave holdings, and setting himself up as a petty tyrant, complete with purple cloak and diadem. He murdered his creditors and soon found himself in command of some 700 men, later to swell to 3,500. Lucullus' father is said to have succeeded in confronting the threat by a promise of immunity to one of Vettius' commanders; Vettius in the end committed suicide with his comrades.

18. With whatever family enmities there existed between the Luculli and the Servilii, we may compare the conflict between the Luculli and the Pompeii that, as we shall see, was at the heart of the Archias episode.

19. Exactly what Lucullus' father was guilty of has been lost to history. Diodorus blames him for not following up on what would have been an easy opportunity to crush the slave revolt for good and all; this failure leads directly to Lucullus' being worsted in a subsequent engagement. Diodorus asserts that Lucullus' failure to succeed was the cause of the charges later imputed to his indolence or avarice. His successor – Gaius Servilius – is said by Diodorus also to have failed in achieving any real success (some have argued that this Servilius may be Servilius Augur, but there is no good reason for the speculation). Lucullus is said to have disbanded his army and burned his equipment to prevent any chance of Servilius winning where he had lost. Curiously, Diodorus also notes that Lucullus was suspected by some of wishing to broaden the scope of the war (this admittedly does not accord well with the charge of indolence); the burning of his camp and supplies, the historian observes, was a way both to harm Servilius and to dispel the charge.

20. Keaveney, 2009, pp.6–7.

21. Cicero, *Pro Archia Poeta* III.5.

22. Cicero dates the voyage to *Interim satis longo intervallo*, which indicates some considerable time after 102 BC, but without specification.

23. He became Aulus Licinius Archias.

24. It seems that Archias lived long enough to see the assassination of Caesar in 44 BC.

25. The significance of Hellenism in Lucullus' life is the subject of the second chapter of Tröster, 2008, with particular reference to the narrative of this quality in Plutarch's life.

26. We have no way of judging the merits of Archias' work, since his poetry has all but vanished from record; Keaveney, 2009, p.15, concludes that 'The loss to literature is not, perhaps, all that great', noting that Archias was best known for laudatory works on his patrons. Keaveney' 2009, pp.292–93, 303, considers the theory of some that Archias' poem on the Third Mithridatic War was an important source for Plutarch's life of Lucullus (the theory is based on the allegedly significant amount of fantastic material in the biography, which to some points to a poetic

source). Keaveney rightly notes that Plutarch does not cite Archias as a source – not a definitive argument against influence, to be sure – but we can only speculate.

27. Keaveney, 2009, p.287, mentions the detail in Pliny, *Naturalis Historia* XXXV.200 that Lucullus had a freedman named Hector who had certain literary talents: 'How far this man may have helped in the composition of Lucullus' history of the Social War … is a moot point.'

28. On this episode, note the edition with full commentary of D.R. Shackleton Bailey, *Cicero's Letters to Atticus, Volume I, Books I-II* (Cambridge, 1965).

29. The complete *testimonia* and evidence for the question of Lucullus' historical compositions is conveniently assembled by T.J. Cornell, ed., *The Fragments of the Roman Historians* (3 vols) (Oxford, 2013). Volume I provides an introduction to Lucullus *Historicus* (p.287), and Volume II the texts and translations of the surviving evidence (pp.492–93). The last volume contains the extensive commentary on the historical fragments. In general, Cornell's work is an outstanding reference for the study of Roman history and the remains of the 'minor' Roman historians. For how Lucullus seems not to have had anything to do with the editing or completion of the memoirs that Sulla left unfinished at the time of his death, see Keaveney, 2009, p.49, which takes Sulla's comment to be purely honorific and not at all as a serious invitation for Lucullus to 'meddle' in the production of the autobiography.

30. Hence some editors speak of the *Academica Priora* and the *Academica Posteriora*.

31. *Academica* II.2.4.

32. Indeed, we know that Lucius was born in either 118 or 117 BC on the basis of the story that he waited to hold office until his younger brother came of age; we know that Marcus was a curule aedile in 79 and that he held the office in the first year in which he was eligible – and so he was born in 116. Working from this, we can postulate a date for the birth of his older brother. See further Keaveney, 2009, p.4.

33. On the particular importance of Greek culture in the Plutarchan account of Lucullus life, note S.C.R. Swain, 'Plutarch's Characterization of Lucullus', *Rheinisches Museum für Philologie*, Neue Folge, 135. Bd., H. 3/4 (1992), pp.307–16, and more generally the same author's 'Hellenic Culture and the Roman Heroes of Plutarch', *The Journal of Hellenic Studies* 110 (1990), pp.126–45.

34. The best edition of this fascinating collection of biographies is the 'Budé' text of Paul Marius Martin, *Les hommes illustres de la ville de Rome* (Paris: Les Belles Lettres, 2016), with French translation, full introduction and copious commentary notes. There is a so-called 'bilingual edition' by Walter K. Sherwin (Norman: The University of Oklahoma Press, 1973), which offers a *deterior* comparison with Martin's Budé. There is no Loeb edition.

35. *Vita Luculli* I.4.

36. One may note, for example, that even the exemplary Loeb Classical Library edition of Suetonius' lives of the Caesars – in which Lucullus is mentioned but once, and not for luxurious habits – has an index note on Lucullus in which he is noted for

his decadent ways, as if this were the defining characteristic of his life. The survey of many republican history and biography texts will often reveal the same judgment when Lucullus is cited in passing.

37. For Arthur Keaveney, 2009, p.20, Lucullus was already of a 'kindly disposition', and Greek literature and the arts served to refine and polish someone who was already more or less refined and polished by nature. Comments of this sort easily descend into generalization; it may well be that Lucullus was not very different from other leading men of his day, with the exception that he took a greater pleasure and consolation in literature than they did – a consolation that would certainly find ample ground for indulgence in the final years of his life.

38. On Sulla's life and military/political career, note especially A. Keaveney, *Sulla: The Last Republican* (Oxford/New York: Routledge, 2005), second edition of the 1982 Croom Helm original publication, and L. Telford, *Sulla: A Dictator Reconsidered* (South Yorskhire: Pen & Sword Military, 2014). The latter book is an unabashed attempt to rehabilitate the reputation of its subject; at the very least, it offers interesting perspectives on certain aspects of Sulla's career. Keaveney's book is essential reading for a scholarly appraisal. Not surprisingly, the controversial Sulla has occasioned a controversial scholarly tradition.

39. For the convenient overview of the so-called *Bellum Italicum*, see P. Matyszak, *Cataclysm 90 BC: The Forgotten War That Almost Destroyed Rome* (South Yorkshire: Pen & Sword Military, 2014). The Social War remains one of the more poorly studied conflicts of the Republic, in part for lack of extensive ancient evidence.

40. Plutarch, *Vita Luculli* IV, 4.

41. Cf. here P.J. Thonemann, 'The Date of Lucullus' Quaestorship', *Zeitschrift für Papyrologie und Epigraphik*, Bd. 149 (2004), pp.80–82; note also the foundational work of E. Badian, *Studies in Greek and Roman History* (Oxford, 1964), pp.153, 220. Thonemann's paper on the date of the quaestorship is the subject of 'postscript' additional material in Keaveney, 2009, pp.287–90, with the author's customary detailed appraisal of the evidence and sober judgment.

42. For general remarks on the aristocrats who supported Sulla (especially those who remained more or less constant and loyal to him throughout), see E.S. Gruen, *The Last Generation of the Roman Republic* (Berkeley/Los Angeles/London, 1974), pp. 6–7.

43. Cf., e.g., the review of Keaveney, 1992, by Boris Rankov, 'The Life of a Rotted Sponge?', *The Classical Review*, New Series, Vol. 43, No. 2 (1993), pp.341–43.

44. M. Crawford, *The Roman Republic* (Cambridge, Massachusetts: Harvard University Press, 1992) (second edition of the 1978 original), p.146. The relationship between the quaestor Lucullus and his mentor Sulla was certainly quite different in its outcome from that between the quaestor Sulla and *his* would-be mentor Marius. Crawford's book is among the best English-language treatments of its (vast) subject.

45. For the episode see Keaveney, 2005, pp.55–56, 201.

46. On such figures note especially Wiseman, 1971, with comprehensive consideration of the problem of who exactly these 'new men' were, and whence they tended to come.

47. The consular Lucullus of 151 BC is cited by Aulus Gellius at *Noctes Atticae* XI.8.2.

48. Cf. van Ooteghem, 1959, p.8.

49. Most of what we know about the consular Lucullus of 151 BC comes from Appian's account of the Roman wars in Spain. For a brief overview note P. Matyszak, *Sertorius and the Struggle for Spain* (South Yorkshire: Pen & Sword Military, 2013), pp.41–44. Lucullus' grandfather campaigned in both Hispania Citerior and Hispania Ulterior; if we can believe Appian, he was more distinguished for greed than for military strategy; for the ancient historian's account of the whole affair, see J.S. Richardson, *Appian: Wars of the Romans in Iberia* (Warminster: Aris & Phillips Ltd., 2000), with Greek text, translation and helpful commentary). Cf. also A. Goldsworthy, *Pax Romana: War, Peace and Conquest in the Roman World* (New Haven, Connecticut: Yale University Press, 2016), pp.39 ff.; 58–59.

50. 'It was with good reason that the Roman noble appealed to custom and precedent. His whole way of life depended on them. In the ideology of the aristocracy … the standards and achievements of the ancestors formed the criteria by which those of the present generation were judged', D. Earl, *The Moral and Political Tradition of Rome* (Ithaca, New York: Cornell University Press, 1967), p. 30.

51. *Naturalis Historia* XIV.96.

52. The (Augustan Age) inscription is from Arezzo, Italy; the original is in the National Archaeological Museum there, a museum that is named after the Augustan patron of the arts, Gaius Cilnius Maecenas.

53. On the similar attitudes and behaviours of Roman aristocrats in the execution of both their political and military duties, see A.K. Goldsworthy, *The Roman Army at War, 100 BC–AD 200* (Oxford, 1996), p.148. On the army reforms of Marius, see de Blois, 1987, pp.11–13. 'In the two decades following Sulla's abdication (79–60) Roman armies operated in an area which stretched from Spain to Armenia.'

54. Normally a *tribunus* was required to have had at least five years of service in the army.

55. See further W.V. Harris, *War and Imperialism in Republican Rome, 327–79 BC* (Oxford, 1979, new printing 1991, with additional material), p.257. Harris considers the question of Roman magistrates who came to office with less than a decade of military experience.

56. We should note that Lucullus was a first cousin on his mother's side to Sulla's wife Metella (see on this Keaveney, 2009, pp.22–23); at least the initial formation of the relationship between Lucullus and Sulla may well have owed something to this familial/marital connection.

57. A detailed, comprehensive account of the life and times of Rome's inveterate eastern enemy is the lengthy volume of A. Mayor, *The Poison King: The Life and Legend of Mithridates, Rome's Deadliest Enemy* (Princeton/Oxford: Princeton University Press, 2010); cf. also P. Matyszak, *Mithridates the Great: Rome's Indomitable Enemy* (South Yorkshire: Pen & Sword Military, 2008); and R. Evans, *Roman Conquests: Asia Minor, Syria and Armenia* (South Yorkshire: Pen & Sword, 2011). There is a brief and useful overview of Mithridates' conflicts with Rome in P. Matyszak, *Enemies of Rome: From Hannibal to Attila the Hun* (London: Thames & Hudson Ltd., 2004), pp.81 ff. McGing, 1986, offers a full appraisal of Mithridates' foreign affairs, including valuable treatment of his propaganda efforts. McGing focuses more on Hellenistic affairs than strictly Roman material.

58. *Vita Sullae* 11. There is a helpful edition of the Greek text of the life with notes in H.A. Holden, *Plutarch's Life of Lucius Cornelius Sulla* (Cambridge, 1886), of use both for reading the original Greek and for the historical problems (there is no English translation).

59. 12.29.

60. And so the annotations of the Loeb edition of Plutarch's *Cimon* opts for as late as 74 BC.

61. Another problem is the question of the legal authority of Lucullus to remove the troops.

62. For a convenient overview of the matter, see Telford, 2014, pp.117–18. 'Lucullus, commanding an advance force, met with Sura and ordered him to withdraw, as the sole command had been given to Sulla, an order which he had no choice but to obey.'

63. Not surprisingly, financial problems were a serious threat to Sulla's success in Greece; cf. the narrative in Plutarch, *Vita Luculli* XII. Lucullus would earn just praise from some for his financial and economic reforms in Asia; he would ultimately incur the undying enmity, however, of the *publicani* or public contractors and their supporters in Rome. It was those very *publicani* who would back the eventual place of Pompey in settling the Eastern wars: regarding the Manilian Law that gave Pompey command in the war against Mithridates and Tigranes, Leach, 1978, p.75, notes: '[I]t had overwhelming support from the people and from the *equites*, whose financial interests in Asia were once more in jeopardy. The threat of war and the collapse of confidence were as fatal to the commercial world in 66 as they are today.' Leach, we might note, argues that the Eastern threat was not as great as Cicero presents it in his speech *Pro Lege Manilia*; still, 'The Pompeians had a strong case.'

64. Plutarch, *Vita Luculli* II.1–2. The coinage is discussed by Keaveney, 2009, p.27, citing M.H. Crawford, *Roman Republican Coinage* (2 vols) (Cambridge, 1974), Vol.1, p.80 n.1. Van Ooteghem, 1959, provides convenient illustration opposite p.23.

65. Cf. the detail recorded by Cicero (*Academica* II.1.3) that Mithridates was the great-est king since Alexander, and that said king considered Lucullus to be a greater general than those of whom he had read in works of military history.

Chapter 2: The First Mithridatic War

1. A helpful overview of the progress of the Mithridatic wars is A.N. Sherwin-White's chapter in *The Cambridge Ancient History*, Volume IX, *The Last Age of the Roman Republic, 146–43 BC*, Chapter 8a, 'Lucullus, Pompey, and the East', pp.229 ff.
2. *Vita Sullae* II.2.
3. For an overview of the relatively little we know about Roman naval warfare prac-tices in this period, see W.L. Rodgers, *Greek and Roman Naval Warfare: A Study of Strategy, Tactics, and Ship Design from Salamis (480 BC) to Actium (31 BC)* (Annapolis, Maryland: Naval Institute Press, 1937/1964), pp.424 ff.
4. XII.33.
5. See further Keaveney, 2009, p.18, with particular reference to the clear friendship between the two men.
6. The embassy of Lucullus to Cyrene is also referenced at Josephus, *Antiquitates* XIV.114.
7. *Vita Luculli* II.3–4.
8. *Vita Luculli* II.5–6.
9. For the problem, note Keaveney, 2009, p.33 n.20.
10. II.2.4.
11. Philo of Larissa (154/3–84/3 BC) is celebrated as the last Academy philosopher who could claim direct lineage from Plato.
12. McGushin, 1994, pp.213–14, provides a convenient overview of the pirate prob-lem in the context of the Third Mithridatic War, with consideration of the 'acts of audacious arrogance' of the pirates in launching raids on Italy, and in threaten-ing the Roman grain supply. McGushin highlights the extraordinary extent of the command that was eventually awarded to Pompey according to the provisions of the *Lex Gabinia*: proconsular *imperium* over the sea east of the Pillars of Hercules, the territory of all islands and even up to 50 miles inland on all coasts, Italy not excepted.
13. *Vita Luculli* III.2–3.
14. *Vita Luculli* III.3.
15. *Vita Luculli* III.3.
16. The exact status of Fimbria is in question. See further A.W. Lintott, 'The Offices of C. Flavius Fimbria in 86–5 BC', *Historia: Zeitschrift für alte Geschichte* 20.5/6 (1971), pp.696–701.
17. The historian Memnon (chapter 24) notes that the senate had sent both Flaccus and Fimbria to make war on Mithridates (on Memnon cf. below on n.122). They were commissioned to work with Sulla, if he was willing to listen to the senate

– otherwise, they were to attack him before they engaged the king. Flaccus was annoyed with Fimbria because his men preferred his leadership; Fimbria was credited with being a more amenable, tractable commander. While attacking Fimbria in words, two of his soldiers murdered Flaccus. The senate is said to have been angry with Fimbria on account of the whole matter – but they arranged for his consular election all the same, and allowed him to command the entire force.

18. There seems to be no compelling reason to assume with some that the 'real' reason for Lucullus' unwillingness to join Fimbria was the fear that his forces would not be adequate to the task of a blockade of Pitane.

19. Cf. Spann, 1987, p.102.

20. 'Indeed, had Sulla done his job properly in the first there would have been no third Mithridatic war. So if Sertorius allowed the Pontic king to occupy Bithynia this was hardly more treasonable than the kiss of Sulla at Dardanus or the far greater gift of life and liberty which the recalcitrance of Lucullus bestowed on Mithridates at Pitane', Spann, 1987, p.102. Memnon (chapter 25) makes clear that Sulla sent envoys to Mithridates to propose a truce precisely at a time when he expected that he might need to tend to domestic, civil affairs.

21. See further here L. Keppie, *The Making of the Roman Army: From Republic to Empire* (Norman: The University of Oklahoma Press, 1998), pp.76 ff. (original edition, B.T. Batsford, 1984). 'The "Valerians" were … a group of near professionals who joined in the aftermath of the Social War, and by wish or circumstances prolonged their service. It seems clear that their service was, and continued to be, extremely profitable financially.'

22. On the role of Lucullus in the diplomatic wrangling, see Telford, 2014, pp.143–45. '[T]he two antagonists [i.e., Sulla and Mithridates] finally met face to face at Dardanus. Mithridates had come in from his hiding place at Mytilene, while Sulla had been taken over by Lucullus to the meeting place in Asia, in the ships he had brought for Sulla's use.' Lucullus would soon be commissioned to serve not so much as diplomatic aide as financial executor of Sulla's dispositions for Asia.

23. Memnon also notes that neither side scrupulously followed the edicts of Dardanus; the Romans imposed ruinous fines and taxation, while Mithridates almost at once started trying to rebuild his lost empire.

24. On certain aspects of the financial initiatives and practices of this time and place, note P.A. Brunt, 'Sulla and the Asian Publicans', *Latomus* 15.1 (1956), pp.17–25.

25. See further Keaveney, 2009, pp.39–40, on how Lucullus' loyalty to Sulla was placed above his natural instinct to make fewer demands on the inhabitants of Asia than his mentor was inclined to impose.

Chapter 3: The Aftermath of War

1. For a laudable effort to provide a coherent and logical timeline of events in Asia from 81–79 BC, see Keaveney, 2009, pp.245–53 (a detailed appendix on the many

problems of chronology). Keaveney also has an appendix (pp.255 ff.) on the problem of when exactly the Third Mithridatic War commenced.

2. *Vita Luculli* IV.2–3.

3. The siege is also cited in *Epitome* LXXXIX of Livy's history.

4. Keaveney, 2009, p.251 n.30 argues that the slaves could have been taken from the territory of Mytilene, not the city proper. But what was the population of the island at this time?

5. Suetonius, *Divus Iulius* II.

6. Plutarch's life of Caesar makes no mention of his military experience on Lesbos.

7. Allen M. Ward argues that Thermus left the 'field command' of the siege to Lucullus in his brief paper 'Caesar and the Pirates', in *Classical Philology* 70.4 (1975), pp.267–68.

8. *Vita Luculli* IV.4.

9. For how Pompey would prove something of his own loyalty to Sulla in the matter of the latter's public funeral, see Keaveney, 2009, p.51. When the consul Marcus Aemilius Lepidus – a reconciled Marian – was of a mind to deny a state requiem, Pompey was instrumental in guaranteeing that Sulla would be buried with full republican honours.

10. 'Given the heterogeneous nature of the coalition which Sulla led to power it is hardly surprising to discover that there was a corresponding diversity of opinion among those who now made up the ruling oligarchy of Rome. Leaving aside those disaffected or about to disaffected, we find, at one extreme, men like Lucullus who were passionate partisans of the dictator, at the other, the likes of Pompey, who, despite quarrelling with Sulla, were prepared to work his system for his own advantage', Keaveney, 2009, p.50.

11. Dio's history is a major source of information for the Lucullan age. Dio was born c. AD 150 and died in 235; his father was the governor of the province of Cilicia, which may have made the region of special interest to his historian son. Dio would eventually become governor in his own right, of Pergamum and Smyrna; he would serve in other major posts before meeting his death in Nicaea. Dio's history was written in eight books; the surviving portion starts in Book XXXVI, just where we may begin to read of Lucullus' adventures in the East (there are gaps, however, in Books XXXVI and LV-LX). The most convenient edition of Dio for anglophone readers is the Loeb Classical Library edition in nine volumes, with translation and some brief notes. The Budé volumes that have been prepared to date offer a French translation and more extensive commentary, as well as a critical text of the Greek original.

12. It is uncertain whether Lucullus' refusal of Sardinia had anything to do with the revolt of Marcus Aemilius Lepidus. After the death of Sulla, Lepidus had supported anti-Sullan rebels in Etruria; after he failed in his revolutionary initiatives, he eventually made his way to Sardinia, where he died of illness. Most of his followers joined the Sertorian cause.

13. 'Plutarch's silence probably indicates he found nothing to report', Keaveney, 2009, p.54 n.18.

14. On Lucullus' wife and her family, note W.C. McDermott, 'The Sisters of P. Clodius', *Phoenix* 24.1 (1970), pp.39–47; also T.W. Hillard, 'The Sisters of Clodius Again', *Latomus* 32.3 (1973), pp.505–14.

15. Cf. the passing references at *Vita Luculli* XXI, XXXIV and XXXVIII; also Dio 36.14.4.

16. Cicero alludes to his charge of Lucullus at *Pro Milone* 73. The oration is a *tour de force* of rhetorical skill, all at Clodius' expense; the crime of Clodius in desecrating the rites of the Bona Dea is rehearsed, as well as the appropriateness of Clodius meeting his end at Bovillae near a shrine of the goddess. Clodius is depicted as a petty criminal, a thug and a vandal.

17. On this most famous Clodia, note M.B. Skinner, *Clodia Metelli: The Tribune's Sister* (Oxford/New York: Oxford University Press, 2011).

18. See further here Keaveney, 2009, pp.64–65, with consideration of both political and amatory possibilities.

19. For a convenient overview, note the aforementioned P. Matyszak, *Sertorius and the Struggle for Spain* (South Yorkshire: Pen & Sword Military, 2013). Also useful is Christopher F. Konrad's *Plutarch's Sertorius: A Historical Commentary* (Chapel Hill: The University of North Carolina Press, 1994), with much helpful information. Philip O. Spann's monograph *Quintus Sertorius and the Legacy of Sulla* (Fayetteville: The University of Arkansas Press, 1987) is good on explicating the Sertorius phenomenon in light of the larger realities of Sullan Rome.

20. 'Lucullus had been allotted Cisalpine Gaul as his province, an appointment that would deprive him of his chance for glory. When Octavius, governor of Cilicia, died early in 74 … Lucullus realized the opportunity it presented', McGushin, 1994, p. 74.

21. See Keaveney, 2009, p.87, for Cotta's own ambitions in the East; he remained more or less loyal to Lucullus, and was perhaps all too aware of the limits of his talents for war. A harsh but reasonably fair critic would conclude, in fact, that Cotta was incompetent in the military arts, and ultimately more possessed of avarice than of tactical or strategic brilliance. 'Cotta was content to let his colleague conduct the main fight while he conducted a side-campaign. This, it is fair to say, was characterized by incompetence, cruelty, treachery and an unslakable thirst for loot. A fitting climax was reached on his return to Rome when Cotta had to face a charge of *repetundae* and expulsion from the senate in consequence.' On this and other 'classic' criminal charges of republican Rome, Riggsby, 1999, is helpful. 'The Roman plan for the opening campaign of the war was that Cotta should hold Mithridates in check in Bithynia, and with the help of a fleet collected from allies, close the Bosporus against Mithridates' navy. Lucullus was to add the veteran legions of Servilius in Cilicia and the Fimbrian legions in Asia to the fresh

legion he brought with him and advance through Phrygia against Mithridates' flank. Delayed by problems in Asia, Lucullus had only reached the river Sangarius when news reached him that Cotta, who had been foolish enough to offer battle to Mithridates' main force and had suffered total defeat, had been forced to fall back on Chalcedon', McGushin, 1994, p.75.

22. Fr.2.86.11–12 Ramsey.

23. *Vita Luculli* V.3.

24. For commentary on the decision, see especially Telford, 2014, pp.237–38, with ample catalogue of all the reasons why Lucullus' loyalty commended itself to Sulla. Enemies of Lucullus might long have remembered that he was also to give the eulogy for his mentor (cf. Telford, 2014, p.240).

25. On this theory, see Keaveney, 2009, pp.69–70.

26. For how Lucullus was 'creditable and more than creditable' up to this point in his career, were one only to judge him by the standards of the 'mass of his contemporaries' and not Pompey, see Keaveney, 2009, p.57. It is reasonable to speculate that Lucullus felt increasingly overshadowed by the brilliant young Pompey; what is more difficult to assert definitively is how much of their relative achievements were the result of innate talent *versus* opportunity and luck.

27. Cf. Keaveney, 2009, p.71.

28. Appian X.68.

29. Sertorius also had a mystical side, even if affected; cf. Plutarch, *Vita Sertorii* XI.2 ff., for the story of the white doe that allegedly communicated the wishes of the goddess Artemis to Sertorius. See further Konrad's commentary *ad loc.* for Plutarch's thinly veiled admiration and enthusiasm for someone who was so skilled at manipulating the superstitutious beliefs of those around him.

30. X.67.

31. X.68.

32. We may compare the account of the Greek historian Memnon of Heraclea, who notes that war initially broke out between Rome and Mithridates because of the king's seizure of Cappadocia. Memnon's account (chapter 22 of Jacoby's standard edition, see below) emphasizes Mithridates' brutality: he killed his nephew, mother and brother. We are indebted to the Byzantine polymath Photius for his preservation of precious remains of Memnon; the ninth-century scholar's *Bibliotheca* is a vast treasure trove of passages and epitomes of otherwise lost works. Memnon is conveniently found in the Budé edition of Photius' *Bibliotheca*, Volume IV (René Henry, ed., *Photius: Bibliothèque, Tome IV: Codices 223–229*), where what remains of Memnon is given in codices 225–227 (with French translation and a few notes of commentary). Memnon is also contained in Felix Jacoby's monumental *Die Fragmente der griechischen Historiker* (1923-), a work left incomplete at the time of the editor's death in 1959, but which new editors have sought to finish (Memnon is found in t. III B, pp.337–68); the Jacoby chapter numbers are generally considered

standard for citation. Photius notes that he was not able to find a copy of Books I-VIII of Memnon's work, or of anything after Book XVI; Memnon would be unknown to us were it not for Photius' preservation of the remains.

33. *Vita Luculli* VI.1.

34. *Breviarium* VI.6.1–2. Eutropius was a fourth-century AD historian who wrote a compendium of Roman history in ten books; the most convenient edition is the Budé text of Joseph Hellegouarc'h, with critical text, French translation and brief commentary, *Eutrope: Abrégé d'histoire romaine* (Paris: Les Belles Lettres, 1999). Eutropius accompanied the Emperor Julian against the Persians, and dedicated his Roman history to the Emperor Valens. His work is in ten books, and the simplicity of the Latin style has made it a popular choice for early readings for students of the language.

35. Keaveney, 2009, pp.72 ff., considers the domestic landscape on the eve of Lucullus' departure for what would be the Third Mithridatic War.

36. Quinctius focused on the question of jury reform and alleged bribery of jurors; Lucullus apparently tried at first to persuade Quinctius not to pursue the matter, and then stood firm against him in public debate. There were no jury reforms in 74 BC – but Lucullus would pay a heavy price for his political and oratorical victory.

37. Helpful on this topic is the article of B. Marshall and J.L. Beness, 'Tribunician Agitation and Aristocratic Reaction 80–71 BC', in *Athenaeum* 65 (1987), pp.360–78.

38. Leach, 1978, p.55.

39. Modern scholars have debated the significance of the Praecia episode, with particular attention to the question of whether or not Lucullus is deserving of criticism for the means by which he won his Cilician appointment. What is clear enough is that for Plutarch, the whole affair was to Lucullus' discredit; it was an expeditious way to achieve what he wanted, but in no way deserving of merit or credit. Of Praecia we know nothing other than what is recorded in Plutarch. We do well to remember that it would have been easy to read back into the story something of the criticism that Lucullus would suffer later in the accusations of hedonism and ill-timed pursuits of pleasure and decadent living.

40. Cf. Keaveney, 2009, p.94: 'Acknowledging that Lucullus benefited by the advice of an alleged whore, we should be equally ready to admit that many a man has come to grief because of the advice of a good woman.' Keaveney interprets the episode as an example of the 'indirect influence' of otherwise disenfranchised women in Roman politics. It is important to note that Plutarch does not specify if Lucullus had a sexual liaison with Praecia, even if one might be tempted to assume that he did; see further here A.K. Strong, *Prostitutes and Matrons in the Roman World* (Cambridge, 2016), p.71. Strong comments on certain aspects and features of Plutarch's language that point to the emphasis on the example of female agency in traditionally male political endeavours. The Praecia affair is exactly the sort of salacious, gossip-laden tale that appeals to some students of social history; in point of fact, that

matter may have been quite boring indeed, and merely an example of Lucullus taking careful note of who had influence over Cethegus. We do well to remember, too, that the Romans were not particularly bothered by liaisons with 'courtesans' – but they were more than happy to ridicule those (like Cethegus?) who were especially infatuated with a given high-priced call girl. In the end, what mattered most to Lucullus was securing his Asian command. It is interesting to note that for all the criticism we know that Lucullus received throughout his career, the Praecia episode does not seem to have been used against him.

Chapter 4: The Third Mithridatic War

1. On the vexed question of when the war started, note B.C. McGing, 'The Date of the Outbreak of the Third Mithridatic War', *Phoenix* 38.1 (1984), pp.12–18, with argument in favour of the 'negative conclusion that the spring of 74 is impossible'. Most valuable is Appendix II of Keaveney, 2009, pp.255 ff., with exceptionally detailed appraisal of all the surviving evidence (both literary and numismatic). Keaveney concludes that the two consuls, Lucullus and Cotta, both departed for Asia in 74, with the war perhaps already in progress. Cotta left first, then Lucullus.

2. Cotta's duties are neatly described by McGushin, 1994, p.163: 'As his specific task in the campaign against Mithridates the proconsul M. Aurelius Cotta had undertaken in 73 the reduction of the Pontic coast and the siege of Heraclea, in which he was to be assisted by Lucullus' naval commander C. Valerius Triarius when the latter had finished his tasks in the Aegean (Memnon, 42–3). The siege of Heraclea lasted two years.' Cotta was essentially responsible for the Heraclea operation, and Triarius for actions in the Aegean. Some of Mithridates' naval forces consisted of units returning from his earlier reinforcement of Sertorius; historians debate exactly why the ships were on their way back to the king now – possibly because Sertorius had died. Memnon (chapter 27.5) notes that when Mithridates sailed past Heraclea, he was not admitted to the city, though the inhabitants did provide supplies. His naval commander eventually arranged for the kidnap of two leading citizens, and the Heracleans were forced to provide the king with five triremes. The Romans were thus disposed to consider the Heracleans to be enemies; when the tax collectors arrived in Heraclea, they attemped to impose harsh indemnities on the residents. The Heracleans are said to have been persuaded by some of the more daring men of the city to kill the Romans and to make sure that the bodies were well hidden.

3. *Historiae* III, fr.16 Ramsey.

4. Orosius is the fourth-fifth-century AD author of the *Historiarum adversus Paganos Libri VII*, an important, late source of information for historiography. Book VI preserves significant details of Lucullus' dealings with Mithridates. The most convenient edition is the three-volume Budé set of *Orose: Histoires contre les Païens* (with critical Latin text, French translation and brief commentary), edited by

Marie-Pierre Arnaud Lindet; the second volume contains Books IV-VI (Paris: Les Belles Lettres, 1991).

5. *Vita Luculli* VII.
6. *Historiae* III, frr.19–20 Ramsey.
7. X.71.
8. For the Bastarnae, see especially McGing, 1986, p.61. 'The most powerful peoples to the north and north west of the Black Sea were the Sarmatians and the Bastarnae … In connection with the Third Mithridatic War the Bastarnae are called the bravest of his troops and specific Sarmatian tribes are named among his forces.' Cf. Appian XII.69 and 71.
9. See Lavery, 1994, p.270, for the argument that *dignitas* was perhaps an 'overdeveloped' quality in Lucullus' personality. Lavery, p.273, concludes that 'Lucullus suffered truly egregious injustices, but even this kindly biographer [i.e., Plutarch] cannot always see him as victimized.'
10. Cyzicus was remembered for its loyalty to Rome; it became a prominent city of Mysia, and one of the greatest cities of Asia Minor.
11. *Historiae* III, fr.21 Ramsey.
12. Some of these events are recorded in *Epitome* XCIII of Livy. Livy was inevitably epitomized in antiquity; his original work was 142 books in length. We have the so-called *Periochae* of the entire work; these epitomes are actually summaries of what was already an abridged version of Livy.
13. XI.72.
14. *Vita Luculli* IX.1.
15. For the Magius affair, see especially Keaveney, 2009, p.105.
16. Sallust, *Historiae* fr.III.25 Ramsey; Frontinus, *Strategemata* III.3.16; Florus, *Epitome* I.40.16; Orosius, *Historia* VI.2.14.
17. Orosius has a similar story: *Lucullus Mithridatem Cyzicenos obsidentem fossa cinxit eumque quod faciebat pati compulit atque ad ipsos Cyzicenos, ut bono animo essent, nuntium misit unum ex militibus natandi peritum, quo duobus utribus suspensus mediam ipse regulam tenens plantisque subremigans septem milia passuum transmeavit* (VI.2.14). Cf. also Frontinus, *Strategemata* III.13.6, amid the author's discussion of inventive ways to send and to receive messages.
18. XI.73.
19. Cf. Sallust, *Historiae* fr.III.36.
20. And for the story of how noise was heard on Mount Dindymon that sounded like a Bacchic revel, as if the gods were making their departure from the cause of their former favourite, see Keaveney, 2009, pp.110–11 – another example of alleged divine intervention and commentary on events.
21. Appian XII.76.
22. *Historiae* fr.III.31 Ramsey.
23. *Historiae* fr.III.32 Ramsey.

24. Memnon provides a straightforward account (chapter 29) of subsequent developments. Cotta proceeds from Chalcedon to face the king at Nicomedeia; Triarius comes of his own accord. Mithridates manages his escape, though a storm wrecks some of his vessels. Mithridates gains control of Heraclea by a subterfuge of alcohol and feasting to cover his *de facto* conquest. A garrison is established in the city of 4,000 of the king's men under Connacorex. Mithridates proceeds to Sinope. Lucullus, Cotta and Triarius prepare to invade Pontus. After hearing about the situation at Heraclea, Lucullus decided to turn against Cappadocia and leave Heraclea to Cotta; Triarius would manage naval affairs and block any attempt of the king's allied ships to arrive from Spain and Crete. Mithridates, meanwhile, planned for his own alliances, of which only his overtures to the Armenian Tigranes would be received favourably. Diophantus and Taxiles were the king's generals in ground operations against the Roman armies, with a force of 40,000 infantry and 8,000 horse. There were nearly daily skirmishes, and two larger-scale cavalry engagements; the Romans won the first, the king's men the second. Lucullus sends men for supplies in Cappadocia; the king's two generals send 4,000 infantry and 2,000 cavalry to check them. The Romans won handily, and the generals eventually fled the rout of their camp, bringing news of the defeat to Mithridates. The bad tidings were followed at once by the king's decision to have the women of the royal household slain.

Memnon, chapters 32 ff. detail the aftermath of events for Cotta and Triarius. Cotta eventually marched against Heraclea, where he met with limited success in his siege operations. Triarius set out from Nicomedeia to confront the king's naval forces; Roman fortunes were significantly better on water than on land. Cotta continued to prosecute his siege of Heraclea, with some unsuccessful attempts at securing diplomatic alliances from the kings of the Bosporus. Trirarius eventually arrives with naval support to aid in the operations. Mithridates' commander Connacorex eventually decided to betray the city not to Cotta (whom he considered untrustworthy and oppressive), but to Triarius. The plan was eventually common knowledge in Heraclea; Connacorex was able to escape by sea, but not before engaging in successful deception of the Heracleans – he told them all would be well, and that Mithridates would soon appear with Tigranes to save them. The Heracleans essentially awoke to the news that the city had been betrayed to the Romans; Triarius' forces arrived *en masse*, and there were atrocities as the Romans took revenge for the long and difficult siege operations. Those who could flee made their way to Cotta, and he learned of the disaster from them. There was nearly an outbreak of civil war, as Cotta's forces felt cheated of their rightful glory. Cotta was no kinder to the Heracleans than Triarius; he ransacked even the contents of sacred precincts and temples, including a statue of Heracles. Cotta eventually sent his infantry and cavalry to Lucullus, dismissed his allies and prepared to return to Rome by ship; in a detail that no doubt gave Memnon pleasure to record, some of the ships were sunk under the weight of the stolen treasures of Heraclea. Triarius meanwhile went in pursuit of Connacorex, who had captured Tius and Amastris; Connacorex was allowed to flee, with the cities taken without a blow being struck.

Cotta would eventually be hailed as *Ponticus imperator* (Memnon, chapter 39) for his efforts at Heraclea. Cotta was criticized, however, for his plunder of the city; even after he handed over much of the loot to the treasury, he was still accused of avarice. The prisoners of Heraclea were released; Cotta was accused in the assembly by the Heraclean Thrasymedes. Cotta was spared exile, but he was expelled from the ranks of the senators. The Heracleans were given back their land, and exempted from any threat of slavery. Thrasymedes would eventually become instrumental in the attempt to rejuvente Heracles (Memnon, chapter 40); he is credited with having gathered together some 8,000 settlers.

25. Cf. Orosius VI.2.15, where he begins a grim catalogue of the king's losses: *Mithridates inopia laborans partem copiarum instructam atmis domum abire praecepit; quam Lucullus excipiens universam disperdidit: nam amplius quindecim milia hominum tunc interfecisse narratur* (Plutarch says 20,000, not 15,000, were slain). At VI.2.19, Orosius notes the plague and pestilence, and the general lack of supplies; vast numbers are citied as having died in consequence (*nam plus quam trecenta milia hominum fame et morbo in eadem obsidione amisisse fertur*).

26. XII.76.

27. *Vita Luculli* XII.1–2.

28. Orosius: *Marius postera die de spelunca, ubi latebat, extractus meritas hostilis animi poenas luit* (VI.6.22).

29. XII.77.

30. For an overview of the entirety of the post-Cyzican operations, note especially McGushin, 1994, pp.98–100, with coverage of how after Cyzicus, Mithridates went by sea to Parium, while he sent a land contingent to Lampsacus; the king's subsequent attempt to create a diversion with the forces of the Sertorian general Marius; his failed attempts to regain access to the Mediterranean and communication ultimately with his allies in Spain and elsewhere; the storm that nearly destroyed him and his subsequent building up of new forces; and Lucullus' preparations to invade Pontus.

31. *Vita Luculli* XIII.

32. XI.78.

33. *Vita Luculli* XV.

34. *Vita Luculli* XV.3–4.

35. XII.80.

36. XII.79.

37. *Stratagemata* II.5.30.

38. On how the Romans managed to find the manpower for the conflict with Spartacus, cf. McGushin, 1994, pp.146–47.

39. Eutropius is a source for the Spartacus War (*Breviarium* VI.7), which is otherwise not as fully documented as we might wish; while quite specific in some regards – e.g., there were seventy-four escaped gladiators from the school at Capua, and an eventual servile army of almost 60,000 – the account credits Crassus with the final victory, with no mention of Pompey's aid, or of the forces of Marcus Lucullus. Otherwise Eutropius is careful to note the ongoing Macedonian operations of Lucullus' busy brother. For how it would have been more appealing to the Romans to credit the ultimate victory over Spartacus to Pompey precisely because he was returning from other campaigns – in other words, the defeat of the slaves was achieved as if it were some minor footnote to 'real' campaigns – see Greenhalgh, 1980, p.64: '[A]nd if it was Crassus who erected an impressively macabre monument to his victory by crucifying six thousand captives along the Appian War from Capua to Rome, it was Pompey who was the hero of the day.'

40. XII.81.

41. The story is also mentioned by Memnon (chapter 30 of Jacoby's edition), who notes that after Mithridates had ordered the princesses of the royal house to be slain, he was pursued in his attempted escape by some Gauls, who did not realize who he was. They stopped to plunder the treasure mule, and Mithridates was able to escape. Mithridates was able to reach Armenia, though Lucullus did send Marcus Pompeius after him.

42. 'Then, since he recognized that Pontus was now lost, the half-Hellenized king revealed the oriental side of his character in his determination that his women-folk should not fall into the victors' hands', Keaveney, 2009, p. 122. Scholars who emphasize the humanity of Lucullus are fond of citing episodes such as this in praise of their subject.

43. Of course for all things Heraclean we have the evidence of the historian Memnon.

44. *Vita Luculli* XVIII.6.

45. *Vita Luculli* XVIII.6.

46. *Epistulae* II.2.26–40. There is a full commentary in C.O. Brink, *Horace on Poetry, Epistles Book II, The Letters to Augustus and Florus* (Cambridge, 1982). Brink takes the poet's reference to a *miles* or 'soldier' to refer to a specific individual in Lucullus' army; he offers notes on the evidence of the passage in terms of the question of Lucullus' relationship with his soldiery.

47. *Vita Luculli* XXII.1.

48. Memnon (chapter 31 of Jacoby's edition) notes that Mithridates was treated with the customary signs of hospitality, and received a bodyguard – though Tigranes refused to meet him.

49. On the vexed question of the year of Sertorius' death, see e.g. Spann, 1987, pp.129 ff.

50. Memnon (chapter 22.10) notes that Sulla would have destroyed Athens, had senatorial forces not intervened to check his intention.

51. Keaveney, 2009, p.124 n.49, makes the important point that where Sulla was obeyed in the matter of the plundering of Athens, Lucullus did not enjoy the same command over his men – that Sulla was the one who determined just how savage the seizure of the city would be, not his men. It is impossible to determine for certain how much of this difference between the men depended on their respective command abilities and the relative loyalties of their men, and how much was a concomitant of just how long Lucullus' men had spent under arms. Sulla's had certainly been away from home for far shorter and less difficult a time.

52. The business of the fire and the wish of Lucullus to save the city from the flames is also cited by Orosius: *Lucullus miserorum hostium intestina clade permotus celeri occasu inmissum restinxit incendium. Ita misera civitas versa vice hostium sociorumque unde defendenda disperdita et unde disperdenda servata est* (VI.3.2).

53. *Vita Luculli* XXIII; XII.82.

54. Chapter 37 of Jacoby's edition.

55. Memnon also notes that Mithridates had entrusted Sinope to one Leonippus, who had offered to betray the city to Lucullus. Leonippus was himself betrayed to the people of Sinope by his colleagues Cleochares and Seleucus; the people did not believe the report of Leonippus' treachery because of his generally good reputation – and so the other officers had him ambushed and slain in the night. The people were annoyed by the murder, but Cleochares and his associates seized control of the city government and acted in a tyrannical fashion in the hope of maintaining order. Their tyranny only increased in savagery and cruelty after they defeated a Roman fleet of fifteen triremes under the command of Censorinus (the ships were bringing grain from the Bosporus to feed Lucullus' forces). Eventually, Cleochares and Seleucus disagreed over strategy; the former wanted to maintain the war, while the latter opined that they could kill all the citizens of Sinope and hand over the city to the Romans for a handsome profit.

56. Cf. Rawson, 1975, p.53: 'There are echoes in the speech [i.e., the Ciceronian *Pro Lege Manilia*] of the reform programme of 70, especially on the need for clean provincial government: Pompey is irreproachable in such matters (so, it seems, had Lucullus been, but Lucullus had been too intent on defending the provincials against Roman tax-farmers and businesses to please that class).'

57. Lavery, 1994, p.265, argues that 'History's verdict must highlight, even in preference to Lucullus' notable military conquests, his rescue from almost total economic collapse of the Roman province of Asia.'

58. XII.83.

59. *Vita Luculli* XXIV.1.

60. Cf. Eutropius: *Ergo Lucullus, repetens hostem fugatum, etiam regnum Tigranis qui Armeniis imperabat ingressus est* (Therefore Lucullus, seeking his enemy who had fled, also entered the kingdom of Tigranes who was ruling over the Armenians) (*Breviarium* VI.9.1). Eutropius moves at once to the capture of Tigranocerta.

Chapter 5: Armenia

1. For the problems of timeline, see Keaveney, 2009, p.135.
2. XII.84.
3. For the situation in Syria at the time, note T.C. Brennan, *The Praetorship in the Roman Republic, Volume II* (Oxford, 2000), p.410.
4. Josephus briefly mentions the need for Tigranes to return to Armenia in the wake of Lucullus' invasion of his kingdom (*Bellum Iudaicum* I.116); cf. *Antiquitates* XIII.421.
5. See further here J.D. Grainger, *The Fall of the Seleukid Empire, 187–75 BC* (Barnsley: Pen & Sword Military, 2015), pp.195–97. Grainger's volume is the third and final in his series on the mighty successor state to Alexander's kingdom in the Near East.
6. There may have been an implicit challenge in this remark, at least in the way it would likely have been interpreted by Lucullus. Lucullus had certainly not merited the title *imperator* for anything having to do with Armenia. The story after Tigranocerta would be different.
7. Keaveney, 2009, p.138.
8. Cf. Tigran Vartanovich Petrosian (1929–1984), the Armenian/Soviet world chess champion.
9. Memnon (chapter 31 of Jacoby's edition) also notes the salutation problem; in his account, Tigranes wrote a letter to Lucullus that contained the same substance as his conversation with Clodius: he would be censured universally if he handed over his father-in-law. One wonders if Lucullus was moved at all by the *pietas* that Tigranes was displaying toward his relative by marriage.
10. *Vita Luculli* XXI.6.
11. *Vita Luculli* XXII.4.
12. *Vita Luculli* XXIII.7.
13. *Vita Luculli* XXIV.3.
14. Cf. Sallust, *Historiae* fr.IV.52 Ramsey.
15. *Historiae* fr.IV.32 Ramsey.
16. Cf. Sallust, *Historiae* fr.IV.53 Ramsey.
17. The alleged favour of heaven is also attested at Sallust, *Historiae* fr.IV.54 Ramsey.
18. 'From Tomisa Lucullus marched south-east to Amida on the upper Tigris. The news of his advance was greeted with incredulity', McGushin, 1994, p.171.
19. Cf. Eutropius' insightful account: *Susceptus tamen est Mithridates post fugam a Tigrane, Armeniae rege, qui tum ingenti gloria imperabat, Persas saepe vicerat, Mesopotamiam occupaverat et Syriam et Phoenices partem* (Nevertheless Mithridates was taken up after his flight by Tigranes, the king of Armenia, who then was ruling with great glory, who had conquered the Persians often, who had seized Mesopotamia and Syria and part of Phoenicia) (*Breviarium* VI.8.4).

20. *Vita Luculli* XXV.1.
21. XII.84; *Vita Luculli* XXV.2.
22. XII.84.
23. On the vexed question of the exact location of Tigranes' showcase city, note especially T. Rice Holmes, 'Tigranocerta', *The Journal of Roman Studies* 7 (1917), pp.120–38; also T. Sinclair, 'The Site of Tigranocerta. I', *Revue des études arméniennes*, n.s., 25 (1994–1995), pp.183–254; L. Avdoyan, 'Tigranocerta: The City "Built by Tigranes"', in R. Hovannisian (ed.), *Armenian Tigranakert/Diarbekir and Edessa/Urfa* (Costa Mesa, California: Mazda, 2006), pp.81–95.
24. *Naturalis Historia* VI.9.26; cf. VI.31.129 (on the local River Nicephorius as a tributary of the Tigris); also B.W. Henderson, 'Controversies in Armenian Topography: 1, The Site of Tigranocerta', *The American Journal of Philology* 28 (1903), pp.99–121. At *Annales* XV.5.2, Tacitus locates Tigranocerta with reference to Nisibis: *apud oppidum Nisibin, septem et triginta milibus passuum a Tigranocerta distantem* – Nisibis is said to have been 37 miles from Tigranocerta.
25. XII.85.
26. Cf. here Keaveney, 2009, p.146.
27. XII.85.
28. See Keaveney, 2009, p.139, for the argument that Lucullus was generously disposed toward Greeks – like a true phihellene or lover of Greek culture and art – but fundamentally contemptuous of eastern potentates like Tigranes, who were expected simply to obey Roman orders. I would argue that the salient point in the Armenian war is that Tigranes was in a position where the surrender of Mithridates must truly have seemed impossible. The king may have been less than competent in the prosecution of his war against Rome – too slow, too inexperienced and ultimately ineffective – but one imagines that Lucullus realized that Mithridates would not simply be shipped off to the Romans with nary a question, and that if the king could be provoked into a 'traditional' battle in open country, then total victory would be achieved. Tigranocerta was the obvious place to head to test fate.
29. On this cf. Keaveney, 2009, p.142 n.12.
30. *Vita Luculli* XXVI.6.
31. The sources strongly emphasize the importance of the cataphracts to the power of Tigranes' force; cf. Sallust, *Historiae* fr.IV.57 Ramsey.
32. Some scholars argue that the battle was fought on 7 October (cf. the *Cambridge Ancient History*).
33. Cf. Keaveney, 2009, p.148 n.18.
34. XII.85.
35. *Vita Luculli* XXVIII.3–5.
36. Matyszak, 2008, p.135.
37. *Stratagemata* II.1.14. Frontinus also credits Lucullus with excellent wisdom in the matter of choosing a place for battle, noting that he was able quickly to seize an

elevated point with a portion of his force, from which he could launch a devastating flank attack against enemy cavalry. The cavalry broke and were thrown into confusion, and Lucullus was able to chase them down and to achieve a significant victory.

38. Memnon (chapter 38 of Jacoby's edition) notes that Lucullus was careful and skillful in the arrangement of his army, and that he gave encouraging words to his men before battle. He proceeded to rout the right wing of the enemy, and once those troops gave way, there was a domino effect as the army took general flight. The Armenians were soon in full panic, and the army was destroyed. Memnon gives a figure of 80,000 men for the force that Tigranes brought to his besieged city; he also preserves the contemptuous comment about there being too many Romans for an embassy, and too few for a war. The story of the rescue of the concubines is also related, with the detail that the Romans and Thracians attacked bravely, and that there was a widespread slaughter of the Armenians, with as many captured as were killed – but that the convoy with the women did reach Tigranes safely.

39. For a detailed account of this episode, note A. Mayor, *Greek Fire: Poison Arrows & Scorpion Bombs, Biological and Chemical Warfare in the Ancient World* (Woodstock/ New York/London: Overlook Duckworth, 2003), pp.243 ff.

40. XXXVI.1b.1–2.

41. *Historiae* fr.IV.55 Ramsey.

42. XII.86.

43. *Vita Luculli* XXIX.2–3.

44. XXXVI.1.3 ff.

45. *Vita Luculli* XXVIII.5–6.

46. Memnon (chapter 38 of Jacoby's edition) notes that Tigranes handed over the diadem to his son; he also records the report that Mithridates soon enough appeared to console his son-in-law and to boost his spirits, complete with new royal apparel and words of encouragment. But it is at this juncture that Tigranes agreed that his father-in-law should take overall command of the operation. Memnon records that the two kings had not been in each other's presence for a year and eight months after Mithridates first arrived as a fugitive in Armenia; the Pontic king had risen once again in his fortunes.

47. See Mayor, 2010, pp.307–09, for commentary on how the Romans failed to appreciate the 'guerrilla tactics' of their foes in the aftermath of such defeats as Tigranocerta.

48. *Vita Luculli* XXIX.1–2.

49. VI.3.6.

50. *Breviarium* VI.9.1. Frustratingly, Eutropius characteristically gives no insight or detail into how Lucullus achieved his victory; at once, the Roman force is off to the conquest of Nisibis. A breviary, after all, is a breviary.

51. See especially Keaveney, 2009, p.152, on the question of the legality of Lucullus' war on Tigranes. Keaveney argues cogently and persuasively that the war was

indeed legitimate; Tigranes was guilty of offering aid and comfort to an avowed enemy of Rome.

52. Keaveney, 2009, p.153, gathers the evidence for a charge he considers unfair.

53. For what little we know precisely of Lucullus' actions in the immediate wake of his departure from Tigranocerta, see McGushin, 1994, pp.199–201.

54. On Parthia, the work of Debevoise, 1938, remains valuable.

55. The king's dynastic name was Arsaces XII; his personal name was Phraates III. He ruled Parthia from 70–57 BC; he would be murdered by his two sons, Orodes II and Mithridates III. The brothers would eventually have a falling out (to put it mildly); Mithridates III would be killed in 54 on orders of Orodes. Orodes would see the great victory over Crassus and last in power until 37 BC; he would be slain by his son Phraates IV, who also took care to kill his thirty brothers. As for the present overtures to the Parthians, Memnon (chapter 38 in Jacoby's edition) once again provides more confirming evidence; Tigranes sent an embassy to the Parthians, promising Mesopotamia, Adiabene and more in exchange for an alliance; Lucullus also approached the Parthians, who perhaps wisely played both sides against the other. Keaveney, 2009, pp.156–57, makes the reasonable argument that Lucullus never planned a war against Parthia, even in the face of legitimate provocation in the matter of Parthian double-dealing; 'to embroil Rome in a war with yet another great power would amount to nothing less than an act of breathtaking folly.' Lucullus no doubt realized that the Parthian question would need to be settled sooner or later.

56. On the subject of espionage in the ancient world, note especially N.J.E. Austin and N.B. Rankov, *Exploratio: Military and Political Intelligence in the Roman World from the Second Punic War to the Battle of Adrianople* (London/New York: Routledge, 1995).

57. A helpful popular overview here is G.C. Sampson, *The Defeat of Rome in the East: Crassus, the Parthians, and the Disastrous Battle of Carrhae, 53 BC* (Philadelphia, Pennsylvania: Casemate, 2008).

58. *Historiae*, fr.IV.60 Ramsey.

59. See further here F. Ahlheid, 'Oratorical Strategy in Sallust's Letter of Mithridates', in *Mnemosyne* 41.1/2 (1988), pp.67–92; also E. Adler, *Valorizing the Barbarians: Enemy Speeches in Roman Historiography* (Austin: The University of Texas Press, 2011), pp.17–36; cf. the same author's article 'Who's Anti-Roman? Sallust and Pompeius Trogus on Mithridates', *The Classical Journal* 101.3 (2006), pp.383–407. The commentary of McGushin, 1994, pp.173 ff. offers a detailed appraisal of what it concludes is 'an extremely skillful exercise by Sallust in the genre of deliberative oratory ... the letter conforms to the principles of ancient rhetorical theory'.

60. *Vita Luculli* XXIX.6–8.

61. 'This was a venal age, a time when bribery was virtually commonplace in public life. So the financiers simply dipped into their large money-bags and bought

themselves some tribunes to add their voices to the initial protests', Keaveney, 2009, p.154.

62. For a good overview of the Alexander question, with consideration of contemporary attitudes toward Lucullus, Pompey and Crassus in terms of their respective reminiscences (real or imagined) of the Macedonian conqueror, see Keaveney, 2009, pp.306–07. It could be argued that while Lucullus was certainly no dreamer with monarchical ambitions in the mold of an Alexander, he was likely all too well aware that his Roman army was treading in much the same country and direction as the storied Greek monarch; it would have been impossible not to remember the lore of Alexander as one entered the territory of Mithridates and Tigranes. And this would have been the case even for someone of such steadfast republican sentiments as Lucullus. Alexander imagery would be all the more poignant in retreat; in the case of both Alexander and Lucullus, army decisions played a significant part in the decision to return home.

63. XXXVI.2.1.

64. *Historiae* fr.IV.62 Ramsey, *imperi prolatandi percupidus habebatur, cetera egregius.* Fr.61 goes so far as to refer to alleged bribery on the part of Lucullus to see to it that he would have no successor in Cilicia. Certainly some of the discontent about Lucullus came from no other source than his own men, who were tired of spending multiple winters in distant Asia – or at least tired of spending them under Lucullus.

65. XXXVI.2.4–5.

66. II.33.1.

67. We are in fact uncertain who made the celebrated (not to say notorious) quip; it may have been the Stoic philosopher Tubero. There may have been a deliberate play on the notion of Lucullus as Alexander – his enemies and critics may have preferred to compare him to the Persian monarch.

68. For an appraisal of such charges, and more generally of the significance of the appellation to an understanding of Lucullus, see Evans, 2007, pp.104 ff., 'as *Xerxes togatus* Lucullus embodies foreignness: an easterner in a thin veneer of Romanness. The joke then is particularly barbed, as it suggests that Lucullus' inner core is not Roman at all, and that if he were to remove his toga, his Romanness would disappear. But clearly Lucius Licinius Lucullus' ethnicity is fixed by his name, his lineage and his role as a public figure, so that the corollary is that even in his native Roman dress, Lucullus perverts the national costume by acting as a foreign tyrant in a toga.'

69. Keaveney, 2009, pp.151–53, offers an extended account and analysis of the process by which gossip reached Rome and was amplified into anti-Lucullan slander.

70. *Vita Luculli* XXXI.3.

71. *Vita Luculli* XXXI.1–2.

72. XIII.87.

73. XXXVI.4.2.

74. See further here Keaveney, 2009, pp.158–59. Keaveney assigns the narrative of Dio XXXVI.5.2 to earlier in the campaign, arguing that 'it looks like the skirmishing tactics of Mithridates'.

75. *Vita Luculli* XXXI.4–8.

76. XII.87; *Vita Lucullli* XXXII.1–2.

77. Despite his victory there, it would in fact be the locus of the reception of more bad news. 'Great as his achievements had been, he had failed to capture the enemy kings, and he was worried by the disturbing reports which had been filtering to him from Rome. In 70 Lucullus had been proconsul in Asia, Cilicia, Bithynia and Pontus, but as a result of tribunician agitation Asia had been taken from his control in 69. And now news reached him in Nisibis that Cilicia had been transferred to the control of his brother-in-law and rival, the consul Quintus Marcius Rex', Greenhalgh, 1980, pp.75–76. By the time Rex would refuse to aid him, and his men would show little interest in defending Cappadocia, the fugitive kings would have achieved much in their efforts to run amok unfettered.

78. *Vita Luculli* XXXII.2.

79. Mayor, 2010, p.309, speculates that the gold caches that Mithridates had hid – and that Callimachus promised to reveal to Lucullus – may still await discovery. If Lucullus really did ignore the pleas of Callimachus to spare his life on condition that he reveal the treasure hoards, it is another example of the ability of the Roman to stand fast against the temptation of luxury. Evidently, Callimachus' life would not be spared by recourse to bribery. No doubt episodes such as this explain why Lucullus would have been so resentful of the accusation that he was prolonging the war merely to enrich his own coffers.

80. XXXVI.8.

81. Spann, 1987, p.104, notes indignantly, 'High treason should be made of sterner stuff' as part of his general argument of questioning the charges made against Sertorius, while men like Lucullus emerged comparatively unscathed in the court of legal and public opinion.

82. *Breviarium* VI.9.1.

83. XII.88.

84. XXXVI.9.1 ff.

85. *Vita Luculli* XXXV.1.

86. There is dispute over the question of why Triarius engaged Mithridates. The evidence of Plutarch and Appian is that Triarius wanted to steal the glory from Lucullus; this is exactly the sort of ancient argument that causes some modern scholars pause. See further Keaveney, 2009, p.167 n.48. The main objection to the ancient narrative is that Triarius asked for aid – but it is not entirely clear when the call for help went out, and it is also possible that Triarius may have summoned 'help' in the form of an audience to witness the aftermath of his own victory. It was hardly the first time that Lucullus had responded to a distress call; he may well have felt that he rarely received proper credit for the speed and efficacy of his responses.

87. XXII.89.
88. *Vita Luculli* XXXV.1.
89. XII.89.
90. 'One wonders whether Lucullus gave any thought to the masses of wandering Cappadocian refugees, who had been transplanted to Tigranocerta by Tigranes, and now had been liberated by Lucullus and sent back to their homeland – just in time to meet Tigranes' reinvasion', Mayor, 2010, pp.311–12.
91. XXXVI.14.
92. *Epitome* XCVIII.
93. *Historiae* fr.V.2 Ramsey.
94. Dio XXXVI.17.1.
95. Cf. the assessment of C. Steel, *The End of the Roman Republic, 146 to 44 BC: Conquest and Crisis* (Edinburgh, 2013), p.142.
96. *Vita Luculli* XXXIII.1–3.
97. On this oft-repeated judgment of Lucullus, cf. McGushin, 1994, pp.202–03.
98. Keaveney, 2009, p.162.
99. XXXVI.15.1–3.
100. A valuable look at Lucullus' relationship with the masses is the essay of N. Tröster, 'Struggling with the Plêthos: Politics and Military Leadership in Plutarch's *Life of Lucullus*', in Nikolaidis, 2008, pp.387–402.
101. XXXVI.14.4.
102. XII.90.
103. Keaveney, 2009, p.230.
104. See further the commentary note of Jacques André in his Budé edition of Book XV, *Pline l'Ancien: Histoire Naturelle, Livre XV* (Paris: Les Belles Lettres, 1960). The cherry may well have been taken from the modern Giresun in Turkey, the ancient Cerasus, although it is open to question whether the name of the place originally had anything to do with the fruit – the city was not known as Cerasus when Lucullus was in the region. For an interesting study on the role of botany and plants in ancient political life, see L. Totelin, 'Botanizing Rulers and Their Herbal Subjects: Plants and Political Power in Greek and Roman Literature', *Phoenix* 66.1/2 (2012), pp.122–44. Tertullian (*Apologeticus* XI.8) sarcastically laments that it is a pity for Lucullus that he was not made a god on account of introducing the (sweet) cherry to Italy, given that Liber was essentially made a god for introducing wine.
105. *Vita Luculli* XXXV.7.
106. *Historiae* fr.V.13 Ramsey; cf. Dio XXXVI.15.1. 'Lucullus had been replaced by the senate in his military command and in his provinces by Q. Marcius Rex (*cos.* 68) and by M' Acilius Glabrio (*cos.* 67), both of whom arrived in their respective provinces in 67. Even though Marcius Rex brought three fresh legions to his province Cilicia, and Acilius Glabrio, proconsul in Bithynia and Pontus, had

been appointed army commander against Mithridates, neither was anxious to be involved in a perilous campaign', McGushin, 1994, p.210.

107.Cf. Dio XXXVI.14.4; 17.1.

108.'Pompey's patience rivalled that of the spider. He ... knew well how to create a situation and then stand back from it until it had matured to the point where others would call upon him to apply a remedy', Keaveney, 2009, p.163). Glabrio would never be able to do what Lucullus had failed to achieve, and so Pompey would be able to swoop in and save the Roman predicament. Pompey, for his part, had good reason to be confident in his abilities; he had achieved success in Spain, Italy and the Mediterranean, and he no doubt assumed that Asia would be yet another victory.

109.Scholars do well to note that the Fimbrians were, by and large, more than happy to sign up for an extended tour of duty with Pompey. They may well have been little more than opportunists at this point; they despised Lucullus and his expectation of work and duty, but they had no interest in returning to Italy to till the soil. A new commander always meant a hope of donatives and prizes; the question of whether Pompey could do any better than Lucullus against Mithridates and Tigranes may not have been of paramount concern. Some of the more thoughtful Fimbrians may have also realized that the kings were not nearly as powerful as Lucullus' enemies might have wanted to project.

110.*Vita Luculli* XXXVI.1.

Chapter 6: Early Retirement?

1. *Pro Lege Manilia* IV.9.10.

2. *Pro Lege Manilia* VIII.20.

3. Lucullus' *virtus* is also cited by Florus, the second-century AD epitomist who refers to this quality of the general in his account of the *Bellum Mithridaticum* (I.40), where he notes that the King of Pontus was subdued by the *felicitas* or good fortune of Sulla, the *virtus* or courage of Lucullus and the *magnitudo* or greatness of Pompey (a play on his title Magnus) – a powerful, ascending tricolon of homage to the three great generals. Lucullus' work at the time of the siege of Cyzicus is also detailed by Florus in complimentary fashion. *Virtus* implies both courage and manliness, and perhaps also endurance and perseverance; Lucullus shows no signs of having succumbed to impatience in his long sojourn in Asia, in the face of enemies who were masters at taxing the patience of their adversaries. If anything, it could be said that Lucullus deserved better soldiers – or better abilites in dealing with the sort of men he had under his command.

4. *Pro Lege Manilia* IX.25.

5. *Pro Lege Manilia* IX.26.

6. J.R. King, *M. Tulli Ciceronis: Pro Lege Manilia* (Oxford, 1917), commentary note *ad* 26.

7. *Vita Luculli* XXXVI.1–2.
8. There is a splendid account of the meeting of Lucullus and Pompey by Greenhalgh, 1980, pp.106–07, with commentary on the character of the former. 'Lucullus played the last, unhappy scene in the drama in which he had held the stage for so long.'
9. XXXVI.46.
10. Dio XXXVII.49.3–5. Lucullus' insistence was ultimately futile; cf. XXXVIII.7.5.
11. 'There was some justice in Lucullus' demands, for Pompey had so far disposed with any senatorial advice, but the real purpose behind them was more sinister – to prolong discussion as long as possible and to delay final acceptance indefinitely', Leach, 1978, p.120.
12. For the attitude of the 'professional' army of Lucullus' day, see Keaveney, 2009, pp.238–42. Keaveney correctly places the ultimate emphasis on the relative unpopularity of Lucullus by the end of the campaign.
13. On the Memmian prosecutions of Marcus Lucullus and (soon after) Lucius, see Gruen, 1974, pp.266–67.
14. On scythe-bearing chariots, note McGushin, 1994, pp.74–75.
15. The captured ships were no doubt also an implicit challenge to the Pompeian achievements at sea. Lucullus, of course, had done more than his fair share at sea; he had won significant naval victories and had done much to ensure the security of Roman sea lanes during troubled times in both the Mithridatic Wars and under the pirate scourge.
16. See Keaveney, 2009, pp.184–86, for the propaganda use of the god Hercules by Lucullus in celebrating his victory.
17. *Vita Luculli* XXXVIII.1.
18. Skinner, 2011, p.63, finds the story of incest rather improbable. 'It suited Lucullus' vengeful purpose well, for it blackened his former brother-in-law with the stain of precocious degeneracy; at the same time, it imputed aristocratic exclusivity and was therefore an underhanded thrust at a proud patrician house ... Whether factual or not (in my opinion, almost certainly not), charges of incest soon became indelibly attached to the Claudian name'; cf. p.56, 'While the accusation was primarily intended to blacken her brother's reputation, as we shall see, and most likely had no basis in fact, it became firmly attached to the family name; in his subsequent attacks on Clodius, Cicero widened it to include all three sisters and even the two older brothers.'
19. There is a letter of Cicero to Atticus (I.18.3 Shackleton Bailey) that preserves the stinging remark that after having treated Marcus Lucullus like Menelaus, Memmius decided to attack both Menelaus (i.e., Marcus Lucullus) and Agamemnon (i.e., Lucius Lucullus) with the same contempt. The adulteries of Memmius are thus regarded as if they were pathetic attempts to recall the world of the Trojan War.
20. Cf. Telford, 2014, p.248.

21. *Ep. Ad Quint. Frat.* 14.3 Shackleton Bailey.
22. Ernst Badian's entry on Lucullus in the *Oxford Classical Dictionary* takes it for granted that Lucullus was an Epicurean: 'He was an able soldier and administrator, an Epicurean, a lover of literature and the arts, and a generous patron. But he lacked the easy demagogy that was needed for success in both war and politics in his day.'
23. The fact that the Athenians would set up a statue in her honour on the Acropolis in 49 is a token of the esteem in which they held her father. But we know practically nothing about Licinia, let alone her ultimate fate. See further Keaveney, 2009, pp.181–82, with dismissal of the theory that Licinia was actually the daughter of Clodius. Keaveney concludes that the statue was a sign of honour for Lucullus, who was evidently hailed as a benefactor of the Greeks; certainly Lucullus' reputation as a phihellene endured in Athens long after the departure of Sulla. Whatever the case of children, it is clear that Lucullus derived no political benefit from his union with Clodia – on the contrary, the marriage brought him nothing but grief. For the statue and inscription (*Inscriptiones Graecae/IG* II.2 4233), see also Skinner, 2011, p.57. For a rather different reception of Lucullus in Greek culture, we may compare the evidence of the letters ascribed to Apollonius of Tyana (71.72), where Greeks are criticized for taking Roman names such as Lucullus, Lucretius, Lupercus and Fabricius (where the names of Lucullus and Lucretius, we might note, are closely associated).
24. Lucius Lucullus – the son of Lucius Lucullus, that is – is sometimes confused with his cousin, the son of Marcus (cf. Osgood, 2006, pp.100–01). See further Keaveney, 2009, p.182. The cousin is apparently mentioned at Valerius Maximus 4.7.4, as part of his commentary on friendships; he was slain on the order of Mark Antony after Philippi for having been a partisan of Brutus and Cassius (republican sympathies ran in the family).
25. Keaveney, 2009, p.183 n.17, comments on the admirable self-restraint of Lucullus, if the story of Servilia's affair with Memmius were true.
26. On this, see further L. Fratantuono, *A Reading of Lucretius' De Rerum Natura* (Lanham, Maryland: Lexington Books, 2015), pp.467 ff.
27. *Vita Luculli* XLI.2–3; XLII.4–5.
28. The most convenient edition of the speech is that of Elaine Fantham, *Cicero's Pro L. Murena Oratio* (Oxford: American Philological Association, 2013), with introduction, Latin text and commentary.
29. See further here Gruen, 1974, pp.267–68.
30. *Pro Archia* VIII.21.
31. There is a detailed appraisal of the problem, with full commentary on the poems, in A.S.F. Gow and D.L. Page, *The Greek Anthology: The Garland of Philip, Volume II: Commentary and Indexes* (Cambridge, 1968), pp.432 ff. No fragments survive of any epic poetry on Lucullus' deeds; we can be sure, however, that Archias composed many verses.

32. *Pro Archia* III.5.

33. *Pro Archia* V.11.

34. We do possess a letter of Cicero to Atticus (I.16.15 Shackleton Bailey, dated to 61 BC; see further the editor's commentary *ad loc.*) in which Archias is cited for having finished his Greek poem on the Luculli, and for commencing a new work on the Metelli. This is the last we hear of Archias from contemporary sources; some have speculated that Cicero's reference confirms that an acquittal must have been won, and some have argued that Archias died in 61. But we have no proof for either conclusion. Archias also commenced a poem on Cicero's own exploits, a work that was apparently left unfinished – no doubt at least in part a reward for Cicero's splendid oratorical defence. On the larger problem of Roman citizenship and related questions posed by the trial, see Sherwin-White, 1939/1973. Cicero had hoped for a treatment of his consulship by Archias; on this note Dugan, 2005, p.46: 'That Archias does not reciprocate Cicero's artfully crafted speech with a poem in the consular's honour, but instead offers his services to the Luculli and Metelli (those figures responsible for the legal basis of his case for naturalization), underscores both the collapse of the *Pro Archia*'s self-fashioning strategies and Cicero's misplaced confidence in the power of literary polish to compete on the same level as long-standing political alliances.'

35. The best overview of the evidence for the incest charge is Appendix II, 'Clodius' Incest', in R.A. Kaster, *Cicero: Speech on Behalf of Publius Sestius* (Oxford, 2006), pp.409 ff. For ancient citations, note Cicero, *Pro Milone* 73; Plutarch, *Vita Caesaris* 10.5. The charge cannot be definitively adjudicated; for how Clodia would not participate in the public mourning for her brother after his death (possibly because of the humiliation she had suffered on account of Cicero's accusations against her), see Skinner, 2011, pp.72–73.

36. For an appraisal of the Ciceronian evidence for the scandal, see especially A. Lintott, *Cicero As Evidence: A Historian's Companion* (Oxford, 2008), pp.254 ff. Helpful too is the article of J.W. Tatum, 'Cicero and the Bona Dea Scandal', *Classical Philology* 85.3 (1990), pp.202–08; also D.F. Epstein, 'Cicero's Testimony at the Bona Dea Trial', *Classical Philology* 81.3 (1986), pp.229–35. 'To mention Bona Dea is to invoke the name of Publius Claudius Pulcher, Clodius, who interrupted the celebration in December 62 BCE and was tried for the offence … in the spring of 61 BCE', S. Takács, *Vestal Virgins, Sibyls, and Matrons: Women in Roman Religion* (Austin: The University of Texas Press, 2008), pp.98 ff.

37. For a good example of the attempt of some to rehabilitate Clodius, with particular emphasis on the Bona Dea episode and the charge of mutiny, see D. Mulroy, 'The Early Career of P. Clodius Pulcher: A Re-Examination of the Charges of Mutiny and Sacrilege', *Transactions of the American Philological Association* 118 (1988), pp.155–78.

38. Plutarch, *Vita Caesaris* X.5; cf. Skinner, 2011, p.64.

39. *Vita Luculli* XXXIX.1.

40. Cf. here K. von Stackelberg, *The Roman Garden: Space, Sense, and Society* (New York/London: Routledge, 2009), with material on what the author considers the 'apolitical' nature of the gardens as places not where political colleagues and allies could gather, but as a haunt of quasi-Epicurean retreat and reflection. Von Stackelberg also considers the political significance of the construction of the gardens; the issue of rivalry with Pompey and his own private/public spaces; and the question of Lucullus' alleged retirement from public life. It is important to note, however, that we have absolutely no evidence for the assertion that Lucullus was an Epicurean; on this important point, note Keaveney, 2009, p.211 n.52. Those who would subscribe to the view that Lucullus was an Epicurean would argue that in the latter stages of his life, he had decided that the pursuit of honour and glory was an act of folly; of course the blind pursuit of riches would also have been problematic for an Epicurean, and Lucullus' critics seem ready enough to indict him for that vice in the final decade or so of his life.

41. Cf. Tacitus, *Annales* 11.26–38; also K.T. von Stackelberg, 'Performative Space and Garden Transgressions in Tacitus' Death of Messalina', *The American Journal of Philology* 130.4 (2009), pp.595–624. On the gardens of Lucullus as the eventual locus of 'Julio-Claudian melodrama', note R. Evans, *Utopia Antiqua: Readings of the Golden Age and Decline at Rome* (New York/London: Routledge, 2007), p.203. It is conceivable that at least some of the Lucullan reputation derived from more sordid events that took place in the gardens long after his death; the Messalina episode may have been an especially tawdry case of posthumous guilt by association for Lucullus. Indeed, we may note the 1981 novel of John A. Schmidt, *The Gardens of Lucullus*, a work of historical fiction that concerns itself with the reign of Caligula. Schmidt's novel extends its coverage of Julio-Claudian Rome into the Claudian years, and associates Messalina with the assassination plot that spelled the end for Caligula; one may well think that Lucullus would be disgusted at the association of his name and his gardens with these more salacious, scandalous episodes of Roman history (especially this fictionalized account thereof).

42. *Vita Luculli* XXXIX.4–5.

43. *Vita Luculli* XXXIX.3.

44. Plutarch does note that there were some who said that these words were indeed spoken with reference to Lucullus, though not by Cato.

45. Today, in the French Quarter of New Orleans, Louisiana, there is a 'Lucullus Culinary Antiques, Art and Objects' that specializes in dining-related *objets d'art* from the seventeenth, eighteenth and nineteenth centuries – a popular place for lovers of food culture and *haute cuisine*. From ancient anecdote to contemporary antique shops, Lucullus' reputation for gastronomic luxury has perdured. The New York City-based 'Lucullan Foods' – which offers corporate events, 'curated dinners' and the services of a private chef – advertises that it 'collaborates with

select artists who wish to engage their audience with food in an art context'. Promotional materials highlight 'Lucullus … Roman general and consul, famous for his luxurious banquets'. We do well to remember in all of these survivals of Lucullan decadence that we know precious little about what one might find on Lucullus' Roman table; Keaveney, 2009, p.198 n.7, speculates that something like the 'pastry eggs' of Petronius, *Satyrica* 33, might have been typical, and he argues that the cherry must have been prominent in Lucullan desserts. But Keaveney does well to note that we have no definitive evidence that Lucullus' guests even enjoyed his feasts.

46. A fascinating article on the life of Lucullus, of particular interest for the question of what exactly happened to cause his apparent decline and fall, is the paper 'Lucullus Daemoniac' by Graham J. Wylie in *L'Antiquité classique* 63 (1994), pp.109–19.

47. On the lengths to which *pietas* could drive a man like Lucullus, see Keaveney, 2009, pp.234–35: 'When his own or his family's position or honour was threatened then Lucullus proved implacable. This mild mannered man conducted a feud with the Servilii that was said to be the most intense in Roman history, and pursued Pompey relentlessly for the wrongs done him in Asia. It is behaviour like unto that of his friend Sulla.'

48. 792B.

49. *Moralia* 785F, for commentary on which see Keaveney, 2009, p.210, who notes the Loeb's questionable rendering of one of the charges as 'sexual intercourse in the daytime', and the possible influence of the inaccurate translation on modern thought about Lucullus' alleged hedonistic tendencies. Daytime leisure activities were of course to be frowned upon, but the charge is perhaps not as salacious as some might have it. Plutarch's passage indicts Lucullus in the context of an argument between Pompey and him (likely the Galatia conference), where Lucullus is said to have upbraided Pompey for a pursuit of office and honour that was unsuited to his age – with the retort from the younger man that it was more inappropriate and out of season for an older man to pursue luxury when he should be pursuing the work of his office and duty.

50. III.30–31.

51. *Controversiae* IX.2.19.

52. VI.274e-f; cf. XII.543a.

53. A useful volume on the problem of luxury and the Greek attitude thereto = R.J. Gorman and V.B. Gorman, *Corrupting Luxury in Ancient Greek Literature* (Ann Arbor: The University of Michigan Press, 2014), with material relevant to an understanding of the views of Plutarch and others on the problem.

54. Cf. Dix, T. Keith, 'The Library of Lucullus', *Athenaeum* 88 (2000), pp.441–64.

55. *Vita Luculli* XLII.4–5.

56. Cf. here T.P. Hilman, 'When did Lucullus Retire?', *Zeitschrift für alte Geschichte* 42.2 (1993), pp.211–28.

57. XXXVII.49–50.1.
58. *Vita Pompei* XLVI.3 ff.
59. *Vita Pompei* XLVIII.1–3.

Chapter 7: Twilight Time

1. Cf. Greenhalgh, 1980, pp.222 ff., with full text of the most relevant Ciceronian evidence.
2. *Vita Luculli* XLII.7–8.
3. XXXVIII.9.
4. Cf. J.W. Tatum, *The Patrician Tribune: Publius Clodius Pulcher* (Chapel Hill: The University of North Carolina Press, 1999), p.112.
5. Keaveney, 2009, p.216, argues that the inclusion of Pompey's name was evidence in itself that Lucullus was still a force to be reckoned with – but the name of the old general might have been all too easy to supply given past, all too public history.
6. We may note here in passing that Lucullus does not make particularly many appearances in Cicero's extant correspondence.
7. For the theory that Lucullus succumbed to Alzheimer's disease, see Keaveney, 2009, pp.222–23. Speculation is all we have, though Gerard Lavery is right to consider the theory intriguing.
8. 792B–C.
9. XXV.25.
10. Love potions or philtres are discussed by Cyril Bailey in the introduction to his edition of Lucretius, *Titi Lucreti Cari De Rerum Natura Libri Sex* (Oxford, 1947), Vol.I, pp.8–11. The truth is that we do not know the origin of the Lucretian story; it may rest ultimately on a misintepretation of a passage in the imperial Roman poet Statius, *Silvae* II.7.76 *docti furor arduus Lucreti*, where *furor* may refer to poetic madness (i.e., inspiration). Our earliest certain source for the story is Saint Jerome's additions to Eusebius' chronicles, or in other words a testimony that classical scholars would consider late (not to say inherently unreliable). In the absence of further evidence, we cannot be sure if Statius' *furor* or 'madness' is to be taken literally. If Callisthenes administered an *amatorium* to Lucullus, it is not clear exactly what the point was; either the freedman wanted Lucullus to fall madly in love with himself, or he was seeking to have Lucullus fall in love with someone else. Plutarch seems to point to a less salacious rationale, namely that Callisthenes simply wanted greater control over Lucullus and his affairs, and in general a more pliant patron. There certainly was a market in such potions and drugs in the late Republic, and there is no good reason to dismiss the story out of hand. Given the penchant of Mithridates for poisons, there is an added reason, however, for the story to have been invented; one might imagine that some at Rome would have commented on the seeming irony of Lucullus' being driven mad by a potion, given the long years he spent in pursuit of the 'poison king'. On the theory

that Jerome misread the Lucullus story and took it to be of the poet Lucretius, see, e.g., L. Wilkinson, 'Lucretius and the Love-Philtre', *The Classical Review* 62.3 (1949), pp.47–48; also A. Betensky, 'Lucretius and Love', *The Classical World* 73.5 (1980), pp.291–99. It is certainly possible that the Lucullus story gave rise to the Lucretius, but the tale of the *poculum amatorium* arguably fits better with Lucretian lore than Lucullan, unless one is to conclude that the story arose as part of the general report and condemnation of the alleged decadence of Lucullus' last days. More generally on love potions, with reference to the alleged circumstances surrounding Lucullus' death, see M.W. Dickie, *Magic and Magicians in the Greco-Roman World* (London/New York: Routledge, 2001), p.133; cf. also C.A. Faraone, 'Agents and Victims: Constructions of Gender and Desire in Ancient Greek Love Magic', in M.C. Nussbaum and J. Sihvola (eds), *The Sleep of Reason: Erotic Experience and Sexual Ethics in Ancient Greece and Rome* (Chicago, 2002), pp.405–06. Lucullus is called 'the model of prodigals and voluptuaries' in part on the claim of the *amatorium* by 'P.L. Jacob' in his *History of Prostitution among All the Peoples of the World: From the Most Remote Antiquity to the Present Day, Volume I*, p.342.

11. For the Caligulan story, see Juvenal, *Satire* VI.615–620; also chapter 50 of the Suetonian life of the emperor. The love potion in Caligula's case was allegedly administered by his wife Caesonia. Certainly the story fits with the general tenor of Caligula's reign, and scholars are right to question the story. But far stranger things were true in his brief principate.

12. Cf. Keaveney, 2009, p.211, with reference to the critical verdict on Lucullus by Sir Ronald Syme in his magisterial *The Roman Revolution* (Oxford, 1939), p.23. On the problem of determining who exactly was an Epicurean, note, e.g., C.J. Castner, 'Difficulties in Identifying Roman Epicureans: Orata in Cicero *De Div.* 2.22.70', *The Classical Journal* 81.2 (1985–1986), pp.138–47.

13. We cannot date Lucretius' death with precision: 55 or 54 BC is often cited on account of, e.g., the aforementioned passage of Cicero to his brother Quintus; most would date Lucullus' death before the poet's, but there is no definitive evidence to support this chronology. It appears likely that the two men died fairly close together in time; as for the story of the *amatorium*, we cannot be sure of whom it was first related.

14. But for caution, cf. A. Palmer, *Reading Lucretius in the Renaissance* (Cambridge, Massachusetts: Harvard University Press, 2014), pp.127–28. In the present instance, the case is perhaps more, however, than one of two men with vaguely similar names, both said to have died as a result of *amatoria*.

15. Cf. Greenhalgh, 1980, p.75: 'With success so nearly in his grasp Lucullus was defeated by the weather and the temper of his troops. However much booty they had amassed and however much more they could expect to find at Artaxata, there was little consolation in carrying it further and further from home into unknown

country beset by the ice and snow of autumn. They refused to advance further, and Lucullus had no option but to turn south again.'

16. Keaveney, 2009, p.237.
17. Keaveney, 2009, p.243.
18. Finley Hooper writes in *Roman Realities* (Detroit, Michigan: Wayne State University Press, 1979), p. 221: 'Centuries before, the mighty Alexander had found that no army could defeat him save his own. Like Alexander, too, it was Lucullus' own self-confident determination that had taken him so far. He was a brilliant man of good intentions, who treasured the satisfaction of a job well done. He was especially proud that his campaign had not cost the government a single sesterce. Did a man need more than virtue and skill for success? His officers and men thought so. Having worked hard and risked their lives, they wanted something to show for it. Lucullus forgot that they had hearts and minds of their own. Whether that particular lapse was a fault or not, it ruined him.'

Selected Bibliography

The following titles represent but a sampling of the books that have been used in the composition of this work; it makes no pretense to comprehensiveness. Other sources (including scholarly articles) appear in the end notes to the volume. For definitive survey of the Lucullan bibliography, recourse should be made to Keaveney, 2009.

Adler, Eric, *Valorizing the Barbarians: Enemy Speeches in Roman Historiography*. (Austin: The University of Texas Press, 2011).

Antonelli, Giuseppe, *Lucullo: La vera storia* ... (Roma: Newton Compton Editori, 1989).

Arnaud-Lindet, M.-P., *Orose: Histoires contre les païens: Tome II, Livres IV-VI*. (Paris: Les Belles Lettres, 1991).

Badian, Ernst, *Foreign Clientelae (263–70 BC)* (Oxford: 1958).

Badian, Ernst, *Studies in Greek and Roman History* (Oxford: 1964).

Badian, Ernst, *Roman Imperialism in the Late Republic* (Ithaca, New York: Cornell University Press, 1968).

Bennett, Charles E., *Frontinus: Stratagems, Aqueducts of Rome*, Loeb Classical Library (Cambridge, Massachusetts: Harvard University Press, 1925).

Brennan, T. Corey, *The Praetorship in the Roman Republic, Volume II* (Oxford: 2000).

Brunt, P.A., *Social Conflicts in the Roman Republic* (New York: W.W. Norton & Company, 1971).

Brunt, P.A., *The Fall of the Roman Republic and Related Essays* (Oxford: 1988).

Cary, Earnest, *Dio's Roman History, Volume III, Books XXXVI-XL*, Loeb Classical Library (Cambridge, Massachusetts: Harvard University Press, 1914).

Chaplin, John D., (tr.) *Livy: Rome's Mediterranean Empire, Books 41–45 and the Periochae*, Oxford World's Classics (Oxford: 2007).

Crawford, Michael, *The Roman Republic* (Cambridge, Massachusetts: Harvard University Press, 1978; second edition, 1992).

Crook, J.A., Lintott, A., and Rawson, E., (eds) *The Cambridge Ancient History: Volume IX, The Last Age of the Roman Republic, 146–43 BC*, Second Edition (Cambridge: 1994).

Debevoise, Neilson C., *A Political History of Parthia* (Chicago: 1938).

de Blois, Lukas, *The Roman Army and Politics in the First Century BC* (Amsterdam: J.C. Gieben, Publisher, 1987).

Dugan, John, *Making a New Man: Ciceronian Self-Fashioning in the Rhetorical Works* (Oxford: 2005).

Earl, Donald, *The Moral and Political Tradition of Rome* (London: Thames and Hudson, 1967).

Edwards, Catherine, *The Politics of Immorality in Ancient Rome* (Cambridge: 1993).

Evans, Rhiannon, *Utopia Antiqua: Readings of the Golden Age and Decline at Rome* (London/New York: Routledge, 2007).

Evans, Richard, *Roman Conquests: Asia Minor, Syria and Armenia* (Barnsley: Pen & Sword Military, 2011).

Flower, Harriet I., *The Cambridge Companion to the Roman Republic* (Cambridge: 2004).

Forster, Edward Seymour, *Florus: Epitome of Roman History* (Cambridge, Massachusetts: Harvard University Press, 1929; with the Loeb Nepos, separate edition, 1984).

Fratantuono, Lee, *A Reading of Lucretius' De Rerum Natura* (Lanham, Maryland: Lexington Books, 2015).

Gärtner, Hans, (ed.) *Plutarchus: Vitae Parallelae, Volumen I, Fasciculus I* (Stuttgart: K.G. Saur Verlag, 2000), fifth revised edition of the first volume of the Bibliotheca Teubneriana edition of Plutarch's lives.

Gelzer, M., *Caesar: Politician and Statesman* (trans. Peter Needham) (Cambridge, Massachusetts: Harvard University Press, 1968).

Goldsworthy, Adrian, *Caesar: Life of a Colossus* (New Haven, Connecticut: Yale University Press, 2006).

Goldsworthy, Adrian, *Pax Romana: Peace and Conquest in the Roman World* (New Haven, Connecticut: Yale University Press, 2016).

Gorman, R.J., and Gorman, V.B., *Corrupting Luxury in Ancient Greek Literature* (Ann Arbor: The University of Michigan Press, 2014).

Grainger, John D., *The Fall of the Seleukid Empire, 187–75 BC* (Barnsley: Pen & Sword Military, 2015).

Greenhalgh, P.A.L., *Pompey, the Roman Alexander* (London: Weidenfeld and Nicolson, 1980).

Greenhalgh, P.A.L., *Pompey, the Republican Prince* (London: Weidenfeld and Nicolson, 1981).

Gruen, Erich S., *The Last Generation of the Roman Republic* (Berkeley/Los Angeles/London: The University of California Press, 1974).

Gruen, Erich S., *Culture and National Identity in Republican Rome* (Ithaca: Cornell University Press, 1992).

Harris, William V., *War and Imperialism in Republican Rome, 327–70 BC* (Oxford: 1985).

Hellegouarc'h, Joseph, *Eutrope: Abrégé d'histoire romaine* (Paris: Les Belles Lettres, 1999).

Henry, René, *Photius: Bibliothèque, Tome IV: Codices 223–229* (Paris: Les Belles Lettres, 1965).

Hooper, Finley, *Roman Realities* (Detroit, Michigan: Wayne State University Press, 1979).

Kaster, Robert A., *Cicero: Speech on behalf of Publius Sestius* (Oxford: 2006).

Keaveney, Arthur Peter, *Lucullus, A Life* (London/New York: Routledge 1992; second edition, with a new postscript, Piscataway, New Jersey: Gorgias Press, 2009).

Keaveney, Arthur Peter, *Sulla, the Last Republican* (London/Canberra: Croom Helm, 1982; second edition, Routledge: 2005).

Keppie, Lawrence, *The Making of the Roman Army: From Republic to Empire* (Norman: The University of Oklahoma Press, 1998; original edition, London: B.T. Batsford, 1984).

King, J.R., *M. Tulli Ciceronis: Pro Lege Manilia* (Oxford: 1917).

Konrad, Christopher F., *Plutarch's Sertorius: A Historical Commentary* (Chapel Hill: The University of North Carolina Press, 1994).

Leach, John, *Pompey the Great* (London: Croom Helm, 1978).

Lintott, Andrew, *Cicero As Evidence: A Historian's Companion* (Oxford: 2008).

Martin, Paul Marius, *Les hommes illustres de la ville de Rome* (Paris: Les Belles Lettres, 2016).

Matyszak, Philip, *Mithridates: Rome's Indomitable Enemy* (Barnsley: Pen & Sword Military, 2009).

Matyszak, Philip, *Sertorius and the Struggle for Spain* (Barnsley: Pen & Sword Military, 2013).

Matyszak, Philip, *Cataclysm 90 BC: The Forgotten War That Almost Destroyed Rome* (Barnsley: Pen & Sword Military, 2014).

Mayor, Adrienne, *Greek Fire, Poison Arrows, and Scorpion Bombs: Biological and Chemical Warfare in the Ancient World* (New York: Overlook Press, 2003).

Mayor, Adrienne, *The Poison King: The Life and Legend of Mithridates, Rome's Deadliest Enemy* (Princeton: 2009).

McGing, Brian C., *The Foreign Policy of Mithridates VI Eupator King of Pontus* (Leiden: Brill, 1986).

McGushin, Patrick, *Sallust: The Histories, Volume 2 (Books III–V)* (Oxford: 1994).

Nikolaidis, Anastasios G., (ed.) *The Unity of Plutarch's Work: 'Moralia' Themes in the 'Lives', Features of the 'Lives' in the 'Moralia'* (Berlin/New York: Walter de Gruyter, 2008).

Osgood, Josiah, *Caesar's Legacy: Civil War and the Emergence of the Roman Empire* (Cambridge: 2006).

Palmer, Ada, *Reading Lucretius in the Renaissance* (Cambridge, Massachusetts: Harvard University Press, 2014).

Perrin, Bernadotte, (tr.) *Plutarch: Lives, Volume II*, Loeb Classical Library (Cambridge, Massachusetts: Harvard University Press, 1914).

Rackham, H., *Cicero: De Natura Deorum and Academica*, Loeb Classical Library (Cambridge, Massachusetts: Harvard University Press, 1933; revised, 1951).

Ramsey, John T., *Sallust: Fragments of the Histories, Letters to Caesar*, Loeb Classical Library (Cambridge, Massachusetts: Harvard University Press, 2015).

Rawson, Elizabeth, *Cicero: A Portrait* (London: Penguin Books, 1975; revised edition, Ithaca, New York: Cornell University Press, 1985).

Reid, James S., *M. Tulli Ciceronis pro A. Licinio Archia poeta ad iudices: Edited for Schools and Colleges* (Cambridge: 1897).

Richardson, J.S., *Appian: Wars of the Romans in Iberia* (Warminster: Aris and Phillips Ltd., 2000).

Riggsby, Andrew M., *Crime and Community in Ciceronian Rome* (Austin: The University of Texas Press, 1999).

Rodgers, William Ledyard, *Greek and Roman Naval Warfare: A Study of Strategy, Tactics, and Ship Design from Salamis (480 BC) to Actium (31 BC)* (Annapolis, Maryland: Naval Institute Press, 1937/1964).

Salmon, E.T., *The Making of Roman Italy* (London: Thames and Hudson, 1982).

Schlesinger, Arthur C., (tr.) *Livy: Summaries, Fragments, and Obsequens*, Loeb Classical Library (Cambridge, Massachusetts: Harvard University Press, 1959; revised, 1967).

Scott-Kilvert, Ian, and Pelling, Christopher, *Rome in Crisis: Nine Lives by Plutarch* (London: Penguin Books, 2010) (Pelling is responsible for the translation of the *Lucullus*).

Seager, Robin, *Pompey the Great: A Political Biography* (Oxford: 1979; second edition, Oxford: 2002).

Shaw, Brent D., (tr. and ed.) *Spartacus and the Slave Wars: A Brief History with Documents* (London: Bedford/St. Martin's, 2001).

Sherwin-White, A.N., *The Roman Citizenship* (Oxford, 1939; 'new edition', 1973).

Shipley, Frederick W., *Velleius Paterculus and Res Gestae Divi Augusti*, Loeb Classical Library (Cambridge, Massachusetts: Harvard University Press, 1924).

Skinner, Marilyn B., *Clodia Metelli: The Tribune's Sister* (Oxford: 2011).

Spann, P.O., *Quintus Sertorius and the Legacy of Sulla* (Fayetteville: The University of Arkansas Press, 1987).

Strauss, Barry S., *The Spartacus War* (New York: Simon and Schuster, 2009).

Syme, Sir Ronald, *The Roman Revolution* (Oxford: 1939).

Takács, Sarolta, *Vestal Virgins, Sibyls, and Matrons: Women in Roman Religion* (Austin: The University of Texas Press, 2008).

Tatum, W. Jeffrey, *The Patrician Tribune: Publius Clodius Pulcher* (Chapel Hill/
London: The University of North Carolina Press, 1999).

Telford, Lynda, *Sulla: A Dictator Reconsidered* (Barnsley: Pen & Sword Military,
2014).

Tröster, Manuel, *Themes, Character, and Politics in Plutarch's Life of Lucullus:
The Construction of a Roman Aristocrat* (*Historia Einzelschriften 201*. (Stuttgart:
Franz Steiner Verlag, 2008).

van Ooteghem, Jules, *Lucius Licinius Lucullus* (Bruxelles: Palais des Académies,
1959).

White, Horace, *Appian's Roman History, Volume II*, Loeb Classical Library
(Cambridge, Massachusetts: Harvard University Press, 1912).

Wiseman, T.P., *New Men in the Roman Senate* (Oxford: 1971).

Index